S0-BRH-366

AARON COPLAND

AARON
COPLAND

HIS WORK AND CONTRIBUTION
TO AMERICAN MUSIC

JULIA SMITH

E. P. DUTTON & COMPANY, INC.

PUBLISHERS : 1955 : NEW YORK

The musical examples in this book are reproduced by permission of the following
copyright owners:

Copland's "Ukelele Serenade," copyright 1928 by B. Schott Söhne, Mainz; "Sentimental Melody," copyright 1929 by B. Schott Söhne, Mainz; both excerpts
used by permission of Associated Music Publishers, Inc., New York.

Copland's *Concerto for Piano and Orchestra,* copyright 1929; *Dance Symphony,*
copyright 1931; *First Symphony,* copyright 1931; *Music for the Theatre,* copyright 1932; *Piano Variations,* copyright 1932; *Vitebsk,* copyright 1934; "Song,"
copyright 1935, all by Cos Cob Press, Inc. Used by permission of Arrow Music
Press, Inc., New York.

Copland's *Two Pieces for String Quartet,* copyright 1940 and 1948 by Arrow
Music Press, Inc., New York.

Copland's "As It Fell upon a Day," copyright 1929 by Aaron Copland. Used by
permission of New Music Edition, Inc.

Copland's *The Second Hurricane,* copyright 1938 by C. C. Birchard and Company, Boston.

Stravinsky's *Octuor,* copyright 1924 by Edition Russe de Musique (Russischer
Musikverlag); copyright 1952 by Boosey and Hawkes, Inc., New York.

Copland's *Sextet,* copyright 1948; *Statements,* copyright 1947; *El Salón México*
(version for two pianos arr. by Leonard Bernstein), copyright 1943; *Billy the
Kid* (arr. for piano solo by Lukas Foss), copyright 1944; *Rodeo,* copyright
1946; *Appalachian Spring,* copyright 1945; *Our Town* (Three Piano Excerpts
from the Film Score), 1945; *The Red Pony,* copyright 1951; *The Tender Land,*
copyright 1954; *Piano Sonata,* copyright 1942; *Sonata for Violin and Piano,*
copyright 1944; *Third Symphony,* copyright 1947; *In the Beginning,* copyright
1947; *Concerto for Clarinet and String Orchestra,* copyright 1950; *Twelve
Poems of Emily Dickinson,* copyright 1951; *Quartet for Piano and Strings,*
copyright 1951, all by Boosey and Hawkes, Inc., New York.

LIBRARY OF CONGRESS CATALOG CARD NUMBER: 55–9659

TO FIVE FRIENDS OF MUSIC:

To my father, *James Willis Smith,* amateur musician, educator, and businessman, who believed that in education lies the hope of the world and that in music is to be found its happiness;

To *Carl Friedberg,* master pianist, eminent artist-teacher at Julliard, and dear friend, whose recognition of my creative talents resulted in my subsequent devotion to the cause of the American composer;

To *Frederick Jacobi,* American composer, with whom I studied Composition at the Juilliard Graduate School (1935–1941), who, when asked which American composer I should choose as the subject for a doctoral dissertation, replied in his characteristically modest and unassuming way: "Choose Copland," he said, "for he has accomplished more than any of the rest of us. Not that we haven't all tried hard—very hard—but somehow or other Copland has struck the 'American' note";

To my husband, *Oscar Albert Vielehr,* whose help, infinite patience, and encouragement has given me the leisure to bring this study to completion—a task that has encompassed more than six years of research and writing;

To the *National Federation of Music Clubs*—which through the years has steadily fostered our serious native music—and its president, Ada Holding Miller, 1951–1955, whose dynamic emphasis on the performance of American works throughout the United States during 1954–1955 has made both her name and that of the organization she has so nobly served synonymous with the term "American music" and guardians of its brilliant future.

Acknowledgments

IT IS a pleasure to express my gratitude for the help given to me in the preparation of this biographical-critical study to my Sponsoring Committee at New York University, especially to Dr. Jack Watson, who instructed me in the Principles of Musical Research and guided me in the plan of my study and to Dr. Aaron Schaffer, of the University of Texas, friend of Aaron Copland, who not only provided me with three early songs of the composer but made detailed criticism of this manuscript. I also wish to thank my aunt, Dr. Ruby Cumby Smith, for her valuable help in the cutting and shaping of the final version of the study and for her assistance in the translation of the Spanish critical reviews. For the reading and expert criticism of the manuscript I am also indebted to Beverly Barkesdale, Musical Director of the Toledo Museum of Art, to Alene Jean Treanor, music and art critic of the Toledo *Blade,* to Ross Parmenter, music critic of the New York *Times;* and to Albert J. Elias, free-lance music critic and executive member of the New York Music Critics' Circle. Acknowledgment must also be made to John Hjalmar Kober and to John Kirkpatrick for Copland letters, newspaper reviews and, for the loan of the "Pastorale" song manuscript.

Recognition must be given to the Music Librarians at the New York Public Library both forty-second and fifty-eighth street branches, to Anna Harriet Heyer, Librarian of the School of Music at North Texas State College, Denton, Texas, and to Robert A. Hug, in charge of the newspaper microfilms at the New York (forty-second street) Public Library, for their assistance over a long period of time.

To Mr. Copland's publishers grateful acknowledgment is made of their permissions to use quotations, both of words and music: Arrow Press, Boosey and Hawkes, C. C. Birchard Company, Cos Cob Press, New Music Press, and B. Schott Söhne. Acknowledgment is also made to Julius Mattfeld, of Columbia Broadcasting System, and to the American Music Center for the loan of orchestral manuscripts.

Finally, my grateful thanks are offered to Aaron Copland himself for biographical and musical (including critical) material, for his reading and checking of the manuscript for accuracy of fact, and for numerous personal interviews granted me as well as letters containing information without which this study would not be comprehensive.

J. S.

Contents

Contents

Foreword

AN OCCASION that will be long cherished by those present as an evening memorable for great music-making and for its expression of affection and high esteem accorded the man and artist was the League of Composers' concert in celebration of Aaron Copland's fiftieth birthday, on November 5, 1950, at New York City's Museum of Modern Art. Exhibiting various facets of the composer's growth, the following representative chamber music works of Aaron Copland were heard: "As It Fell upon a Day" (1923), from the Paris Study Years; *Sextet* (1937), from the Second, or Abstract, Period of his work; and three compositions from the Third, or Folksong, Period—"Seven Songs" from *Twelve Poems of Emily Dickinson* (1949–50), *Quartet for Piano and Strings* (1950), and the large choral work *In the Beginning* (1947).

A tall, commanding, still youthful-looking figure, lovable and grave of mien, Copland himself appeared in the concert, playing sensitively and beautifully the expressive piano accompaniments to the Dickinson songs. One deeply felt the presence of this simple and great man in our midst, whose powerful personality and spiritual strength projected through a lifelong devotion and ministration to his chosen art have made him, at the half-century mark, one of the leading composers and musical figures of the contemporary world.

The music press made much of Copland's attainment of his fiftieth milestone, synonymous, in many respects, to the gains of American music as a whole, with Olin Downes, senior music critic of the New York *Times*, voicing the following evaluation of the composer's quarter century of work:

> By the quality of his workmanship, the sincerity and adventurousness of his progress, Copland made himself the spearpoint of the development of the modern American school. And he has

done this in an unostentatiousness and a desire for service to his art that will leave their mark on this whole period of native composition and open the way for a greater future to come.[1]

Believing that an artist's work ought not be separated from his life, a principle enunciated by Plato, I have not followed the present-day practice of most musical-critical studies, which generally are divided into two main parts: (1) The Man (biography); (2) The Music (analysis of techniques). Instead, I have traced the development of Aaron Copland, the individual, and his work simultaneously for, in reality, his work is a reflection of his life.

This procedure offers several advantages, of which these are the most important: (1) a chronological or historical growth in life and art is clearly viewed; (2) although Copland, the artist, is a complex creator, in observing each successive step of his musical development, one is able to comprehend the really simple and logical processes through which his work has become art; (3) a greater number of readers may glean a knowledge and understanding of twentieth century music-compositional techniques which will enhance their enjoyment not only of the music of Copland but that of other contemporary composers.

The following pages reveal, at least in some measure, "the adventurousness of [Copland's] progress" as an artist, his vigorous and healthy efforts in pursuit of his own musical destiny and that of American music in general, which combined purpose has earned him in the opinion of many, including the present writer, the appellation, "America's First Great Composer."

[1] New York *Times*, "Copland at Fifty," Sunday Music Page, Oct. 29, 1950.

Preliminaries

IT WAS in the fall of 1935 that I first heard the name of Aaron Copland. The occasion was the memorial service held for Rubin Goldmark, in the theater of the Juilliard School of Music. Afterwards, several of the Goldmark pupils (of whom I am one), congregated in the back of the hall, conversing in hushed tones, when one of our group suddenly asked the question then uppermost in our minds: "With whom shall we study now?" Rae Rabinowitz, youthful "star pupil" of Goldmark's Fugue Class, unhesitatingly replied: "I'm going to study with Copland, if he'll accept me. He's tops!" "Who's Copland?" I naïvely inquired. "Of course *you* wouldn't know, being from Texas," was her withering reply, implying that my native state lay beyond the cultural pale. Within a few moments she enlightened me on the subject of "Copland": as a youth he had studied with Goldmark, who regarded him as a "radical"; he continued his studies abroad with Nadia Boulanger, who thought him a "genius"; he was the most "advanced" in outlook and technique of all the American composers of his time, et cetera, ad infinitum.

In spite of Rae's glowing words about Copland's talents, I chose to continue my studies with Frederick Jacobi, to whom Ernest Hutcheson, then Dean of Juilliard, at Goldmark's instance, had directed his pupils during the master's last illness. Jacobi continued his teaching, at Juilliard, along the classical lines adhered to by Goldmark, whose pupil he had been, though Jacobi's musical language was more "up to date" and his sense of form more "modern" than that of Goldmark.

By 1938, the name of Aaron Copland began to register as a musical personality upon my student's consciousness, for the premier performances of his high school opera, *The Second Hurricane,* in New York City during the previous year and of *Billy the Kid* in 1938 earned him his first important successes in the theater. I shall never forget the effect that one of the first New

York performances of the ballet had upon me, for I—hailing from the Southwest where the cowboy songs Copland employed in *Billy* sprang into being—was completely touched by the sincerity and authentically expressive emotional content projected by the happy union of music and choreography. "This is real American art," I thought, "the genuine article!"

In 1940, Jacques Singer, then conductor of the Dallas Symphony Orchestra, invited me to appear as guest conductor of my *Episodic Suite* (orchestral version), in Dallas. The pair of concerts also included Copland's *El Salón México*—perhaps that composer's most popular orchestral piece—which I heard for the first time. I distinctly recall that the work struck a responsive ear with its direct, simple, and uninhibited folk style.

By 1945, I was searching about for a suitable subject for a doctoral dissertation. I wanted to write about contemporary American music, for, to me, it seemed time that the work of our native "serious" composers be recognized as subjects deserving of musicological research. Which one of several outstanding composers' life and work should I study—Ives, Copland, Harris, or Sessions—to mention only a few?

Following the best musical advice to be had on the subject (which was North-South-East-West overwhelmingly in favor of Copland) and my own inclination (based on my preference for his music), I wrote to Aaron Copland, asking his permission to develop a critical biography of his work, on a Ph.D. level, to which he gave his consent. Five years were spent in the preparation of this study, with the result that the completed dissertation extended to 649 pages. The present volume is a condensation of the study's most salient features.

I regard the time spent in the research and writing of this study as being exceedingly fruitful, for I have seen what one man has been able to accomplish within a time span of approximately thirty years and I have glimpsed the direction in which American music must inevitably develop, a course which Aaron Copland, more than any other composer to date, has helped to chart.

J

The Background, Childhood, and Early
Music Study of Aaron Copland
Brooklyn
(1900-1917)

ALTHOUGH Aaron Copland was born in Brooklyn during the first year of the twentieth century, his maternal grandfather, Aaron Mittenthal, was one of seven million new persons who came to the United States in the decade following the Civil War.

News of America's welcome to immigrants spread as far as the little village of Shavel, Lithuania, near Kovno, the county seat, where Aaron Copland's father, Harris Kaplan (pronounced Kŏplan), was born around 1860.* Harris was the oldest child of Sussman and Freda Kaplan, the others being Sadye, Becky, Alfred, Fannie, Abraham, Rose, and Lillian, all born in Shavel.

A cousin of the Kaplan family, a Mr. Sussman, had gone to America, settled in Brooklyn, and had written letters home telling of the opportunities to be found in the United States.

Harris, the eldest son, in order to escape the indignities of the ghetto and the compulsory seven-year Russian military service, decided to come to America, if possible, by way of England. At the British port of entry, the immigration official, a practical man apparently not versed in languages, wrote on Harris Kaplan's papers the English equivalent of his name—HARRIS COPLAND—a transcription which Harris was to keep permanently. The lad took small menial jobs in London and Manchester, remaining in the latter city about a year until he had saved enough money for his passage to America.

Into an atmosphere of aggressive business competition in Brooklyn came the sixteen-year-old Russian-Jewish boy, about

---

* Biographical facts in this chapter have been corroborated by members of Aaron Copland's family.

the year 1877. With the help of his cousin Sussman, Harris Copland established a dry-goods business in Brooklyn in partnership with his cousin.

Plucky, resourceful, and extremely devoted to his family, Harris, as he was able, brought over his brothers and sisters one by one to this country. All took the name of Copland. Harris assisted his brothers in establishing themselves in business and found desirable husbands for his sisters. Finally the last to come over were his father and mother, who left their Lithuanian homeland behind forever.

Seeing his immediate family launched on independent lives of their own in the newly adopted country, Harris also began to wish and plan for a home. It was not to be long before he would meet his future wife.

As in the case of the Copland family, cousins of the Mittenthal family had earlier settled in America and had written home telling of the opportunities to be found in the United States.

Aaron Copland's mother, Sarah Mittenthal, was born in 1862 in the small village of Vistinich, Lithuania, a border town opposite Koenigsburg, Prussia. This little town was not far from the village of Shavel where Harris Kaplan, Aaron Copland's father, was born. Sarah's father, Aaron Mittenthal, had married Bertha Wittstein and the following children had been born in Vistinich: Annie, Fannie, Louis, and Sarah.

In 1867 or 1868 Sarah's father, acting on the advice of his cousins who had preceded him to America, came to the United States. Though his relatives had settled in Jefferson, Texas, Aaron Mittenthal chose instead to settle in Chillicothe, Illinois, where he established a small general store. His business prospered sufficiently for him to be able by 1869 to send for his wife and four children. Sarah then was seven years old. The family remained in Chillicothe about two years, Samuel being born there in 1870.

Aaron Mittenthal next moved his family westward to Peoria, Illinois, where Lillian was born in 1872. By now Sarah and the oldest children were attending public school and were learning our American language and customs, which they found to be quite different from their Yiddish mother tongue and Jewish traditions.

Persuaded by the Jefferson cousins that Texas offered greater opportunities, the family soon moved to Dallas, where Aaron Mittenthal opened a large wholesale and retail dry-goods store. The older children, in Dallas as in Peoria, attended the public schools and helped in the store after school hours. Here Jacob was born in 1874 and Abraham,* next the youngest, in 1877.

In 1881 the Mittenthal family, with the children from Sarah down, moved to New York City. The two older girls and the older boy had, by this time, married and settled permanently in Texas, the girls residing in Waxahachie and the boy in Dallas.

In New York City the Mittenthal family first resided on East Broadway, then later moved to 413 East 122 Street, where Nathan, the youngest, was born. The children attended the New York public schools and, in addition, Sarah and Lillian took piano lessons, practicing on the family Kranich and Bach grand piano. As Sarah grew older she developed a pretty singing voice, often accompanying herself at the piano, much to the enjoyment of both family and friends.

Harris Copland and Sarah Mittenthal met at some family social gathering. Almost immediately Sarah was attracted to the handsome, successful, dapper young man. Unable to resist her appealing singing of "I Await Thee, My Love," Harris asked Sarah to become his wife. They were married in 1885 in Pythagoras Hall, located on Canal Street at what is now the entrance of Manhattan Bridge. Harris took his young wife to Brooklyn to live.

About 1887, severing partnership with his relative, Harris opened his own department store in a spacious new building located on the corner of Washington Avenue and Dean Street. While the new building was being completed, Harris and Sarah occupied an apartment across the street, where Ralph, their first child, was born. The new building was located at 626-628 Washington Avenue. The upper stories of the building, called

---

* In the absence of records, Abraham Mittenthal (deceased, 1954) was regarded by the Copland family as being its most reliable historian.

a "taxpayer," were to remain the family home until 1924. Here Leon, Laurine, Josephine, and the youngest child, Aaron, were born. Aaron was born November 14, 1900.

Washington Avenue, described as "drab" by Aaron Copland, resembled one of the lower-middle-class London streets, with the exception that it was peopled largely by Italians, Irish, and Negroes.[1] On this street Aaron lived the first twenty years of his life.

Harris Copland, Aaron's father, spent most of his life on Washington Avenue, living the brisk, painstaking existence of a small businessman trying to get ahead. In his own business world Harris was supreme; he was able to serve the interests of his neighborhood, meet his competitors on an equal basis, and provide more than the necessities of life for a family whom he adored. Speaking English with a fairly strong accent all his life, Aaron's father always seemed much more foreign to the boy than did his mother, Sarah, who spoke without a foreign accent.

Coming to America at such an early age, the mother retained scarcely any memory of Russia, and, having lived her childhood and young womanhood in the West, she reflected only an American background. She was also more artistic in nature than was her husband, who was business-minded. However, she preferred to assist in the business rather than to be concerned with housekeeping duties. A cook always took care of the family meals and managed the housekeeping. A sweet-natured woman, patient and gracious, Sarah always found time to listen to the small problems of her children. Harris also valued Sarah's wise counsel regarding the conduct of business affairs. It is said of him that he never made an important financial or family decision without first having discussed it with his wife.

There was a lapse of seven years between next to the youngest child, Josephine, and the youngest, Aaron. As a stage of parental exhaustion had been reached by this time, Aaron was left principally to his own devices. All of the family lived very close to the business downstairs, and the small boy was quite conscious of that larger world.

The street in front of the Copland business-home, as is typical of most large cities in a neighborhood of this sort, was the children's playground. Their sports were constantly being interrupted by a stream of traffic, which included hand-delivery carts, wagons and buggies drawn by fast horses, and an occasional motor vehicle. Combining the various nationalities of the neighborhood, a group of small boys of all ages frequently played baseball in the street.

Aaron, named for his maternal grandfather, was more often a spectator than a participant in these sports. The youngest child and rather delicate, he did not attempt to compete with his older brothers in games, but was content to watch them play from the vantage point of the front steps. Sitting there quietly, sometimes with one of his favorite Horatio Alger books open on his knees, he presented the picture of a shy, meditative, sensitive child.

By the time he was nine years old Aaron began to go to summer camps as the older children had done. He went four successive years, from age nine to thirteen, to Camp Carey, near Wilkes-Barre, Pennsylvania. The boys he met there became his friends during the winter, and most of his social life began to date from that time. While there were other Jewish boys at the camp, the clientele was not exclusively Jewish, and Aaron enjoyed the companionship of boys who reflected a wide range of American homes. He enjoyed sports such as baseball, hiking, and swimming with the other boys, but felt he was not proficient in them. Though he did not excel in athletics, in any matters requiring judgment and risk the boys always depended on Aaron for guidance and advice. The expression of leadership which was to prove so characteristic of Copland in later years was already present and being exercised during the childhood period.

If there is anything significant in the idea of inheritance, the available evidence tends to show that Aaron Copland inherited his musical gifts and artistic sensitivity from his mother, while from his father emanated qualities of forcefulness and sureness of decision, once decisions were made. There seems to be expressed in his travels over both North and South America as well as over Europe a reflection of his parents', particularly his mother's, earlier American migration and settlements. Finally, Aaron Copland appears to be a composite of the most striking traits possessed by both his parents.

Though he did not come from a family which, as far as is known, had ever produced a professional musician, nor from a home where any one of its older members might be classified as more than a competent amateur, Aaron Copland, through his family, through the synagogue, and through various social activities, was subjected to a number of early musical influences.

Ralph and Laurine, the oldest boy and girl, studied violin and piano, respectively, for a number of years with Mr. and Mrs. Henry Schradieck, who were among the leading teachers of Brooklyn. Ralph, who applied himself more to music than did his sister, studied a good part of the violin literature, including sonatas, concertos, and, of course, the shorter violin pieces. Laurine, more interested in dancing and singing, learned enough piano to accompany her own songs, and also Ralph, in the playing of shorter violin pieces. Together they often played potpourris from *Traviata* and *Faust*, occasionally for gayer moments indulging in ragtime.

The Copland family frequently gathered around the piano in the evenings after supper for informal "sings," Laurine always playing the accompaniments. The music they sang was generally the popular music of the day. Aaron, described by Laurine as "an adorable little brother," was often present listening to whatever was being played or practiced.

The children's Uncle Alfred was recalled as being the only one of the Copland line who particularly enjoyed music. An amateur violinist in his younger days, he used to bring over such songs as Schubert's "Serenade" and "Four Leaf Clover," a ballad, for Laurine to play and sing for him.

The family attended Beth Israel Anshei Emes, on Harrison Street, the first synagogue to be established in Brooklyn, of which for many years Aaron's father was president. As it was situated quite a distance from the Copland home, the family did not attend regularly except on Jewish holidays. However, all the children were graduated from its Sunday school.

The synagogue was modified orthodox and contained no organ. The cantor's music had real oriental flavor, consisting of pure, unaccompanied Jewish melody handed down from previous centuries. The music of the chorus, on the other hand, originally monody (single-lined melody), had, in the course of history, been set to conventional harmonies in order to provide separate parts for choral singing. These ancient melodies, now garbed in harmonic settings of the style of Mendelssohn and other early nineteenth century composers, had lost their Jewish characteristics. Actually, except for his trio, *Vitebsk* (a study on a Jewish melody), and a setting of the Jewish folksong "Dance-Hora," Copland has not turned to Jewish sources for music materials.

As a child, Aaron heard much music at Jewish weddings, which the entire family frequently attended together. At these functions, though ensembles usually played American dance music such as ragtime, waltzes, and schottishes, yet an occasional Jewish dance was thrown in for local color.

Both the older boys were graduated from Boys' High School in Brooklyn. Ralph went on to study at Columbia University, where he was graduated in law; Leon, being of a more practical turn of mind, went into business in Brooklyn.

Laurine, after graduating from the Manual Training School (for girls), went to Manhattan to study at the Metropolitan Opera School located in the Metropolitan Opera Building. The school had a box at the Metropolitan, and the young girl went almost every week to a performance. Laurine always brought home her programs and librettos to Aaron, who insisted that she tell him all that occurred.

Aaron attended Public School No. 111 and Public School No. 9, as had the older children before him. In Public School No. 9, which Aaron entered when he was about eleven, the boy made good grades consistently until he began to develop other interests, such as music. By the time he reached the Boys' High School his marks in both Latin and mathematics had lowered.

When he was seven and was recovering from a slight illness, Aaron wrote a poem, "Dorothy," on the name of a young lady he greatly admired at the time. Dorothy Levy (for it was she who inspired what was probably his very first creative effort) later became the young man's sister-in-law when she married brother Ralph.

When Aaron was about eleven, Laurine, one day noticing that he was watching her practice with unusual intensity, said, "Come on, Aaron; sit down and I will show you how to play the piano." His sister had a graded series out of which she had begun her study with Mrs. Schradieck. This became the basis for Aaron's first lessons.

The lessons with Laurine lasted about six months. Finally one day she told him, "You know more now than I learned in eight years of study. I can't teach you anything else!"

For a year and a half Aaron worked at the piano by himself, reading and studying whatever music he came across. Being a methodical worker, one who had practice in thinking things out for himself, Aaron eventually arrived at the moment when he decided he wished to study with a professional teacher.

He had considerable trouble persuading his mother to let him take piano lessons, for she recalled the substantial sum she had spent on music lessons for the older children, and nothing had come of it. Aaron persisted in asking for lessons until finally she said, "All right, if you want to find the teacher yourself, we don't have any objections to your studying."

Taking his mother at her word, after making a number of inquiries, Aaron knocked on the door of Leopold Wolfsohn's studio at 345 Clinton Avenue and announced he wished to take piano lessons. Annually, Wolfsohn's advanced pupils played in recital at the Wanamaker Auditorium in Manhattan. It was at one of the Wanamaker recitals that Aaron made his first public appearance as a pianist when he played a "Polonaise" by Paderewski.

The boy heard his first concert when he was about fifteen years old. Paderewski was playing at the Brooklyn Academy of Music and, as no one else at home was interested in hearing a piano recital, Aaron went alone. The fact that Paderewski was both pianist and composer began to stir Aaron's imagination with thoughts of his own future.

As soon as the Copland children were old enough, they began to help in their father's business, downstairs. Aaron followed this same pattern, beginning when the store had its busy hours. At an early age he graduated to cashier at mealtime, when the regular employee was at lunch or supper. He worked at odd hours after school and on Saturdays until he was about fifteen, for which work his father always paid him. By the time he went to Paris he had several hundred dollars saved up to pay for concerts, operas, trinkets, and other "extras" not provided for in his student's budget.

During World War I, from 1914 to 1918, Aaron attended Boys' High School in Brooklyn. As a contribution to the war effort, he and a group of his high-school chums went to Marlboro, New York, to assist in the harvesting of the berry crops. In a postcard to one of his friends, John Kober (a lad several years younger than himself who did not go along on the project), Aaron has noted briefly some aspects of country life:*

Dear John,

Am back here again—this time picking berries and living in a barn. Will be here about a week longer. Sometimes play a tin pan [piano] thru a farmer's kindness. Write to me up here. After picking berries all day we cook our meal and go for a swim. My regards to your folks. Yours,

AARON

During the summer vacation when school was not in session, the Copland family frequented nearby resorts. It was on one of these vacations in 1916 (in the latter part of the summer) that the youthful musician met a young man whose friendship occurred at a very important and impressionable period of his life. This young man was Aaron Schaffer, some seven years older than Aaron Copland. Dr. Schaffer recalled that he first met the

* Postmark Marlboro, July 8, 1916. The postcard and other Copland letters were made available to this study by John Hjalmar Kober, now an official of the Lincoln Savings Bank in Brooklyn.

future composer at the Hotel Fairmont in Tannersville, New York, when the youth was almost sixteen years old:

> . . . He [Copland] was a very lively and . . . very sensitive lad and was passionately fond of the piano (which was then and has remained my favorite instrument). Thus although I was twenty-two and had received my A.B. degree from the Johns Hopkins University, I was attracted to the youngster at once.
> We became close friends, and we often talked about music. . . . At the time, he was both fun-loving and serious—always ready for a hike or a boyish prank, but convinced that he would one day be famous as a pianist or a composer or both.*

Ross Parmenter notes that Copland remembers, at the age of sixteen, informing a friend (no doubt Aaron Schaffer) that he was going to be a composer. However, at about the age of thirteen he had already decided to compose an opera. Having no text, Aaron decided to reset *Cavalleria Rusticana*, for Laurine had attended the opera and brought home the libretto. "At that time [Copland] did not know he could purchase lined music paper, so he drew his own lines and got as far as re-setting the off-stage women's chorus at the start of the opera."[2]

In "Composer from Brooklyn" Copland himself states: "The idea of becoming a composer seems gradually to have dawned upon me."[3]

The youth's adolescent yearnings and aspirations are discussed in a letter of Aaron Schaffer's in answer to one of Aaron Copland's. Dated Baltimore, August 11, 1916, Schaffer's letter reads as follows:

> Your highly interesting train-letter was to me, to say the least, a source of distinct pleasure. The thought that I should have aroused in one so sensible, and so full of appreciation for the things which really tend to make life beautiful, sentiments such as those expressed cannot but be gratifying to me. If I have stimulated you just the slightest bit towards continuing in the ennobling work for which you seem now so well fitted, I feel that I have accomplished something worthwhile and that my vacation was anything but a failure.

* Excerpt from a letter by Dr. Schaffer to the author, April 18, 1949.

You say that your heart is full of high ideals and great ambitions. I need not tell you that I, too, have certain definite aims which might seem, to the average man, either incomprehensible or useless. For what difference does it make to such a person that a Mozart, a Chopin, a Keats, or a Jehuda Ha-Levi lived, suffered, and produced work which will hand down their names to the end of time? Young men with aesthetic qualities and inspirations have always had, and have today more than ever, a terrific battle to fight against the dogged "horse-sense" (a word I almost detest) of the everyday, work-a-day world. So that when I urge you to be firm in your resolution to enter one of the most glorious professions in the gift of God and not to be deterred by the carping of small-minded people, I am only strengthening myself for the same task.

As regards a correspondence between you and myself, I should be more than delighted to keep up my end of it. I shall always be glad to hear of your progress, in music as well as at school, and to be kept posted on the musical events of New York. I, in turn, shall let you know about the big concerts which take place here, and imagine, when I attend any of them, that you are sitting beside me. Although I expect to be exceedingly busy this winter, I shall always find time to read and answer your letters. . . .*

It was Leopold Wolfsohn, his piano teacher, who helped young Aaron find a harmony teacher when, at this time, the youth realized that to be a composer one must study harmony. At first he had had the notion that harmony could be learned from a correspondence course, but a few trial lessons cured him of such an idea.

So it came about, in the fall of 1917, that Aaron was to cross to Manhattan weekly to study harmony and composition with the noted Rubin Goldmark. Although unaware of its true import at the time, with this momentous step forward the Brooklyn-born lad was now to embark upon what later proved to be the self-dedicated career of composer.

---

* The letters of Aaron Schaffer were provided the author by Aaron Copland, spring, 1949.

The Years of Study with Goldmark—
Manhattan
(1917-1921)

THE United States was in the midst of the war with Germany when sixteen-year-old Aaron Copland (not seventeen until November) began his theoretical studies with Rubin Goldmark,* September, 1917. Aaron's new teacher was a nephew of Karl Goldmark, composer of the opera *Queen of Sheba*. At this time, Goldmark, who taught privately in Manhattan, lived with his brother, Dr. Carl Goldmark, a physician, at 140 West Eighty-seventh Street.

On Aaron's first visit to Goldmark, he was ushered into a large anteroom and told to wait; after a long interval a door suddenly opened and a distinguished-looking gentleman appeared: " 'Well, young man,' he demanded in a gruff voice, 'what's the matter with you?' I explained I just wanted to study harmony. 'Humph!' he said, turning on his heel. 'I guess you want to see my brother.' I had rung the wrong bell and got the wrong Goldmark."[1]

Aaron's first encounter with the right Goldmark was almost as disconcerting. His first remark to the boy was: "What do you want to become a composer for!"[2]

Aaron studied harmony, counterpoint, and composition with Goldmark, using E. F. Richter's *Manual of Harmony* as the first text. It was Goldmark's procedure to require his pupil to write out weekly assignments according to the Richter rules and practices. Later Foote and Spalding's *Modern Harmony, Its Theory and Practice* was used. In counterpoint, beginning with the Five Species, Aaron continued with the writing of two- and three-part inventions and some fugue. His composition studies

* Goldmark had studied with A. M. Livonius, Door, and Fuchs in Vienna and with Joseffy and Dvořák in New York.

included Song Forms, Variation Forms, and the "good old" (Copland's phrase) Sonata Form, the latter being Goldmark's ideal of perfection in musical expression, a mastery of which he required of all students who remained with him.

In regard to his four-year-period of study with Goldmark, Copland has expressed the following: "Goldmark had an excellent grasp of the fundamentals of music and knew very well how to impart his ideas. This was a stroke of luck for me. I was spared the flounderings that so many musicians have suffered through incompetent teaching at the start of their theoretical training."[3]

About this time Aaron and a friend, probably John Kober, "discovered" a small collection of music upstairs in the Brooklyn Public Library, Montague Street branch, which also contained a number of general books on music, such as histories, biographies, and the like. The music (not often used) consisted mostly of the "classics," which the boys were able to withdraw at intervals and enjoy at their leisure.* This is indicated in the following letter that young Aaron wrote John, dated October 11, 1917, for which he conveniently borrowed the business stationery of the H. M. Copland Department Store:

Although I said something about coming over to your house this Saturday, I'd like to take it back, if you'll let me. If you would come to my house at about 2 o'clock Saturday, we would go immediately to my sister's house, where I am sure we would be able to spend four hours (2-6) in real enjoyment. The slick piano is still there.† I expect to go down to the library and will take out some new stuff that we will play together [four hands]. If I do not hear from you I will take it for granted that you are coming. Please do.

By now Aaron was attending concerts regularly. Walter Damrosch and the New York Symphony played weekly concerts at

---

* Although Mr. Kober is now engaged principally in banking, he continues to perform professionally as organist and choirmaster in a church near New York City.

† Laurine (Mrs. Charles Marcus) was purchasing a new grand piano at the time.

the Brooklyn Academy of Music, the repertoire consisting chiefly of classic symphonies, with an occasional novelty. Aaron attended these concerts, as he was eager to hear for the first time all the Beethoven, Brahms, and Tschaikovsky symphonies. During this time he also attended performances of the ballets *Schéhérezade* and *Le Spectre de la Rose* by the Diaghilev ensemble.

In a note to John Kober, written October 19, 1917, Aaron expressed delight on learning that his friend had bought a ticket for a piano concert at Carnegie Hall for the following Saturday. Making an appointment to meet John at the Fifty-ninth Street subway station (since he would be in New York for his lesson with Goldmark on Saturday morning), Aaron's letter continues:

> I also have the program and in the musical literature that I have are included some of the numbers. These include Beethoven's Sonata Op. 110, the Brahms' Intermezzo, the Chopin Valse and the Ballade in G minor. I also have the original song from which Liszt derived the "On the Wings of Song." It is a song by Mendelssohn and I sing it often. I regret that we have no opportunity to meet before the concert, but Friday is my Military Training Day, so it is hardly possible.

A note on November 9 makes mention of the fact that Aaron is to hear the Philharmonic on the eighteenth "and maybe I can get some of the stuff they will play in duet form. My first opera,* this Wednesday, is *Boris Godounow*. . . . It was not in when I went for it at the library. Too bad, wasn't it?"

Again, on November 19, John is informed of the following:

> Percy Grainger is the soloist at next Sunday's concert at the Metropolitan. . . . If you would like to go and have a half a buck to spare let me know and I'll be delighted to buy two tickets for us. Grieg's Concerto Sunday was ravishing. If you should decide to go we can make arrangements to meet Sunday eve later.

---

* During this time Aaron held a subscription to the Metropolitan Opera.

Since Aaron had studied with Leopold Wolfsohn for several years, Goldmark found it desirable to send his young pupil to Victor Wittgenstein, with whom the youth continued his piano lessons from October, 1917, to the spring of 1919. During this period of study Aaron was able to perform Schumann's *Faschingsschwank* in a highly creditable manner. He was also interested in the playing of the Debussy *Preludes* and studied many of Scriabin's piano works.

Wittgenstein remembers his young student as being "quiet, shy, well-mannered, and gracious in accepting criticism. He had a unique type of mind and his knowledge of harmony was considerable. The boy always analyzed music much more than did the other students." He became a member of Wittgenstein's Artists' Class, performing frequently in student recitals. If Aaron was composing at the time, he never mentioned the fact at his piano lessons.[*]

However, from another note to John Kober, we learn that the young high-school student was composing a song with words inspired by World War I. Dated December 21, 1917, the letter reads:

> Excuse the pencil, but I'm writing between a rush of business in the store. Now that the Christmas holiday is here, I am very anxious to see you. The most convenient time I can think of is Tuesday, Christmas afternoon and maybe evening (?) Will that suit you? Could you get the Tschaikovsky *Pathetique Symphony* No. 6 for four hands through your library? I heard the Philharmonic play it and I am sure I can show you some beauties in it that we missed. It is perfectly ravishing. Can I say more? If you write and let me know immediately whether you are coming (as I hope you are) I will get your card by Monday. Be over at about 2 P.M.
>
> Yours,
> Aaron
>
> P.S. I have 4 piano pieces by my teacher [Goldmark] that I want you to hear. And this confidentially, I have just composed

---

[*] Interview with Victor Wittgenstein on February 23, 1949.

a song that I have not been able to sing to anyone yet, so you will be the first victim. The words, written by a Belgian poet are:

> Sing, Belgians, sing,
> Although our wounds may burn
> Although our voices break
> Louder than the storm, louder than the guns;
> Sing the pride of our defeats,
> 'Neath this bright autumn sun
> And sing the joy of courage,
> When cowardice might be sweet.

They are, in my opinion, very stirring. Sir Edward [Elgar?] has written music which is played as an obligato when the words are recited. However, I have not seen the music. Come, won't you?

By now Aaron was instructing John to some extent in harmony, as his note of April 9, 1918, suggests:

Dear John—I'm writing to ask you to come over SATURDAY, the 13th, between 2 and 2:15. Try and do something in harmony so that we can go on. A woman gave me some piano music and there are quite a few doubles among them. These you may gladly have. I believe Schubert's Impromptus and Moments Musicaux are among them. I bought a subscription ticket for 3 concerts at Carnegie Hall at which Ossip Gabrilowitsch will be conductor of a specially selected orchestra of 100 and also soloist. He will play Mozart's D Minor Concerto, Schumann's Concerto in A Minor and Franck's Symphonic Variations at the 3 concerts. My mother and I are to hear Heifetz on April 28. I am taking up secondary seventh chords, major and minor, as used in modulation, now with Goldmark. No more news and just drop me a line if you can come.

In the spring of 1918 high-school graduation was approaching; it was the time for making decisions which were to shape the lad's entire life. Aaron was exceedingly perturbed by conflicting desires as to whether to pursue a musical career, or to do as his parents wished, go to college. Aaron believed it would be impossible to do justice to either by trying to combine both;

yet, if he refused to go to college, would his parents continue to pay for his musical studies? He could not offer them the alternative of choosing to study at a professional music school, such as Juilliard, Curtis, or the Eastman Schools of Music, for these institutions had not yet been founded. The conservatories then in existence, with their limited curricula, offered less in the way of noted musician-teachers than New York where many artists and teachers lived and maintained studios. His teacher, Goldmark, was the leading composition teacher in America at that time, and there were a dozen or more noted piano teachers located in the metropolitan area. Aaron had begun to feel disappointed in his progress with Wittgenstein, which fact also added to his unrest. If his parents refused to pay for his professional musical education, would Aaron, in order to pay for his lessons, be able to obtain work in the New York theaters as an orchestral pianist? All these problems kept the boy in a confused state. He did not like to bring matters to a head in a discussion with his family until he had first settled things in his own mind.

As was his custom when important problems arose, Aaron wrote to his friend Schaffer for advice. The latter, since September, 1916, had been serving as a member of the faculty of the Johns Hopkins University in Baltimore. In the same letter Aaron enclosed the vocal line of a song he had composed to one of Aaron Schaffer's lyrics. A letter from the young instructor, dated May 23, 1918, indicated his complete comprehension of the young composer's problems, for which he offered certain opinions regarding their solution; these he supported by an allusion to a similar problem recorded in Rolland's musical novel, *Jean-Christophe:*

> Your plans for your life after graduation from high school are extremely interesting and, in the main, praiseworthy. Might I, however, be allowed to differ with you regarding the advisability of your taking work at one of the New York theatres? Many a talented young musician like yourself has gone into this kind of work to use it, as you propose, merely as a stop-gap while continuing his studies and developing virtuosic perfec-

tion, and most of them have soon succumbed to the deadening
atmosphere of the theatre and ended as mere musical wrecks.
I know a number of concrete instances of this very thing. You
will remember how Jean-Christophe detested that kind of work
and that he gave it up as soon as he could. There ought certainly
to be some ways for you to earn money to enable you to continue
your studies under Goldmark and a ranking piano teacher—
one like Stojowski or even Gabrilowitsch himself (does he give
lessons?). I agree with you that you cannot go to college and
devote yourself to music at the same time, and your plan of
educating yourself from now on is a very commendable one,
if you stick to it, as I am sure you will.

I was highly delighted to receive the advance indication of
your musical composition for my "Summer Vacation." I shall
wait anxiously and eagerly for the completed piano score, and
then, when I have learned the song by heart and made everybody else in the family learn it, I shall treasure it up amongst
my most valued possessions. The idea has occurred to me that
the two of us might publish a volume of "Lieder'" . . . . the
poems to be written by me and the musical scores by you. Isn't
that a splendid, foolhardy notion?

A letter from Aaron Copland to John Kober, dated June 10,
1918, reveals that the two high-school lads were having difficulty arranging their recreational hours, and that Aaron was
making consistent musical progress:

Dear John:
I tried to get you on the phone this evening, but you were
out unfortunately. It appears that you have become a regular
business man, with enough to do to almost crowd out our pleasant afternoons together. But we won't give up as easy as all that.
On Sunday afternoon I am always needed to drive the car, so
that time is ruled out. We might see each other on Sunday eve.
and one week from this Sunday, June 22, would be fine. . . .
Consider June 22 as the day, since next Tuesday I will be taking regents.

Musically I've been quite busy myself. I have completed two
more songs to some words by my poet friend Aaron Schaffer.*

---

* These songs were "My Heart Is in the East" and "Night," listed among
Copland's "Juvenilia" (see Appendix I).

You heard the substance of one of them, which I have already
sent to Baltimore to my friend. The other one is finished, but
not written [out]. I'm anxious to have you hear both. I am working on a theme which I think I will eventually use for a violin
and piano selection. I could not resist the temptation of buying
that volume of Debussy's Songs. I have also bought the second volume of Russian Piano Music which you had out of the
library and includes "Polichinelle" by Rachmaninoff. It also has
an Intermezzo by Moussorgsky and some Preludes by Scriabin
which are exceptionally fine. . . .

Aaron

Besides Aaron Schaffer, another friend, Arne Vainio, had an
effect on young Copland's intellectual awakening. When Aaron
was about eighteen, he secured a position as piano player at the
Finnish Socialist Hall (Brooklyn), in a group of three or four
boys near his age. Vainio, the clarinet player, was a young "left-
ist" intellectual who first interested Aaron in socialism and its
leaders, particularly in Eugene V. Debs. Through his friend,
Aaron began to read *The Dial,* the chief literary magazine of
that time, the boys often discussing its contents. (*The Dial* was
comparable to today's *Partisan Review* or *Kenyon Review.*)
Vainio, about two years older than the other boys, was the leader
of these youthful discussions and a convincing spokesman for
the "new" ideas.

Besides the clarinet, Vainio also played the cello in a respectable fashion. Together he and Aaron played through most of
the cello literature, including the Beethoven cello sonatas. The
cello pieces in Copland's list of "Juvenilia" (see Appendix I)
were written for and played by Vainio. The young Socialist had
both a literary and a musical influence on Aaron, though the
literary influence predominated.

Aaron's father, a staunch member of the Democratic party
during his life, took little stock in his son's socialistic views. One
day, regarding the Russian Revolution then going on, Aaron
commented that perhaps there was a new idea in the struggle
which might have value for the world. His father quickly answered: "America has the only real idea when it comes to gov-

ernment." He and all of Aaron's uncles always felt that America had made them whatever they were and had given them a chance to "be somebody." They insisted that America was the only country in the world where such a chance could happen to the "little people."

In June, 1918, Aaron was graduated from high school and, with the consent and aid of his parents, was able to devote all his energies to music. Though they still desired their son to select a more practical profession, they were wise enough to feel that in another year or two of musical study Aaron would convince himself of the futility of becoming a composer.

For the second successive summer, Aaron and a group of his high-school chums contributed their "bit" to the war effort by assisting with the harvesting of the large berry crops upstate. On returning to Brooklyn, he took a job as runner for a Wall Street brokerage concern, holding this position for two summers, both in 1917 and 1918. Between deliveries of stocks and bonds he often browsed in an old bookshop around the corner from his work. It was here that he purchased his first French book, when the thought of going eventually to Paris began to occupy his mind.

In regard to the subject of modern music, a term with which Copland has long been identified as one of the "avant-garde," he has stated that, as far as he could remember, no one had ever told him about "modern music" and that apparently he had happened on it in the course of his musical explorations. "It was Goldmark, a convinced conservative in musical matters," he declared, "who first actively discouraged this commerce with the 'moderns.' That was enough to whet any young man's appetite. The fact that the music was in some sense forbidden only increased its attractiveness."[4]

Because of the war the "new" music was difficult to obtain. Published only in foreign editions, the works of Scriabin, Debussy, and Ravel fetched high prices, beyond the means of most music students. It was at the Fifty-eighth Street Music Library (Manhattan) that Aaron found the modern scores, which could be withdrawn for two-week intervals of study. Making good use of this source, he read much of the available modern literature. Aaron also went at least once a week to the Forty-second Street library, where he read, with "excitement," Paul Rosenfeld's articles in *The Dial* "about the young Stravinsky and Ernest Bloch." It was in a Rosenfeld article that he first saw mention of Roger Sessions.[5]

It was during 1918 at the Metropolitan Opera House that Aaron heard the opera *Marouf* by Henri Rabaud. It was during the same time that he first heard Stokowski in the early days of his career with the Philadelphia Orchestra in Carnegie Hall perform Debussy's *Nocturnes*, "Nuages" and "Fêtes." These performances were among the earliest beginnings in the development of Aaron's preference for French music, which was soon to make a notable imprint upon his career as composer.

At Goldmark's further suggestion Aaron left Wittgenstein to study with Clarence Adler from the winter of 1919 to the spring of 1921. Copland's first "lecture" was in Dr. Adler's studio. "He played the Ravel *Sonatine*, a revolutionary piece at the time; and in order not to shock the ears of the uninitiated, he extemporized explanatory notes. He did it so well that he went on with this activity, and has since become known as a lecturer as well as famous as a composer."[6]

Meanwhile young Professor Schaffer was planning to do graduate study at the Sorbonne in Paris. He planned to leave New York City in July, 1919, for a year's stay abroad. Aaron, whose interest in modern French music was becoming paramount, wrote to his friend, asking him to visit in the Copland home at his earliest convenience and tell him of his plans for Paris.

Aaron shortly received a reply from young Schaffer, who accepted with pleasure the invitation to visit in the youthful composer's home. Dated June 25, 1919, Schaffer's reply continues as follows:

> I have some very flattering news for you. My sister took our three songs to her piano teacher—a lady who is a member of the faculty of the Peabody Conservatory here and who is well qualified to judge—and she expressed herself most warmly both with regard to the music and to the verses. She stated most emphat-

ically that the music showed undoubted genius. (I'll pat you on the back when I see you!) But, best of all, she said that, in her opinion, "Night" is well deserving of publication, and that she has a friend connected with the Ditson Music Publishing Co., who makes it his business to give aspiring young composers a start along the road to fame. With your (and my) permission she would be willing to send the piece to this gentleman, with a warm recommendation that the Ditsons publish it. Or if you have anything else that you would rather have them see, she would be more than willing to use her good offices. What do you think of it? I consider it a splendid suggestion. I'll talk it over with you when I get to New York. If you could only come to Paris with me! Wouldn't we be two happy Bohemians!

During the summers of 1919 and 1920 Aaron performed as a professional musician at various summer hotels in the Catskills. As pianist, he formed a duo with Sydney Rooff, violinist, who later became a medical doctor.

During his student years in New York Aaron greatly missed the companionship of other music students. He had a sense of isolation and of working too much by himself. Yet he maintained an active correspondence with Aaron Schaffer, who continued his warm interest in the young composer's growth. From Paris, young Schaffer wrote enthusiastic letters regarding the intellectual and artistic stimuli of that city, which now held the cultural position formerly enjoyed by Berlin. The thought was beginning to take shape in young Copland's mind that he, too, must go to Paris for further study and development.* But how was he to persuade his parents that this daring step should be taken?

From number 9 rue de Moscou, Paris, a letter from Aaron Schaffer dated November 20, 1919 reads as follows:

I read your last letter with even more than the usual interest because it was so full of "meat." I was particularly pleased to learn of your progress as a piano virtuoso, for you know I have always firmly believed that you ought not neglect your undeni-

---

* In an interview with Mr. Copland (April 22, 1949) he stated: "Aaron Schaffer was the source of inspiration in my desire to go to Paris."

able gifts in that direction. I look forward to the day when I shall have the pleasure of hearing your reading of the *Faschings-schwank* and whatever else you may be in the mood to play. And you'll see to it that I get a box for your "debut" perform-ance, won't you?

Your account of the [Leo] Ornstein recital was interesting because of the fact that that musician-clown seems to have pro-duced rather much the same impression upon you as he did upon me, when I heard him some two years ago. I shall never forget the amused snicker that passed over the audience as he rose completely from his seat to pound the crashing discords of his "Anger." If Leo's real fits of anger are anything like that, I should hate to be in his vicinity when the emotion seizes him. Incidentally, I can assure you that Debussy is one of the idols of Paris musicians—both orchestras and soloists include selec-tions from his work on their programmes.

And now for the music young Schaffer was hearing in Paris in 1919 which, of course, was Aaron's paramount interest:

I know you would find joy in this city if you were here; the concerts are simply countless and of every conceivable char-acter. You can have Moussorgsky, Stravinsky, Scriabin recitals or Bach, Haydn, and Beethoven; you get series of three or four recitals that cover the history of the sonata or the concerto; and the symphony organizations are undoubtedly the best in the world. Personally, of course, I can't devote the time I should like to these various concerts; one a week must, perforce, suffice me, with all my other innumerable interests.

By 1920 Aaron, having explored the "classic" repertory of music very thoroughly, was now attending concerts of the "new" music whenever possible. Interested in hearing as many "first performances" as he could, Aaron was eager to know first-hand the new trends from Europe as soon as they arrived in America. There were several important events outstanding in his memory. Besides the Ornstein piano recital (indicated in the preceding Paris letter from young Schaffer), Aaron heard the first perform-ance of Ernest Bloch's *Violin Sonata* at Aeolian Hall in 1920, performed by Paul Kochanski and Artur Rubinstein. He also heard some of the spectacular concerts of modern composition presented by Edgard Varèse, conductor and founder of the New Symphony Orchestra. The youth also heard for the first time Debussy's *Pelléas et Mélisande,* with Mary Garden in the title role, in a performance by the Chicago Opera Company on tour in New York. Aaron was particularly interested in a piano recital by Cyril Scott, who visited the United States in 1920 as performer of his own music. Among other works Scott played his *Piano Sonata,* a composition in which each measure appeared to have been written in a meter different from the preceding. Aaron was so impressed with the sound of the *Sonata* that he went at once to a music store and purchased a copy of the work.

When Aaron's turn came to go to college he astounded and greatly perplexed his parents with the announcement that he had definitely decided to become a composer, and that instead of going to college he desired to study in Europe in order to achieve his ambition. (Aaron's first idea had been to go to France in 1920, but Goldmark persuaded him to stay on with him another year to insure him a more solid background.) A family conference was called immediately to consider the possibility of persuading Aaron to give up his impractical idea. It was his mother who turned the discussion in Aaron's favor. Realizing that her son would never be happy without having had the opportunity of trying to be a composer, she settled matters by saying, "The boy must have his chance. Let him try and we'll see what happens. After all, Aaron is still young enough to enter a profession if the venture should not turn out well." Thus it was decided that the parents would send their youngest to Europe for a year's study.

One day while reading *Musical America* Aaron saw an advertisement announcing the establishment of a School of Music for Americans at Fontainebleau. Actually Fontainebleau was a French school for Americans founded in conjunction with an American organizing committee, headed by Walter Damrosch. The school was to inaugurate its first session during the summer of 1921. According to the Brooklyn *Eagle* (clipping undated), the American committee awarded Aaron one of nine scholarships at Fontainebleau so that his summer's study was gratis.

No one was happier at Aaron's decision and the family's consent for him to go to Paris than was young Schaffer. In a letter from that city dated January 18, 1920, he wrote:

> I was truly delighted to hear of your resolution to follow in the footsteps of so many of your knowledge-seeking compatriots and spend some time in Paris. I am particularly pleased to feel that my letters have proved of some influence in your decision, and I sincerely trust that you will never have cause to regret your having taken such a step, if you do actually realize your hopes of coming to Europe next July. I shall certainly be more than ready to talk the whole matter over with you or go into as minute detail as you like. . . .

Aaron had previously sent some of his compositions to George F. Boyle, pianist and composer in Philadelphia, for criticism. Boyle warmly praised the youth's work, with which fact Aaron had acquainted Schaffer, who commented in the same letter:

> I congratulate you warmly upon George Boyle's merited compliments of the compositions you submitted to him, although I have known for years the things he said about you, so that I was scarcely surprised. Keep it up, old man—cherish the ideals you have formed and cling to them in the face of all obstacles. What matter if your efforts may not receive the full meed of reward (but they will!) that you anticipate for them; for nothing can compensate for the joy of creation, the relentless pursuit of the ideal. Do I voice your sentiments? I'm sure I do. . . .
>
> Yours for Paris,
> AARON [SCHAFFER]

A list of works composed by Aaron Copland between the years of 1916 and 1921, designated by him as "Juvenilia," may be classified under the following categories: three violin pieces; two cello pieces (one incomplete); eight songs; eight piano solo pieces, one of which is a suite containing three short pieces; a piece for piano (four hands); and a work in the larger forms, a piano sonata. With the exception of the piano sonata, this respectable output of works reveals that young Copland was writing in the smaller forms, mostly two-page songs and piano pieces. A chronological listing of these pieces by title is to be found in Appendix I.

In addition to the list of "Juvenilia," two works which were published in France during the early twenties belong to this period. They are "Scherzo Humoristique: Le Chat et la Souris (The Cat and the Mouse) for piano, and the song "Old Poem," both of which reflect the French impressionist style, with the latter indicating, on the part of the youthful composer, a beginning interest in a frequent change of meter. The unpublished song, "Pastorale,"* bearing the date April 4-12, 1921, also stems from these years. The following chapter reports the first artistic successes in France of these three short works: "The Cat and the Mouse," "Old Poem," and "Pastorale," as well as other compositions written during the Goldmark study years.

During the early part of 1921 a large and elegant dinner party was given to Rubin Goldmark at the Hotel Esplanade in New York. As an "old boy," it was Frederick Jacobi's duty to call for the master and escort him to the affair. Copland was obviously the *enfant terrible* of the group and, as such, the butt of many of the jokes. During the course of the dinner, Jacobi, as toastmaster, rose to announce: "You are now going to hear a performance of one of the best examples of a student's work—the harmonization of a chorale, in the Goldmark manner." The master was supposed to guess who had written it. Far from being "in the Goldmark manner," the setting was full of sharp dissonances and daring innovations of harmony. At its conclusion Goldmark rose and, in mock anger, pointed his finger directly at Copland, saying, "You are the culprit! *You* did it!" But he enjoyed the joke as much as anyone.

Now that it was decided that Aaron was actually to go to Paris, he was busy with final preparations for his journey. What an exciting time, with the purchase of his first steamship ticket,

---

* A photostat copy of the song manuscript was made available to the author by John Kirkpatrick, a fellow student friend of Copland's during the Paris study years.

proper luggage and clothes enough to last a year! He had the foresight to ask for letters of introduction to persons in Paris who might be of help to him as well as to inquire of his friends as to whether they knew any young persons who were going over that summer.

Shortly before Aaron was to sail in June, 1921, his cousin Elsie Abrams Clurman introduced him to her brother-in-law, a young man who was also planning to go to France to study, not music, but literature at the Sorbonne. This young man, later founder of the Group Theatre and director and producer of many plays on Broadway, was Harold Clurman. As neither Aaron nor Clurman knew any Americans in Paris, they decided it would be a good thing to "team up," particularly since their interests lay along kindred lines. As the Sorbonne session did not begin until fall, it was agreed that Aaron, who was going on ahead for the summer session at Fontainebleau, would find living quarters for both of them for the winter.

Meanwhile Aaron Schaffer had returned from Paris at the end of March, 1920. The two Aarons spent considerable time catching up on Copland's musical progress and Schaffer's activities in Paris, which included a thorough "briefing" of the young composer on what to expect, once he had landed in the French capital.*

On June 9, 1921, Aaron Copland sailed for Europe on the ship "La France" with a party of American students who were to attend the Fontainebleau school. They traveled in what would today be called "tourist" class. Aaron participated in the ship's concert of June 14, contributing the first movement of Beethoven's *Sonata*, Op. 90.†

At the students' table in the dining salon sat the French painter, Marcel Duchamp, whose famous painting, "Nude Descending a Staircase," had created a scandal when it was exhibited in New York about 1913. Duchamp proved to be extremely kind and helpful in giving the young American advice as to

---

* Soon after, Dr. Schaffer accepted an appointment to the University of Texas, where he has since become Chairman of the Department of Romance Languages; he and Mrs. Schaffer reside in Austin, Texas.

† From the ship's program.

what to do and where to go when he arrived in the strange, new country. The artist further suggested that Fontainebleau was much too conventional a place for study and that, as Aaron was already enrolled for the summer, it should be regarded merely as a "stepping-off place."

Reversing his family's original migration of traveling from the Old to the New World in pursuit of economic security, our young composer now proceeded from the New to the Old World in search of its greater artistic legacy. Seven days after its departure the ship docked at Le Havre, June 16, 1921.

III

The Years of Study in Paris with Nadia Boulanger, and Other European Influences (1921-1924)

As is generally known, the first score of years of the twentieth century gave evidence of a conscious turning away by the younger creative musical minds from the nineteenth century romantic aesthetic, which had reached fulfillment in the works of Brahms, Wagner, Strauss, and others, in quest of new aesthetic conceptions, such as impressionism, expressionism, dynamism, and nationalism, exemplified respectively in the work of Debussy, Schoenberg, Stravinsky, and Bartók. By the early 1920's, smaller peaks or fads in art, such as futurism and Dadaism, had begun to disappear.

Stylistically, Stravinsky, within a few years' span, had evolved from the fantasy of the Russian fairy tale, *Firebird*, to the realism of *Petrouchka* (1911), in which the "Petrouchka chord" (F sharp major and C major sounded simultaneously) marked the beginning of polytonality, on to his greatest achievement in rhythmic virtuosity, *Le Sacre du Printemps*.

The plan of writing for as few as eleven instruments, as noted in the chamber work "Ragtime" (1918) and other smaller combinations, led to the turning point in Stravinsky's next style development, which occurred when he produced his *Pulcinella* ballet in Paris (1920). This was based on the music of the early eighteenth century composer, Pergolesi, and Stravinsky became so imbued with its spirit and chaste formalism that he immediately adapted the essence of this earlier period to his own original works. In 1923 his first original neoclassic work, *Octet for Wind Instruments*, appeared. In this work Stravinsky adhered to the form of eighteenth century classicism but dressed up his musical ideas in the present-day devices of polytonality, polyrhythms, and dissonant counterpoint.

The victory of the Allies in 1918 brought about a shift in the center of musical activity from Germany to France, so that Paris, not Berlin, became the art capital of the world.

Impressionism, no longer a novelty, had given way to a post-impressionism movement led by Ravel and Roussel. Sponsored by Erik Satie, a group of still younger composers, who believed that music should not be impressive, heroic, or oratorical but simple, direct and sincere, were dubbed "The Six." * These composers decided that by pooling their efforts in a group they could obtain performances of their music more easily than if they worked independently.

The aim of the composers during this postwar period was *originality* at any price. For a time they discarded the classic laws of form, rhythm, and harmony, substituting for them their own formulas and "new" artistic conceptions. Dissonance was the order of the day and engrossed the attention of the creative minds, each trying to outdo the other, though not without protest from the public. The ideal of originality produced all kinds of experiments, including jazz, quarter-tone music, and music for mechanical instruments.[1]

---

* According to Nicolas Slonimsky, *Music Since 1900* (New York: Coleman-Ross Co., 1949), the famous Six was designated as such in an article published in the Paris daily, *Comoedia*, January 16, 1920. The composers Milhaud, Honegger, Poulenc, Auric, Tailleferre, and Durey formed the group.

One of the most enthusiastic champions of the "new" music was Serge Koussevitzky, who in the spring of 1921, after a career as conductor and double-bass soloist in Russia, had come to Paris. In April and May he conducted there a series of three orchestral concerts announced as a Russian Music Festival. In London, he presented another series with the London Symphony Orchestra, conducting on June 10 the first performance of Stravinsky's *Symphony for Wind Instruments.*[2]

Into the cacaphonous, ear-splitting, innovative, stimulating atmosphere that was Paris came Aaron Copland on June 16, 1921. No wonder Goldmark had preferred that his young pupil remain an additional year in New York to pursue the study of classic traditions before allowing the boy to be plunged into this maelstrom! Aaron planned to stay on in Paris at the end of summer school. He felt that Fontainebleau would give him a good chance to get acclimated to French ways as well as to become more familiar with the language. At the same time he could be looking around for a suitable teacher with whom to continue his composition studies.

Stopping at the Hotel Savoy on Rue de Vaugirard, Aaron spent about a week in Paris, before he was due at Fontainebleau, seeing the sights and hearing as many concerts as possible. On June 19, he attended the premiere of Jean Cocteau's ballet, *Les Maries de la Tour Eiffel,* the music of which was composed by *Les Six,* their only work written in collaboration. Aaron was greatly amused at the demonstration on the part of the audience and discovered at first hand the seriousness with which the Parisians took their music—something to be fought for, or against. What he remembers best of those first days in Paris was a performance of Milhaud's new ballet, *l'Homme et son desir.* The audience whistled its disapproval.

June 24 found Aaron at the Fontainebleau School, not far from Paris. It was the only regular music school he ever attended, and he remained there only three months.

The school was housed in a very ornate and decorative palace formerly occupied by the Bourbons. Aaron, however, was more conscious of Napoleon's occupancy during the First Empire, since all of the books in the vast library were marked with a gilt *N*. The girl students lived at the palace and the boys outside, but they had their meals together, dormitory style. Behind the palace were beautiful gardens and beyond, the deep woods of the Fontainebleau forest, where the students often walked.

Aaron's composition teacher, Paul Vidal, a rotund little man, amiable in disposition, proved to be the conservative in musical matters that Duchamp, the artist, had predicted. In addition, Vidal spoke a peculiar French dialect, difficult for the young American to understand after only two years of high-school French. However, Aaron faithfully prepared his daily assignments, though they seemed conventional and routine to him. His work lacked the enthusiasm and excitement of composing which he had thought to find in France.

One of the students, Djina Ostrowska, an attractive young woman who later played second harp with the New York Philharmonic Orchestra, sat next to Aaron in the dining room. The two young musicians daily exchanged news, and it was through Djina that Aaron began to hear about the excellence of a young harmony teacher, Nadia Boulanger. This news at first held little interest for the young man, as he felt he had completed his harmonic studies with Goldmark. Nevertheless, Djina continued her praise of Boulanger's teaching until one day Aaron decided to look in on the class. At that particular lesson Mlle Boulanger was explaining the harmonic structure of one of the scenes from *Boris Godounow*. Aaron had never before seen such enthusiasm and clarity in teaching; he at once suspected he had found his teacher. Yet it was a serious step and Aaron pondered it carefully: "No one to my knowledge had ever before thought of studying composition with a woman. . . . Everyone knows that the world has never produced a first-rate woman composer; so it follows that no woman could possibly hope to teach composition. Moreover, how would it sound to the folks back home?"[3]

Mlle Boulanger taught orchestration as well as harmony at Fontainebleau. Visiting her classes at every opportunity, Aaron gained much from the ideas projected by this dynamic woman. For example, she assigned beginning classes exercises in orchestrating short piano pieces from the classics, and he adopted the practice as his own.

By letter Aaron continued to keep in touch with Goldmark, telling his former teacher of his lack of enthusiasm for the lessons with Vidal and recounting his various European experiences.

In a letter of August 26, 1921, from Woodland, Colorado, where he was to vacation several summers, Goldmark replied:

> I was extremely interested in your nice letter, and in learning all about your experiences and impressions. It was good of you to write me in such detail, and I have gained a pretty good idea of your new life. A first European trip is a thing never to be forgotten—especially when taken at an impressionable age. I am sure it will broaden you and be of great value to you, particularly if you make use of all your faculties to absorb and digest—even outside of music.
>
> Paris is indeed a marvelous place and I often look back for its many attractions. As to the school—you will probably have to wait until the end of the session to take stock of what you have really gained. But as you say, it is only a preparation for the year you are to have abroad. You are indeed fortunate that your parents are willing to grant you this. I shall be eager to know how you are going to put it in. I hope, above all things, you will continue along the lines of acquiring a solid technique in composition, so that you may be able to express yourself with confidence, along the lines [toward which] your talent and your inclinations may lead you. I hope you will make some more progress in the Sonata form. Don't get to despise this, even if you should fall into the hands of some radicals. There is no preparation like it—if you once master it—for doing anything you like afterwards. . . .
>
> Drop me a line whenever you feel like it. It will always be welcome. With all good wishes for your welfare and success, I am
>
> Sincerely,
> Your friend and teacher
> RUBIN GOLDMARK*

---

* The Goldmark letters were made available to this study through the kindness of Mr. Copland.

At the Fontainebleau graduation concert in September, Aaron gave the first performance of the piano piece, "The Cat and the Mouse," written in 1920 while studying with Goldmark. Jacques Durand, the French publisher, was present at the concert and offered the young American five hundred francs (approximately $35) for the world rights to this work, with a promise of immediate publication. Copland was not only delighted to accept the $35 but he also felt exceedingly complimented that the publisher of Debussy's works found merit in his own short piano piece.

On September 23, at the Salle Gaveau in Paris, students of the American Conservatory at Fontainebleau presented a concert for the benefit of l'Association Nationale des Anciens Élèves du Conservatoire de Musique et de Déclamation. In the concert Aaron performed several of his piano works, including his third "Sonnet" and "Trois Esquisses: amertume, pensif, and jazzy" (listed among his "Juvenilia" in Appendix I), and "The Cat and the Mouse." In addition, Miss MacAlister sang his "Melodie Chinoise" (later renamed "Old Poem"), accompanied by the composer. *

Remaining in Paris, Aaron, who had earlier that fall wired Harold Clurman in New York that he had found suitable rooms for the winter, was joined by his friend there. The two students lived at number 207 Boulevard Raspail, off Boulevard du Montparnasse, in a building opposite the Café du Dôme.

Known as the "left bank" (of the Seine), this section of Paris is by tradition one of the two main artistic centers of the city. Sylvia Beach's bookshop, called Shakespeare and Company, was an important gathering place for writers, musicians, and painters. Sylvia Beach was also the publisher of James Joyce's *Ulysses,* and young Aaron used to see Joyce come into the bookshop every evening around six o'clock with the day's proofs tucked under his arm.

Of the French composers, Erik Satie, Florent Schmitt, and Albert Roussel were often encountered. Stravinsky, then the

* From the official program of the concert, provided for this study by John H. Kober.

leading contemporary Russian composer if not the most famous composer in the world, frequently attended concerts of his music or strolled in leisurely fashion along the boulevards.

It was during this time that Ezra Pound, the American poet, "discovered" George Antheil, a young unknown American composer, and was excited enough about him to write a book on his new discovery. The poet attended every performance of Antheil's music, and Copland recalls seeing Pound turn pages at an entire Antheil concert. During these years Antheil lived in an apartment over Sylvia Beach's bookshop.

Ernest Hemingway lived and worked in this section and could always be found at one of the sidewalk cafés, correcting proofs of his early novels. On one occasion Aaron spoke for a time with the celebrated American author. A young Japanese painter, Kuniyoshi, who later became an important figure in the art world, was often around. Virgil Thomson was then living in Paris, having studied organ with Boulanger several years before. Copland believes they first met during these early twenties, perhaps through Antheil.

On December 15, 1921, the Paris edition of the New York *Herald* noted that Stanley Avery of Minneapolis and Aaron Copland of Brooklyn, each of whom had competed for the Prix de Paris at the Institut de Paris, had received honorable mention; but the prize, the grand award in composition for students of the American Conservatory of Music at Fontainebleau, was not given that year. The jury was composed of Blair Fairchild, the American composer; Francis Casadesus, director of the American Conservatory of Fontainebleau; Charles-Marie Widor, Max d'Ollone, Paul Fauchet, Marcel Samuel-Rousseau, and Jean Gallon. The problem presented was the composition of an allegro for string quartet on a theme by Paul Vidal.

Regarding Copland's composition, the *Herald* critic, on the following day, expressed himself thus:

> Mr. Copland gave the problem the fuller development. In straying a little he perhaps less rigorously realized the intention of the problem, but he gave himself the opportunity to show the varied and original character of his talent. Mr. Copland

is very obviously a follower of the modern school. . . . He yielded somewhat to the temptation to favor the first violin to the diminution of the other parts. The result is that while his work is perhaps more appealing than that of Mr. Avery, it is a little less valuable as a solution of the academic problem proposed.

Meanwhile, Aaron, after doing considerable thinking about the matter, became reconciled to the idea of studying composition with a woman. He visited Mlle Boulanger in the fall and asked her to accept him as a pupil. She was about thirty-four years old at the time, and Aaron was her first full-fledged American composition student. Regarding his teacher, Copland has said that she possesses two qualities that make her unique: "her consuming love for music, and. . . . her ability to inspire a pupil with confidence in his own creative powers. Add to this an encyclopedic knowledge of every phase of music past and present, an amazing critical perspicacity, and a full measure of feminine charm and wit."[4] Elsewhere he has stated that what distinguishes Boulanger from the routine professional musician is her enthusiasm and interest in contemporary music.

Asked recently to cite the most important musical event of his life, Mr. Copland enthusiastically replied: "My introduction to Nadia Boulanger and her acceptance of me as a pupil!" With that statement in mind, let us recall briefly the significant events of this remarkable woman's career.

Nadia Boulanger was born in Paris, of French and Russian parents, both of whom were distinguished musicians. At the age of five she read music fluently. A pupil of Fauré and a gifted composer, Nadia won first prizes at the Paris Conservatoire in harmony, counterpoint, fugue, organ, and accompanying. In 1908 she received the second Grand Prix de Rome because, according to Marion Bauer, the committee would not award the first to a woman. "It was ironical, that the first time it was awarded to a woman it was Lili Boulanger, her sister, who received it."*

* From a letter sent from Peterborough, N.H. to the author dated June 15, 1950.

After Lili had won the first Prix de Rome, Nadia voluntarily stopped composing and devoted herself completely to the guidance of her sister's career. Lili's untimely death in 1918 at the age of twenty-four was a tragedy from which Nadia never quite recovered. Time has mellowed her feeling of personal tragedy, though she devoutly believes that the world lost a musical genius in the death of her sister.[5]

Every Wednesday afternoon, except in the month of March, Nadia had a get-together of all her pupils in her apartment. An international group, the students met to sing Bach cantatas (to develop sight-reading) and to familiarize themselves with other choral music. Occasionally the guests included a distinguished artist, composer, or conductor, to whom the students were introduced. Afterwards, in the dining room, Madame Boulanger (Nadia's mother), sitting at the head of the table looking very regal, poured tea from a samovar.

That she has produced so many excellent contemporary composers without having herself composed since 1913 remains another paradox in the phenomenon of Mlle Boulanger's esteemed position in the world of music today.

Aaron's composition lessons were in the late afternoon, from five until about seven o'clock. Clurman used to join him at Boulanger's apartment and the two boys would dine together at some Boulevard restaurant, afterwards attending a concert or the theater (Clurman's interest). Over an apéritif Clurman usually asked Aaron what he had learned at his lesson, and the young man could always tell him quite clearly and accurately everything that had happened.

Aaron studied composition, orchestration, and score-reading with Boulanger. If she felt a pupil needed more practice in the established forms, she would say, "Don't you think you would like to write a Passacaglia?" rather than the usual pedantic, "Next week bring in a Passacaglia!"

Orchestration was studied in class with other private students who met frequently. At various sessions of these group classes a competent flautist, oboist, clarinetist, or other orchestral player would be present to demonstrate the timbre and individual characteristics of his particular instrument. The following week's assignment would then be for each student to compose a short piece for the instrument which had been demonstrated.

In score-reading it was Mlle Boulanger's practice to place an unfamiliar score on the piano and, no matter how slowly the student read it, he was required to proceed to the very end. She also spent a great deal of time in analyzing scores with her pupils from the standpoint of harmony, rhythm, counterpoint, and form. Aaron frequently found a movement from a Mahler symphony, one he had never seen before, on the piano rack in front of him, and he had to play it through to the very last note. Boulanger constantly reminded her students, "Take the musical scores with you when you go to a concert or the opera. Study the music as you hear it. Listen to the same work over and over again, until you know all of the music, every little phrase."

Though Aaron did certain exercises in composing during the day, he preferred to do most of his creative work at night. He also practiced piano seriously several hours a day, studying the first year with Ricardo Viñes, a Spanish teacher, with whom Poulenc also worked. There was a published collection called *Album des 6*, a work Aaron spent considerable time in studying. He was also especially fond of practicing Ravel's *Tombeau de Couperin* and continually looked up new music of all nations, reading and playing it.

With the intellectual stimulus of the "new" music occupying the daytime hours, Aaron turned to the quiet of night for working out his own compositions. If the music flowed out steadily, he often worked late into the night. Aaron did, and still does, all of his composing at the piano, a practice shared by Chopin, Stravinsky, and many other composers.

During the fall of 1921 Aaron completed *Four Motets* for a chorus of mixed voices, *a cappella*. The text, taken from the Bible, was arranged by the composer. Without titles, the tempo markings are indicated thus: *Adagio ma non troppo; Allegro (molto ritmico); Molto adagio;* and *Vivo*. Modal in their linear structure (Hypomixolydian, Phrygian, Mixolydian, and Hypodorian melody respectively), which lends an archaic-modern charm to the short work, contrapuntal devices that are effectively used in the *Motets* are ostinato accompanying figures, imitation, stretto, and open fifth cadences.

Boulanger liked the *Motets* enough to have them sung frequently in class. According to Arthur Berger, she conducted their first performance in Paris, February, 1937.[6] However, a letter from Boulanger to young Copland in the fall of 1924 (see Chapter IV), reveals that she had at that time conducted the *Motets* in a concert of American works at Fontainebleau, thirteen years earlier than the Paris performance.

Koussevitzky, now back in Paris, announced a series of four concerts on Thursday evenings at the Opéra, beginning November 10. Called "Concerts Symphoniques Koussevitzky," the series contained a repetition of Prokofieff's *Scythian Suite*, the first performance of *Horace Victorieux* by Honegger, Russian music not well known in France, as well as standard works from the German and French repertoire.[7] Aaron and Clurman attended the entire series, but it was the aggressive new music which most interested them. Elsewhere they heard *Pelléas et Mélisande* at the Opéra-Comique, Stravinsky's *Concertino* for string quartet performed by the Flonzaleys, a jazz concert arranged by Jean Wiéner, and Bloch's *Schelomo* performed at the Concerts Colonne.

Wishing to see as many European countries as possible during his stay abroad, Aaron decided to spend the Christmas holidays in London. His father, whose first journey away from home had included a visit to that English city, had urged him to visit London when he could spare the time from his studies. Aaron visited Herbert Elwell, with whom he had crossed from New York to Le Havre the previous June, who was now residing in London. The two young Americans spent their time sight-seeing, there being little or no music performed because of the Christmas holidays.

On January 10, 1922, Aaron experienced his first professional Paris première at the Salle des Agriculteurs, when two of his early songs, "Old Poem" and "Pastorale," were sung by Charles Hubbard. The American tenor was accompanied by "the clever young American composer," as Aaron was designated by the New York *Herald*. In a program of forty short songs, by twenty-three authors, "mostly of the advance guard," the *Herald* reported that "Mr. Copland's work may be said to have won the honors of the evening and both author and singer received an ovation at the end of 'Pastorale.' "[8]

Maurice Senart had accepted "Old Poem" and Aaron's recently completed "Passacaglia" for publication earlier in the year. Surely, Aaron's family would now be convinced that he was on the way to being a successful composer!

In a letter to John Kober in Brooklyn, dated February 3, 1922, Aaron gave his friend some insight into his activities in Paris:

> I can't think of doing anything but throwing myself on your mercy. Long ago, I received your first letter. It arrived just at the time of the concert in Paris (recital of Fontainebleau students, September 23) and I had been thinking of answering ever since but one thing and another prevented me. . . . I have been fortunate enough to have had a piano piece published by Durand's and will send you an autographed copy in the near future. I am also enclosing a copy of a program on which two of my songs were sung and which I accompanied. I intend to stay in Europe for more than a year yet, and am continuing my studies, in composition and piano. The summer I shall probably spend in Berlin and Vienna, and come back to Paris next winter. I spent Christmas vacation in London and intend to go to Italy (Rome, Venice and Milan) for the Easter. All this must sound very far away from Norwood Ave., but when one is over here it is best to take in as much as one can, I think.
>
> Naturally, I attend many concerts. The French play a great deal of Beethoven, and never any of the Tschaikovsky or Brahms Symphonies. I have never been able to understand why they don't like the latter two composers. At the Opéra Comique I have heard Mozart's *Don Juan*, Lalo's *Roi d'Ys* and Paul Dukas' *Ariane et Barbe Bleue*. The French also play a great deal of Debussy and Ravel and it is amusing for me to think of the time when we used to imagine they were both *very* modern.

During December 1921 and the end of January 1922, Aaron completed his "Passacaglia" for piano. Consisting of an eight-measure theme (or ground bass), in G sharp minor, and eight variations, the "Passacaglia" is an effective work for solo in serious vein. In spite of the skill and imagination evidenced in the handling of the different variations and the various contrapuntal devices contained therein, as well as the excellent writing for the piano, the "Passacaglia" is a work not unified in style. Its diatonic and chromatic harmonies as well as its style of piano writing show the influences of Schumann, Franck, Fauré, and a Scotch folk flavor. Yet it points the way to a certain grandeur and expansiveness which are to prove characteristic of his orchestral works up to 1929.

In addition to attending Koussevitzky's spring season of concerts, Aaron and Clurman heard a number of other important first performances elsewhere that season, including Milhaud's *Creation of the World,* which caused riots in Paris. Schoenberg's atonal *Pierrot Lunaire,* which Aaron heard for the first time, received a quieter, if not more enthusiastic, reception from the general public. Clurman recalls Aaron's whispering to him at the Schoenberg concert, which Milhaud conducted, "That's the kind of music I want to write!" At the Opéra Comique the two young Americans heard *Pénélope,* an opera by Gabriel Fauré, and *Ariane et Barbe Bleue* by Paul Dukas. Clurman recalls that, while hearing the latter opera, Aaron was so engrossed with the reading of the score that he hardly even glanced at what was happening on the stage.

The two Americans frequently attended foreign-made films, particularly German movies, whose literary and dramatic content they admired. It was a German film that was to prove the source of inspiration for Copland's first ballet, *Grohg.* Soon after seeing the film *Nos Feratu,* Aaron brought to Boulanger some short piano pieces reflecting a macabre and supernatural atmosphere. His teacher, after hearing Copland play them, immediately asked, "Why don't you make a ballet out of this material?" Acting on Boulanger's suggestion, Aaron began to write the ballet, a task in which he was to be engaged for a period of three years (1922-1925) in various European countries and in America.

In April, Aaron sent his parents and Goldmark copies of "The Cat and the Mouse," his very first published work. His parents, pleased with the success of their son's Paris performances of his works, happy to receive his first publication and to learn that two other works were in process of publication, decided that his progress in composition warranted an extension of his stay abroad for at least another year. About Goldmark's reaction to the publication we shall learn later.

Wishing to broaden his knowledge of Europe and to become acquainted with the various countries, Aaron made a short trip to Italy during the Easter vacation. He spent about two weeks there, a few days each in Milan, Florence, and Rome, attending concerts whenever possible. He was accompanied by Melville Smith, also a student of Boulanger at that time and now direc-tor of the Longy School in Cambridge, Mass. The two young Americans traveled together as far as Florence, where Smith decided to prolong his stay while Aaron went to Rome. Aaron lodged near the Piazza di Spagna and spent five days in the Holy City, viewing its religious and historic art treasures. From Rome he sent a postal card to John Kober, with the following message:"Here I am touring thru Italy. I have already been 4 days at Milano, where I heard *Mefistofele* conducted by Tos-canini at La Scala Opera House. Rome seems very fascinating. I received your letter while still at Paris and thank you for it. Regards to your family."*

Wishing to see something of Germany and musical conditions there, Aaron decided it would be helpful to him artistically to spend three or four months in that country. After all, Goldmark was an exponent of the German musical tradition (Vienna School). Not knowing anyone there, he wrote to his former teacher for advice as to whom to see. Goldmark's letter of May 16 proved most helpful.

> I was very glad indeed to receive your last letter and to learn of your fine success. I received the Chat et Souris piece and I

* Dated March 30, 1922.

think it is very good—clever, musicianly and not too extreme
for my taste. The fact that you are bringing out other things
ought also to be a great help to you when you come back. I can
see that your sojourn abroad is doing you a world of good in
every way. I hope it will keep up thus. I was much interested
in all that you wrote about conditions in Paris and elsewhere.
I presume your Italian trip was a revelation to you. My sojourn
there twenty years ago was a truly wonderful thing to me.

I think it is a good idea for you to get an impression of
German musical life etc. I haven't been over there in so long
that I hardly know to whom to recommend you. I am enclosing
two letters—one to Schnabel in Berlin, and the other to my
cousin Karpath in Vienna. The latter is a very prominent music
critic. Either of the above gentlemen will gladly give you advice
and you need not hesitate to call on them. Let me hear from
you, whenever you feel like it.

Armed with the two letters of introduction from Goldmark,
early in June Aaron went to Berlin. He found lodging at the
house of Frau Jurges, Brücken Allee 17, which remained his
residence until the end of September.

If Paris, the citadel of the victors of World War I, was the
epitome of European intellectual stimuli and creative achievement, Berlin, the city of the vanquished, was its direct antithesis.
Germany was not only exhausted economically and militarily,
but its creative springs also appeared depleted.

One day Aaron presented himself, along with the Goldmark
letter of introduction, to Artur Schnabel, the famed German
pianist. Schnabel received the young American most courte-
ously and wished to be of help to him. However, he was in the
depths of despair and saw no hope at that time for Berlin's artistic future.

Aaron began to feel that Berlin was no place for a young composer. If he remained longer he might also be engulfed in these
artistic doldrums. After all, he seemed to be getting from his
lessons with Boulanger what he wanted. Clearly he was not impressed with what he saw of the German "Kultur." With such
thoughts uppermost in his mind, he again wrote Goldmark, who
answered promptly, on August 21:

Your good, most interesting letter reached me in my mountain retreat. . . . in the shadow of Pike's Peak, where I have a most quiet, healthy and restful life. I was glad to have news again and to know of all your doings. You are certainly making the best of your European sojourn. I think it was very wise of you to go into Germany for a while, even tho' its musical lustre may be diminished for one who has sat at the feet of *Les Six*. But then one can become tolerant, when one remembers what that country did in preparation for *Les Six*. And it is a good thing for a well-rounded musician to have experience in many lands and absorb what they can give him. But on one point, you need not apologize, my dear fellow. You cannot trouble me with anything you say about Berlin. I never liked that city. I studied and spent two years in Vienna, and that's quite a different story. It was the Vienna of Brahms and Hans Richter, and Bruckner and a host of distinguished musicians. . . .

I am glad that you met Schnabel and that he was so courteous. You are certainly old enough and advanced enough in your studies, to choose your own teacher with intelligence, and so, if you feel you are getting what you want from Nadia Boulanger, you are absolutely right in sticking to her. I see with pleasure that you are working hard, and along various lines. I shall be still more interested in seeing the compositions themselves. I hope you can stay abroad as long as possible to round out your education. For you are going to have a sinking feeling artistically when you hit Brooklyn again. (Not that B. is any worse than many other places.) . . .

Aaron returned to Paris in October to begin his second season's work with Boulanger, more convinced than ever that she was the right teacher for him.

The second winter the two American boys, Copland and Clurman, lived near the Porte d'Orleans on Villa d'Alesia Street in the upper floor of a private house owned by a singing teacher.

This season indicated that young Copland, both from the standpoint of performance and of writing new musical works, was making steady progress as a composer.

In January, 1923, the Société Musicale Indépendante presented the first performance of his "Passacaglia," played by the pianist Daniel Ericourt. Dedicated "à Mademoiselle Nadia

Boulanger," this work had been published the year before
by Maurice Senart. Truly the young composer was becoming a professional, since he could point to a published work as
having its first performance.

During this year Copland completed three musical scores:
"Rondino" for string quartet; a song entitled "As It Fell upon a
Day"; and a section of his ballet *Grohg*, entitled *Cortège Ma-
cabre*, the latter for orchestra.

"Rondino," completed in the spring of 1923, is based on a
theme which spells the name of Gabriel Fauré, with appropriate substitutions for letters not found in the musical alphabet.
Scored for string quartet, Copland's first (survived) writing for
this combination of instruments, "Rondino" adheres to the following sectional design: A-A-B-C-C-B-A-coda of A material.

A first example of a rather timid use of polytonal harmonies
occurs in the return of the B theme. The polytonal harmonies
are heard between the outer voices (C major implications in
Violin I, C sharp major sustained in the cello), while the inner
voices play, in canonic imitation, a derivative of the A theme in
still another tonality (Example 1). Although somewhat tight
in form and strongly influenced by Fauré, the little work contains an American rhythmic flavor.

Ex. 1

During the Easter vacation in April, Aaron spent a week in
Brussels. In the capital city of the Belgians, the young traveler

was very much impressed with the king's palace, the Théâtre de la Monnaie, which produced the standard operas in magnificent productions, and the Conservatoire Royal. At the last-named place, he heard several remarkable organ concerts played by leading Belgian organists. Thus Aaron's brief visit to Brussels presented another facet of European culture to the impressionable American.

Returning to Paris, Aaron put the finishing touches to his first orchestral score, *Cortège Macabre* (from the ballet *Grohg*), on which he had been at work since early in 1922. A ballet in one act, its origin is indicated on the title page of the score: "Story by Aaron Copland in collaboration with H. E. Clurman." It is scored for full orchestral instrumentation as well as two harps and piano; the characters of the ballet are listed as the following: Grohg, a sorcerer; A young girl; A streetwalker; An opium eater; An adolescent; Major-domo; Servitors of Grohg. The action of the *Cortège* reveals an elaborate stage retinue composed of the servitors of Grohg offering an array of coffins to their master.

Beginning with a short Introduction, which invokes a mood of necromancy, the *Cortège* is significant because it contains the first example of Copland's use of polyrhythms as such. In a section devoted to a brilliant manipulation of polyrhythms used as a kind of ostinato, or ground rhythm, the intensity of the servitors' dance around the coffins is heightened. Copland, realizing the difficulties of the innovation to conductors and orchestras, made the following note at the bottom of the score page at the beginning of this section: "N.B. To facilitate the task of the conductor, a common bar line has been retained in this polyrhythmic section. The small notes indicate the precise rhythm desired" (Example 2).

Ex. 2

While *Cortège Macabre* shows an uncanny instinct for appropriate orchestration as well as a dramatic feeling for a gruesome, fearsome story, it is not a well-fashioned piece of music. In an effort to tighten up its loosely woven structure and make it acceptable, the author has made many cuts throughout the work. An example of Copland's consistent growth from the string quartet "Rondino" to full orchestra, *Cortège Macabre* is important as the forerunner of several successful ballets which Copland has to his credit: *Hear Ye! Hear Ye!*, *Billy the Kid*, *Rodeo*, and *Appalachian Spring*. These works were to place him, without any question, as America's foremost composer of the ballet.

A feature of the Paris 1923 spring season of concerts was Koussevitzky's performance of Ravel's transcription of Moussorgsky's piano pieces, *Pictures from an Exhibition*. Prior to the *Pictures première*, one of Boulanger's assignments to Aaron's class had been to orchestrate the opening bars of the Moussorgsky work. For that reason Aaron had an additional curiosity regarding the first performance, which he attended with Clurman. As Koussevitzky played the opening bars of this work, Aaron turned to his friend and whispered excitedly, "That's the way I orchestrated it!"

In July, Aaron and Clurman went to Vienna to spend the summer, a "foreign" trip that proved most fruitful for Copland. In Vienna they found rooms with Frau Steinhof at Number IX Hörlgasse.

From August 2 to 7 both young men journeyed to Salzburg to attend the first festival of the International Society for Contemporary Music. How excited the two Americans were to be "in" on the birth of international contemporary music! How thrilled they were to see many of the world's leading composers in attendance or performing their music at the festival!

Among the composers whose works were presented were Alban Berg, Schoenberg, Bartók, Florent Schmitt, Ernst Křenek, Honegger, Malipiero, Busoni, Milhaud, Poulenc, and Hindemith.

Regarding the August 6 concert Copland recalls: "I remember being mystified by the sounds of a quartet rehearsing in the hotel room adjoining mine, making sounds I couldn't quite recognize. Later, at the evening concert, I realized it was the Alois Hába quarter-tone quartet. Kodaly's unaccompanied cello *Sonata,* and Ravel's *Duo-Sonata* for violin and cello, both made impressions as instrumental tours de force."

Returning to Vienna after the Salzburg festival, Aaron found a short note (in English) from Boulanger, in answer to an earlier letter of his in which he had reported his progress on *Grohg.* Her reply, on black-bordered stationery, undated, reads as follows:

Les Maisonnettes
Gargenville (S.O.)

My dear Copland:

I am so stupid after having orchestrated five hundred pages, that I have not the smallest hope to be able to write you something which justifies the lost of time you accept to read it.

But, I will first thank you for your interesting letter and after, as an egoist I am (as we all are, no doubt) ask you to bring me a little new works you was interested with (for hundred or hundred and twenty francs).* This manner to be curious of music for a certain price, but no more, pleases one infinitely, it is the true manner to determine our intellectual judgement!

Here was the summer un-musical—but in a certain measure, very nice—I hoped to read very much things I don't know well, but . . . orchestrate was the first obligation and the last.

I am more impatient than I can tell to see your ballet. I would you are finishing it soon, I expect so much of him—and——

I must say that we would also be very glad to see you again. No sentimental at all, but truly sincere, what is much more ridiculous, is it not?

Give my best compliments to your friend [Clurman] and be sure, dear Copland, of my deep personal and musical affection.

NADIA BOULANGER

* Boulanger, in a typical display of French frugality, insists that Copland is not to spend more than eight or nine dollars for some new German music for her to examine.

During the same summer in Vienna, in addition to his arduous work on the ballet, Aaron wrote the song "As It Fell upon a Day," in reality, an exercise in orchestration. One of the assignments given to the orchestration class by Boulanger, after an instrumental demonstration, had been to write a piece for flute and clarinet. On his own initiative Aaron decided to add a soprano-voice part to his composition. Presenting a diversion from the large orchestration of *Grohg*, this song, with only three lines available, requires that every note must sound and appear indispensable.

The setting of a poem by the seventeenth century English poet Richard Barnefield, "As It Fell upon a Day" is a twentieth century madrigal, which through its text and its use of modal intervals and harmonies invokes a sixteenth or seventeenth century English flavor.

The design of the song is loosely the following: Introduction: A-B-C-B-C, with the introductory material used again as a coda. In the first part, written in the Mixolydian mode, every four bars of the madrigal is interrupted by an instrumental interlude. In the middle section the voice imitates the nightingale, a practice characteristic of the early madrigal writers, which, in turn, is imitated by the flute.

Recalling that the first (timid) example of polytonality in a published score was found in "Rondino," a more deliberate and self-assured use of that harmonic development is found where the voice and flute are written in E major, while the clarinet answers in B flat major (Example 3). The final cadence contains the polyharmonies of B flat and E flat.

Ex. 3

A remarkable fact about "As It Fell upon a Day," the earlier *Four Motets,* and the two choral works which follow in the jazz period is that all of these works reflect Copland's *instinctive* use of the old modes, no doubt emanating from his Russian-Jewish origin.* The composer, himself, acknowledges that the above-mentioned works contain a modal flavor, sometimes in conjunction with other contrasting elements.

Nor did Boulanger introduce Copland to the principles of polytonality. As has been noted, much of the new music heard in Paris during the 'twenties, especially that of Milhaud, contained polytonal harmonies. On the basis of what he heard, plus his desire to experiment with all new musical developments, Copland adapted polytonal principles to his own use. In forging ahead "on his own" in these and in other directions, Aaron again exercised his unquenchable thirst to find out everything new for himself, a quality first in evidence during his years of study with Goldmark.

Unsuspected sources frequently offer a creative artist material which he can adapt to his own particular purposes. We have already seen how young Copland, in listening to and studying music containing polyharmonies and polyrhythms, appropriated these new techniques in his latest compositions. His recent contact with quarter-tone music (Alois Hába's quartet performed at the Salzburg Festival) shows its first reflection in his music at the end of the second movement in the *Dance Symphony.* Thus the creative mind is always on the alert for new sounds, ideas, or techniques, some of which may, through contact with the artist's subconscious cerebrations, emerge from him as expressions of stylistic individuality.

Aaron's contact with jazz, as presented in Vienna's popular bars, offers yet another instance of how a composer may cull or select from all types of experiences specific materials which may

* In reply to the question: "Was the study of the old modes an important aspect of Boulanger's teaching?" Copland replied: "My generation didn't learn about modes. All of this is a recent development. I have never consciously written in a mode." To him a mode is "simply music on the white keys." (Ernest Bloch has been influential in America in reviving the old modes as tools of composition.)

serve his creative genius. Though Aaron had been in contact with American popular music since childhood, he has said that it was in a popular bar in Vienna, in 1923, that jazz struck him as brand new in its potentiality:

> The impression of jazz one receives in a foreign country is totally unlike the impression of such music heard in one's own country. Perhaps, because a person is more objectively observant in a foreign country, or because the setting was so completely unlike anything I had seen in America, nevertheless, when I heard jazz played in Vienna, it was like hearing it for the first time. It was then that I first began to realize the potentiality of jazz material for use in serious music.

Aaron was immediately to put his new conception of jazz to use in the last movement of *Grohg*. In the "Finale" of that work are planted the seeds which were to bud forth in a new style, in works designated as belonging to the Jazz Period (see Chapter IV).

After spending the most stimulating summer of their European sojourn in Vienna and at the Salzburg Festival, the two young men returned to Paris in October. What an education it had been to Aaron to come in contact with the advanced musical thought advocated by the different European schools, to listen to new works performed and then debated over by the assembled musicians! Ideas began to take shape in his mind as to what America's part in international contemporary music should contribute. Creatively the summer had been productive, for Aaron brought back to Paris his completed chamber music song and many new pages of *Grohg*.

The third winter, Aaron and Clurman had rooms with a mulatto family at Number 66 Boulevard Pasteur. The husband and father was a judge in the French court. In applying for rooms, the two Americans had been asked if they had any racial prejudice, to which both boys quickly answered "No." The family behaved so discreetly as to give the impression that it never noticed the two American occupants. This conduct both students appreciated exceedingly and it was something they were to miss on their return to America—the European respect for a sense of privacy.

On February 6, 1924, Copland's new song, "As It Fell upon a Day," had its first performance by Ada MacLeish, wife of the poet Archibald MacLeish, at the Société Musicale Indépendante. The concert took place in the Salle Pleyel and included works by Oswald Guerra, Nicolas Tcherepnine, Jean Déré, Albert Roussel, Gabriel Fauré, and two young Americans, Aaron Copland and Leo Sowerby.

The Paris press enthusiastically received Copland's new work, with the *Courrier Musicale* reporting:

It is sufficiently rare to be worthy of remark, the case of the young American musician, who, at an age when his compatriots are still imbued with the Brahmsian religion, deliberately gets away from it and writes in the neoclassic style which seems to attract the best part of the young French generation. Written with a clever, firm and bold pen, this song is full of ingenious and charming details: it, alone, permits us to hope for great things from the author.[9]

Raymond Charpentier, critic for *Commoedia*, stated that Copland's song "shows a sensitive, flexible nature and a technique which is already highly finished. With so few instruments," he continued, "a composer cannot bluff; he must play fair. Therefore every effect is doubly meritorious. . . . With his song, M. Copland has conquered, at the first shot, his diplomas at Paris. I have, besides. . . . his manuscript of four *Motets* . . . which offer like qualities and show that [the song] is no exception."[10]

While in France, in addition to developing his musical gifts in composition and pursuing the further study of the piano, Copland discovered a new talent, the ability to write clear, concise, interesting, and informative musical criticism. Besides Robert Schumann, whose reviews are an important contribution in the development of musical criticism, other composers who were also active as critics are Weber, Liszt, Wagner, Hugo Wolf, and Debussy.

Thus Copland had ample artistic precedent to support his own bent in that direction. The discovery of this new talent, of almost equal artistic stature with his creative gifts, was to augur well in spreading the fame and understanding of the young composer's own music specifically and of American music in general. During this year he was to write and publish two critiques: "Gabriel Fauré, a Neglected Master," which appeared in the *Musical Quarterly*, October, 1924; and "George Antheil," which was published in the *League of Composers' Review*, issue of January, 1925. Because of the number of the critiques (approximately sixty-five) written between 1924 and 1955 and their importance in a study of the composer's artistic development, the final chapter of this study, entitled "Critical Works and Influence," has been devoted to them.

The spring series of orchestral concerts was a fitting climax to Koussevitzky's four years of conducting in Paris. He would soon be leaving for America, where he had been recently engaged to conduct the famed Boston Symphony Orchestra during the coming season. He left his French public in a final blaze of glory with such provocative new music as Honegger's *Pacific 231*, Prokofieff's discordant, rhythmic *Sept, ils sont sept*, and an entire Stravinsky concert with the composer as soloist in the first performance of his *Concerto for Piano.*[11] Clearly Koussevitzky believed in the European composers of the twentieth century. Would he believe in the music of American composers when he became a part of the American culture? That was yet to be seen.

It was during the spring of 1924 that Boulanger, recognizing that young Copland was now ready to launch out on his chosen career as composer, asked Koussevitzky to look at some compositions by one of her promising American students. The conductor consented and invited other friends of his, including Prokofieff, to examine the music while Copland was present. Aaron took his recently completed first orchestral work, *Cortège Macabre*, which he played on the piano for Koussevitzky's hearing. The conductor liked the work and told Copland he would perform it the following season with the Boston Symphony Orchestra. Prokofieff commented, according to Moses Smith, "too many bassi ostinati in it."[12] On returning to his room, Aaron told Clurman, "Prokofieff picked out a phrase that he particularly liked. 'Now that is quite good,' he said. I was amused because that particular phrase resembled one of his own [Prokofieff's]." That Copland's introduction to Koussevitzky was an important step in his development as a composer is shown in the following chapters. Koussevitzky became young Copland's friend and artistic mentor in America, conducting many first performances of Copland's works.

Mlle Boulanger's instrument was the organ and towards the end of Copland's stay she was invited to America for some appearances with the New York and Boston Symphony Orchestras. Deciding to *première* a new work by an American, and believing implicitly in young Copland's musical gifts, she invited him to provide her with such a work. Copland agreed to do so, though up to that time he had written only one work in an extended form, had only a "passing acquaintance" with the organ as a solo instrument, and had never heard a note of his own orchestration![13] During the month of May he made some preliminary sketches of the organ symphony.

Ballet *Grohg* (from which is derived *Dance Symphony*)*

Thirty-five minutes in length, *Grohg* is Copland's most ambitious undertaking, as well as the outstanding achievement of his Paris study years. In spite of the fact that the orchestration was not completed until the summer of 1925, at the MacDowell Colony, its inclusion in this chapter is both chronological and important because of the trends it foretells in Copland's development.

* *cf.* pp. 133–134 and 134f of this volume. The ballet *Grohg*, as such, is not available.

Despite the fact that the *Dance Symphony* is played through without any separating pauses, each of the three dances is in sharp contrast to the preceding. The movements are connected by fragments of transitional material.

Dance No. 1, Allegro, "Dance of an Adolescent," is very French in flavor and comprises three principal sections: these disclose charming polyharmonies, a flowing flute melody accompanied by two harps, a four-voiced canonic imitation between trumpets and trombones, and, following a climax, a return to the introductory material.

Dance No. 2, Andante moderato, 3/4, is the "Dance of a Young Girl Who Moves in a Dream." Near the end of a viola solo there appears an interesting, if not entirely accurate, direction from the composer (Example 4). The direction points to Copland's more accurate symbol, to flat a tone, a quarter step, used in a work written during the jazz period. (See "Ukelele Serenade," Chapter IV.) Further, a more extensive use of flattening a tone a quarter step is found in the trio, *Vitebsk,* a work from the Abstract Period, in which the composer uses still another symbol. Nevertheless, these various treatments of quarter tones all stem from the quotation cited below.

Ex. 4

If the first movement of the *Dance Symphony* is sparkling, elegant, and pointed and the second movement lyrical and sustained, the third movement is feverish and exciting, characterized by violence and syncopation. Designated by the composer as a "Finale," in this movement all of Grohg's servitors and his various victims mock at him. With the tempo marking *Allegro vivo,* the initial jazzy motive is treated to a veritable Stravinskian rhythmical tour de force, with such alternating measure signatures as 5/4, 3/4, 3/8. While the violins, English horn, and xylophone execute a sustained trill, the jazzy first motive is heard *fortissimo* in the wood winds and piano (Example 5).

Ex. 5

It is in the Finale that Copland, by his use of jazz materials (a theme and polyrhythms),* discovered one of the important elements of his musical style, thus pointing the way to *Music for the Theatre*. In that work the major and minor thirds, resulting (as here) from a polytonal harmonic relationship, become a manifestation of the composer's jazz melodic style when applied to jazz materials. The Finale foretells a period of approximately three years in which Copland is to devote himself to experiments in jazz.

In the spring of 1924, when it came time for Aaron to return home, a farewell party was given for him by his fellow students at Boulanger's apartment, on the Rue Ballu, where she still lives. The climax of the party was the performance of a four-hand arrangement of *Grohg,* played by the young composer and his teacher.

With the creations of the Paris study years packed carefully in his traveling bags, Aaron, with Clurman, sailed for New York about the middle of June.

Thus was effected the transition from a student composer to an artist who had received European recognition but who had yet to convince his own countrymen of his musical stature.

---

* Regarding Boulanger's attitude to Copland's first uses of polyrhythms, he recently communicated the following: "She made much of their appearance in my own work, and rather pointed them out to me as one of the new features of music in the '20's, different from what the typical young French student would be producing. She showed great interest in my rhythmic experiments, and made me more conscious of my own potentialities as a rhythmicist."

IV

First Style Period (French-Jazz)
New York, Boston, Peterborough, Europe,
The American West
(1924-1929)

BECAUSE of the number of Copland's musical works from 1924
to 1929, and because they point in two opposite directions, I
shall divide the French-Jazz Period into two parts: the first part,
"Jazz Idiom," including his works from 1924 to 1927; and the
second part, "Experimentation and Recapitulation," his works
from 1927 to 1929.

Nine in number, the jazz-inspired compositions are comprised
of three large works and six smaller pieces, the latter, for the
most part, being offshoots of the former, with the following titles: *Symphony for Organ and Orchestra (First Symphony);*
two short choral works, "The House on the Hill" and "An Immorality"; a chamber orchestra suite, *Music for the Theatre;*
two pieces for violin and piano, "Nocturne" and "Ukelele Serenade"; two piano pieces, "Sentimental Melody" and "Blues";
and *Concerto for Piano and Orchestra.*

The climax of the jazz-style works is the *Concerto for Piano
and Orchestra,* while the peak of the experimental works and,
indeed, of the whole French-Jazz period is the *Symphonic Ode.*
Though the *Ode* reverts to the stylistic manner of Copland's
First Symphony, it also contains elements that are the basis of
a new style, that of Copland's second or "Abstract" period.

Jazz Idiom (1924-1927)

In order to show the jazz ingredients which are the basis of
Copland's style from 1924 to 1927, the characteristics of jazz
must be set forth. In addition to other writers who have contributed to an explanation of jazz, young Copland himself, in a critique entitled "Jazz Structure and Influence," has given us an
early and compact analysis of the new idiom.

Jazz had its origin, Copland surmised, on some Negro's tom-tom in Africa and descended through the spirituals. Ragtime is its closest ancestor, having as its rhythmic foundation the 1-2-3-4 bass in quick tempo. "Over the ragtime bass," he wrote, "is carried invariably one of two rhythms, sometimes both: either the dotted eighth followed by a sixteenth: ♪♪♪, or this most ordinary syncopation: ♫♫♫." [1]

According to Copland, the fox trot was the beginning of modern jazz. The four-quarter bass was considerably slower in pace than in ragtime and was improved by accenting beats on two and four (1-2-3-4). This was combined with another rhythmic element, sometimes (but not always) in the melody and was written thus: ♫♫♫♫. In reality this jazz rhythm is much subtler than that found in the printed arrangements of simple jazz compositions; the correct way of writing it is the following: |♫♫♪♪ ♪♫♪|. "Therefore," explained Copland, "it contains no syncopations; it is instead a rhythm of four quarters split into eight eighths and is arranged thus: 1-2-3: 1-2-3-4-5, or even more precisely: 1-2-3: 1-2-3: 1-2. Put this over the four-quarter bass; and you have the play of two independent rhythms within the space of one measure." Whatever melody is subjected to this treatment comes out "jazzed."

The next step produced polyrhythms, independent rhythms spread over more than one measure or over a series of measures, as typified by the song "Stumbling." Thus the conventional 4/4 fox-trot bass was retained while the melody appeared in 3/4 meter. Copland cited Zez Confrey's "Kitten on the Keys" as an example of the best combination of these rhythms. It was George Gershwin who took most advantage of the discovery made in "Stumbling." Copland was of the opinion that Gershwin's "Fascinating Rhythm" was the most original jazz song composed to that date (1927).

The Charleston rhythm brought about the elimination of the evenly rhythmed bass, at least for the space of a few measures. The Charleston used the upper fox-trot rhythm: 1-2-3:1-2-3-4-5 in the bass as well as the treble.

(Charleston Rhythm)

The unchanging 1-**2**-3-**4** bass was broken in another way by Gershwin in "Clap Yo' Hands," published in 1926. In that song he wrote two measures in 4/4 meter followed by two measures in 3/4 meter. This process was already familiar in the Russian folksong, but it was an advance in jazz, in that it offered a relief from the old relentless 4/4 bass.*

Although polyrhythms have been highly developed among primitive races, in the old English madrigals, and in the works of recent European composers, yet the polyrhythms of jazz are different in quality and effect from all previous uses of them. "The peculiar excitement they produce by clashing two definitely and regularly marked rhythms is unprecedented in occidental music. Its polyrhythm is the real contribution of jazz."

Since jazz, in the hands of American composers, is indigenous and not exotic, as is the case with European composers, Copland believed that it would be traceable more and more frequently in American symphonies and concertos and that its chief influence would be shown in the development of the polyrhythm. "This startling new synthesis," he concluded, "has provided the American composer with an instrument he should appreciate and utilize. . . . It may be the substance not only of his fox trots and Charlestons, but of his lullabies and nocturnes. He may ex-

---

*Copland himself varied 4/4 with 3/4 and even 2/4 rhythms as early as 1920 in the song "Old Poem."

press through it not always gaiety, but love, tragedy, remorse."[2]

Returning to New York about the middle of June, 1924, Aaron went to the new apartment located on President Street, Brooklyn, which his parents, upon their retirement from business, had recently acquired. The older brothers and sisters, who had married in the meantime and now maintained homes of their own, gathered at their parents' apartment to welcome Aaron home and to hear of his travels and studies abroad. The family was impressed with the youngest son and brother, who was already something of a celebrity.

Since Copland's travels and studies up to this point had been made possible by the generosity of his parents, he decided it was time he did something about making a living for himself. Hunting up an old friend, Abraham Ginsberg, violinist, with whom he had played chamber music in earlier years, Aaron found that Ginsberg was looking for a pianist to be the third member of a trio to play in a resort hotel for the summer. Aaron accepted the position immediately, since he could thus combine earning a living with composing.

During the same month, June, 1924, Aaron was delighted to receive a letter from his beloved teacher and friend, Nadia Boulanger. Undated (Mlle Boulanger never dated her correspondence), this letter, as are all of the Boulanger letters quoted here, was indicative of her continued attitude of personal loss over Lili's death six years before; it was written on black-bordered note paper. Bearing the letterhead Les Maisonettes, Gargenville (S. et O.), her letter reads:

My dear Copland:

I do not wish to, nor can I let you leave without thanking you for your confidence, without telling you the value that I attach to it, without reiterating my affection. Years have added to the years bringing you nearer, then making more distant the image that I first had formed of you, for you have very quickly surpassed it [the image] in profoundness and personality. Today I well believe that you can no longer astonish me, although each of your stages of progress is to me such a moving joy— And—you cannot comprehend what that means to me; had I never seen you—your music would even so bring me artistically the same sum of beauty—but, when one has uselessly served what one loves best, it is more than a consolation to see a cherished being realize that which one has renounced. . . . Give me quickly news of the brain child [organ work] that I perhaps was wrong in wanting to operate on so cruelly—but the more I think of it the more it seems to me that having let him have his head, his heart, you wish to give him a body [middle section] that is not his, a theoretic body that would not know how to replace the one that the proportion, and even the character of his head [the beginning] has already determined.

You know that there is nothing but admiration in my insistence —and that, if I am mistaken, and that, remaining faithful to your present plan, you succeed in your first part, there will be no regret mixed with my feeling: I ask only to recognize my error. But how beautiful your piece will have to be to convince me!

Don't jump around too much. Enjoy the charms of the sea— and tell yourself—that Mama and I think of you, dear Copland, with a very profound affection.

NADIA BOULANGER*

After about two weeks with his family, Aaron went to the resort hotel in Milford, Pennsylvania, where, beginning the week end of July 4, he played with the trio. During the forenoon he worked on the organ symphony in the local motion-picture theater, the quietest place in town; afternoons and evenings he played at the hotel.

Aaron, who had agreed to play with the trio until Labor Day, began to worry about finishing the organ piece on time. Deciding that that work, above everything else, must come first, he soon left the hotel to go to the home of his sister, Mrs. Marcus, in Brooklyn, where he could work with greater concentration, remaining with her until he could locate a studio for himself in Manhattan. He planned to support himself by teaching and, at the same time, to finish the orchestration of the new organ work, the sketch of which was now complete.

* The Boulanger letters (in French) were made available by Mr. Copland; English translations by the author.

Aaron's first studio was at 135 West Seventy-fourth Street, where he took occupancy on October 1. His first efforts at teaching were disheartening; he sent out cards announcing himself as a teacher of piano and theory, but no pupils presented themselves.

Meanwhile he had sent the first draft of his organ work to Boulanger for approval under the tentatively suggested title of "Little Symphony." The title page read: "Dedicated to NADIA BOULANGER with admiration. A. C." The work consisted of three movements: Prelude, Scherzo, and Finale.

Boulanger, back in Paris after spending the summer at Gargenville, answered promptly:

> Letter and manuscript by the same post! I can't tell you my joy—the work is so brilliant, so full of music. Impossible to write you in detail, I am more rushed these days—but I must at once thank you profoundly for a dedication to which, I assure you, I attach a value that surpasses in everything obvious questions which, often, give importance to such things—This to me is truly a genuine pride of an artist and the real joy of a friend— understand with what sincerity I tell you this.
>
> I am writing by the same mail to Mr. Damrosch to tell him how happy I am to play the work in New York—(I think also in Boston and afterwards, I hope in Paris) certain passages will be difficult in performance, the orchestra having always to accompany the organ—certain accentuations will seem weak to you from the standpoint of rhythm, especially on electric organs, but I do not doubt however the excellent sonorous result which must be judged carefully the first time with someone in the hall.
>
> I have recognized a familiar theme [of yours] in passing and it is good in the place you have used it—and generally speaking, the organ is treated very well—Isn't that paradoxical! I like best the Prélude, Scherzo and Finale which will avoid dogmatic discussions, the search for "Cyclisms"! and other useless difficulties —but, after all, Little Symphony is satisfactory—
>
> Other news will follow soon—thanks with all my heart again— and in haste, to you and Clurman, in deep and faithful affection.
>
> N. B.

Elated over Boulanger's reception of his new score, Copland settled down in earnest to complete the orchestration. As his time permitted, he began to look about for other performances of his works and to make additional professional contacts that would be of help to a young, unknown composer.

Marion Bauer had met Aaron Copland in Paris during the previous season (1923-1924), at one of the many receptions Nadia Boulanger was accustomed to hold in her salon. On returning to New York Miss Bauer wrote a letter to the board of directors of the League of Composers, telling them that young Copland was an American composer who should be heard and who, in her opinion, as well as in the opinions of certain European musicians, held great promise for the future.

It was at the League's audition of his compositions that Aaron first met Paul Rosenfeld, distinguished writer, lecturer, and music critic of *The Dial*. Rosenfeld had a better understanding and appreciation of what the younger composers were attempting to do than had any other critic of his time in New York. He has recorded "certain happy scenes from the mid-twenties," in which is included his first memory of young Copland, on the occasion of his first audition before the board of the League of Composers. The audition took place in Claire Reis's apartment in Seventy-seventh Street:

> . . . at the keyboard, playing and singing one of his own compositions, sways a slim, beglassed, shy and still self-assured young fellow with the aspect of a benevolent and scholastic grasshopper. . . . Swiftly there revives my delight in the fresh, entirely individual sonorities. . . . At last the composer comprehends our pleasure in him and his music. For the first time, he looks at us and openly smiles. It is Aaron Copland: still half-boyish but a personality.[3]

The Board voted to accept two piano pieces for performance at the November (1924) concert, the "Passacaglia" and "The Cat and the Mouse." This was the first performance of any of Copland's compositions in his native land and, in general, his work was well received by both audience and critics.

Money was plentiful in 1924 and art patrons were numerous. Through a mutual friend, Minna Lederman,* Rosenfeld was asked if he could find a patron to assist the young composer for the time being. Rosenfeld persuaded Mrs. Alma Wertheim, sister of Henry Morgenthau, Jr., to subsidize young Copland for a year. This timely assistance enabled the young man to complete his work on schedule and permitted him to focus his best thought and energy towards his first orchestral *première*.

Another letter from Mlle Boulanger brought young Copland up to date on the happenings at Fontainebleau. Her letter told of a first performance of Aaron's "Rondino" (in which she took a hand during rehearsals),† a first performance of his *Motets*, his piano pieces and the song, "Old Poem." But, she asked, where was the finished organ piece and what final title was it to have?

> At Fontainebleau, a new confirmation of my fears on the subject of your rhythm—the conception surpasses at present the (average) means of performance and those who write are isolated from those who perform—nothing to do yet—Discussions with the quartet, useless discussions . . . but lively—by installing oneself near them for a few weeks—either one would have killed them, or they would have killed you—but there was one hope—with the rehearsals as they are done nowadays and the prejudice [for] the "strong beat" [down beat] "eveness of the beat" the situation is desperate—Nevertheless "the audience" though warned judged that this Rondino was "charming." Let's not contradict them!
>
> After the daily rehearsals conducted by "Smiss" [Melville Smith], a really conscientious "conductor," our Paris-American-Gargenville choral has really done marvelously, those motets sound in the voices in a stunning manner and even with the "unprofessional" voices the effect is completely attained.

* Editor of *The League of Composers' Review* and its successor, *Modern Music*.

† This information contradicts Arthur Berger's assertion that the premiere of "Rondino" took place on May 6, 1928, at the Copland-Sessions Concerts and that of the *Motets* took place in February, 1937, in Paris, by a chorus under Nadia Boulanger's direction. See his *Aaron Copland* (New York: Oxford University Press, 1953), pp. 99-100.

McGreggor played the piano pieces with fingers at times insufficiently prepared, but with a musicality, an excellent understanding. . . . Greggor is [a musician] without any doubt—and although there are certain traits in him that lack a little brilliance, he has been an excellent interpreter for you.

Miss Howinson sang, quite well, Old Poem—but we didn't dare risk the piece with the clarinetist [As It Fell upon a Day] who was so nervous and upsetting. . . .

(Ah! I almost forgot—if there is a way, don't have the motets appear before my arrival—there are some small modifications to make for the breath marks—You will see what you think of it but I believe that, without these changes, the performance will not be in accord with what you wish). . . .

I am going to give a letter [of introduction] for you to a young man named Gerald Reynolds who is a young man of the first order—he himself is quite interesting (he was at Fontainebleau this summer) and he knows a group of people that I believe also very interesting. He directs a woman's chorus and wants to ask you to write something for him—Give it some thought, it is important, of that I am certain.

And I—? I am sailing December 27, playing in New York *January 11*—Engles has asked me for my program—I can ask him to be patient for a bit—but will you be ready and what title? When shall I have the music? Will the orchestral parts be ready? There is no more time to lose—above all, don't be too complicated—one cannot rehearse very much and orchestras are not ready to handle certain problems properly.

How much pleasure our little parties will give me—I hope to remain a while in New York since I play there the eleventh, I have my first lecture there the nineteenth—and I hope to have a little freedom—it will be necessary to work, it is true, for your organs are different from ours—and I shall have to give some lessons probably, without counting the appearances in society! . . .

Now, I rather think that I have exhausted all the news and that the resources of my mind are drained dry— . . . I thank you very earnestly for your confidence so warm-hearted, so simple, so comforting, and I assure you, my dear friend, of a devotion full of admiration for the artist and affection for the man that you are.

On his return to America later in the fall, Gerald Reynolds, the young American choral conductor, presented himself, along with Boulanger's letter of introduction, to Copland. Conductor of the Women's University Glee Club in New York, Reynolds invited Copland to write two short contrasting works for performance at the April, 1925, concert of the Glee Club. Aaron agreed to do so immediately after the *première* of the organ symphony.

Symphony for Organ and Orchestra

With Mlle Boulanger as soloist (her first appearance in America), the *Symphony for Organ and Orchestra* received its first performance on January 11, 1925, at Aeolian Hall, with the New York Symphony Orchestra conducted by Walter Damrosch. Begun in May (1924), the *Symphony* had been completed the following November. In addition to the *Symphony*, the program contained two other works for organ and orchestra: Handel's *Concerto in D Minor* (for organ and strings), and Lili Boulanger's *Funerailles d'un Soldat*, as well as orchestral works by Bach, Wagner, and Ravel.[4]

Noting that the Copland *Symphony* could not be dismissed as "another one of those things," the *Times* critic estimated the work as one of very high rank in the ultramodern school, deserving of this place because of the very real power the composer disclosed in dealing with rhythm. He received almost the impression, however, that Copland composed by rhythms instead of by themes and believed that the "motto," which appeared in all three movements, was more notable as a rhythmic pattern than as a theme. He found it difficult to recall any work in this style by an American, which showed great promise of an original and distinctive talent in composition.

The work received considerable applause, which the conductor shared with young Copland, who was seated in an upper box. According to the critic, when the applause had quieted down, Damrosch advanced to the footlights and thus addressed the audience: "Ladies and gentlemen! It seems evident that when the gifted young American who wrote this Symphony can compose at the age of 23, a work like this one," here he paused and the audience expectantly awaited his proclamation of a new genius, but Damrosch smilingly continued, "it seems evident that in five years he will be ready to commit murder."[5]

At this, a loud laugh went through the audience and, up in his box, according to the critic, young Copland laughed as loudly as the rest and applauded the sentiment.

Lawrence Gilman found Copland's *Symphony* contained pages of bite and power, both rhythmical and harmonic, chiefly in the Finale, where he sensed that the young American had the most to say. Observing certain contemporary influences in the composer's work, he described these as follows: "Mr. Copland, even though he does present us with some second-hand Stravinsky—his second movement is redolent of 'Petrouchka'; even though he suggests to us in his first movement a kind of Prospect Park Schoenberg, is . . . working out his own musical destiny in his own way."[6]

While the critics of the *Times* and *Herald Tribune* thus remained calm and dispassionate in their judgments of the new music, Rosenfeld was positively rhapsodic over the new work. Observing that Mlle Boulanger brought honor both to herself and her sensitive pupil by performing his *Symphony for Organ and Orchestra,* Rosenfeld noted that the composition contained two contrasting veins,

> the one a sensitive, contemplative, pastoral vein, whimsical and tranquil in turn, a musical idealogical early April with tender gurglings from the ponds, chirps of a single bird, cool shadows [the vein of the Prelude and middle section of the Scherzo]; . . . the other a bold feeling for strident, breathless, obsessive rhythm as advanced as anything in Stravinsky [the vein of the Scherzo proper and passages of the Finale].[7]

In Rosenfeld's opinion, no American under twenty-five years of age had won artistic spurs more honorably or more certainly than had Copland. The American already stood, Rosenfeld affirmed, with earth-sprung talents to which New York City could look for sustenance.

Thus, with his first orchestral performance, young Copland had scored an artistic success; it appeared that he conquered conductor, audience, and critics, all, with an "ultramodern" work. He had achieved an auspicious beginning in his first year back home.

The next performance of the *Symphony* took place in Boston a month later, February 20, with the Boston Symphony conducted by Koussevitzky, then in his first American season. Copland went up to assist in the rehearsals and to attend his first orchestral performance by that noted group.

Moses Smith tells us that for a week prior to the Boston performance, as Copland played the score on the piano in Koussevitzky's house and as the conductor rehearsed it carefully with the orchestra in Symphony Hall, Koussevitzky gave Copland "the impression that the whole symphonic week centered on his Symphony. Copland walked on air. He found it hard to believe that Koussevitzky should lavish so much attention on an unknown American youth of 24."[8]

Although, according to Smith, Copland's music was poorly received by the audience, some of whom "indulged in discreet hisses," while the critics "blew hot and cold," Koussevitzky's faith in the young man never wavered. On the contrary, he immediately persuaded the League of Composers to commission Copland to write a new composition for the program of modern works he (Koussevitzky) was to conduct for the League the following season.

First Symphony

In 1928, Copland completed a purely orchestral version of this work, omitting the organ part altogether, and gave it the title of *First Symphony*.* This was not too difficult a task because, in the first version of the work, the organ had been treated as an integral part of the orchestra, rather than as a solo instrument with orchestral accompaniment.

* It was performed for the first time in this version by Ernest Ansermet and the Berlin Symphony Orchestra in December, 1931. However, the Scherzo movement had received its first performance on November 4, 1927, by Fritz Reiner and the Philadelphia Orchestra in Carnegie Hall, New York. *New York Times,* Nov. 5, 1927.

Approximately twenty-five minutes in length and scored for large orchestra, the *Symphony* is cyclic in form, having a "motto" based on the tones of the minor triad, which recurs in all three movements. Inasmuch as the cyclic principle of composition was established by César Franck and his French followers, D'Indy, Saint-Saëns, Fauré, and Dukas, it is of interest to see how Aaron Copland applied this principle to his *First Symphony*.

The first movement, called "Prelude" (andante, 6/8), is free in form and intensely lyrical in spirit; there is only one theme, which is introduced by the flute over an accompaniment of strings. The "motto," when it first appears in this movement as a mere accompaniment, seems almost inconsequential (Example 1). As the work progresses, however, its real significance becomes apparent.

Ex. 1

The Scherzo (molto allegro, 3/4), sets forth two themes: the first, a fast, syncopated theme introduced by the oboe; the second, of a more sustained character, is first introduced in the wood winds. Following a full development of the first theme, which arrives at a climax for full orchestra, the "motto" suddenly interrupts, announced by two horns and imitated by a trumpet, with a fragment of the first theme in the clarinets heard over the imitation (Example 2). The middle section, introducing new material, marks the first appearance of "blues," as such, in any of Copland's music to date. It is achieved through the use of the alto saxophone (for "jazz" timbre), plus a syncopated "blues-type" melody written in syncopated (fox-trot)

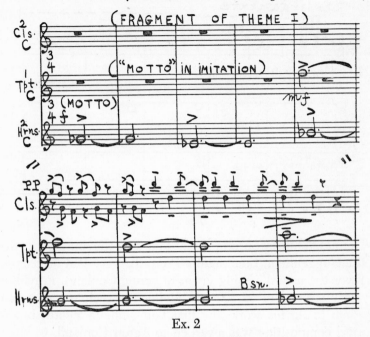

Ex. 2

rhythm: [♫♩ ♪♫]. This section is significant because it is the first evidence of the blues element which, added to the fast jazz rhythmic mood (first encountered in the Finale of the *Dance Symphony*), was shortly afterwards consciously adopted by Copland in order to make his music sound more "American."

The Finale (*lento, allegro moderato*, 4/4), corresponding to the usual first movement of a symphony, is written approximately in sonata form. The quotation below (Example 3) juxtaposes the four main elements of the Finale—three rhythmic versions of the "motto" (tonality of B minor) with Theme II heard overhead (E major tonality with Phrygian mode implications)—and proceeds to a brilliant coda, which brings the work to a satisfying close.*

During the spring of 1925 United States Senator and Mrs. Simon Guggenheim set up the John Simon Guggenheim Foundation in memory of their son, who died in April, 1922.

* Copland was also greatly influenced by Bloch's application of cyclic principles in *Schelomo*, the *Violin Sonata* and *Viola Suite*.

Ex. 3

Thomas Whitney Surette was at that time the musical advisor to the Guggenheim Foundation. From the very first he seemed to favor the award's being given to young Copland. Providing a yearly stipend of $2,500 and giving the recipient complete freedom to do his work, the first Guggenheim Fellowship in musical composition was awarded to Aaron Copland, to begin in October, 1925. The following year it was renewed, thus giving the young man financial stability until the fall of 1927.

On April 24, 1925, the two choral works written by Copland for the Women's University Glee Club and its conductor, Gerald Reynolds, received their first performance at the Engineering Building, in New York City. These works were "The House on the Hill," with text by Edward Arlington Robinson, and "An Immorality," with text by Ezra Pound. Copland appeared in the concert, playing the rhythmically "tricky" accompaniment to "An Immorality." Written in January, 1925, the two choral compositions are in utter contrast, both in mood and in the style of writing.

"The House on the Hill," set for four-part women's voices, *a cappella*, expresses a mood of quiet resignation and lyric sorrow, wherein the music describes the bleak melancholy of Robinson's abandoned homestead. Evidence of the potency of rhythm in underlining the mood and spirit of a work is noted in the opening phrases of the chorus, which show an astounding similarity to the first measure of the Scherzo from the *First Sym-*

phony. In the Scherzo, the extrovert spirit of jazz is evoked by manipulating the original material in a fast rhythm; while, in the chorus, the same material presented in a slow rhythm projects the inner contemplative utterances of the sensitive mind. Thus the economical use of materials is seen to be characteristic of the composer's methods from the very beginning of his professional career. In its use of Lydian and Phrygian modes, the chorus has the archaic modal flavor of a fourteenth or fifteenth century motet, and is completely contrapuntal in texture. Like these motets, the song has neither measure signature nor bar lines; phrases are punctuated by a black, vertical line. A little three-part form, the principal polyphonic device used throughout, is canonic imitation.

Turning to the second chorus, we may say that "An Immorality" is Copland's first consciously written jazz piece. It exudes the spirit of the "snappy number"* in a highly sophisticated setting. The work is scored for women's chorus of sopranos divided and altos, and has an independent piano accompaniment. Jazz materials present in this short work may be identified as follows: a polytonal and polyrhythmic ground-bass jazz accompaniment ("riff style"); a syncopated melodic line featuring flatted intervals of a third and a second which suggest polytonal-jazz implications; a succession of triads in second inversion descending by consecutive whole steps (a favorite "stock-in-trade" radio vocal writing technique during the late twenties and early thirties); and a three-part jazz-canon at the unison. With all voices singing in contrapuntal style and with the piano beating out its jazz polyrhythms, the effect of the composition is that of a "hot" jazz madrigal.

On May 1,† 1925, seven young American composers heard their orchestral works performed for the first time by the Rochester Philharmonic Orchestra at the Eastman Theatre in Rochester, New York. In the nature of a public rehearsal, this first

---

* Copland, in *Our New Music*, notes that the two dominant jazz moods are the "blues" and the "snappy number."

† John Kirkpatrick, in "On Copland's Music," *The Fontainebleau Alumni Bulletin*, May, 1928, erroneously gives the date of the *première* of *Cortège Macabre* as April 1, 1925.

experimental program of American compositions was given under the auspices of the Eastman School of Music.

Conducted by Howard Hanson, the rehearsal, according to F. D. Perkins, "completed with convincing success the first stage of a far-reaching plan designed to free the American composer for orchestra from what is, at present, the chief handicap in his path—the lack of opportunity to hear, and learn by hearing, his works performed."[9]

Three of the composers, whose ages ranged from twenty-four to thirty-five, were from New York: Aaron Copland, the youngest composer, represented by his *Cortège Macabre,* Mark Silver, and Bernard Rogers. Other composers were Donald Tweedy of the Eastman faculty, Adolph Weiss, first bassoonist of the Rochester Philharmonic, Quincy Porter of the Cleveland Institute of Music, and George F. McKay, teacher of music in the public schools of Lead, South Dakota. Compositions by these seven composers were chosen from fifty-four submitted manuscripts by Howard Hanson, director of the Eastman School, and Ernest Bloch. The Eastman School met the traveling and living expenses of the successful composers, thus enabling all of them to attend the rehearsal. In addition, the school undertook the copying of the string parts.

Of Copland's *Cortège Macabre* Perkins wrote that in the composer's use of a "style suggesting a blend of Stravinsky and the radical Gauls he knew, it seemed, what he wanted, and the rather gruesome atmosphere of the plot—a procession bearing four corpses—was vividly suggested in repeated heavy chords."

With the support of his sponsor (Mrs. Wertheim), Copland was able to devote himself completely to composing the new work for the Koussevitzky concert of the League of Composers. After hearing the performances of his two orchestral works, the *Symphony* and *Cortège Macabre,* Copland had begun to think they were too European in inspiration. In his next orchestral composition, he was anxious to write a work that would be recognized immediately as being American in character; but just what was the American idiom?

As has been seen, Copland had experimented to some extent

with the melodic and rhythmic implications of jazz, notably in the choral work "An Immorality." Now he wanted frankly to adopt the jazz idiom, in order to see what he could do with it in a symphonic way. Rosenfeld, always interested in the young composer's artistic progress, suggested the MacDowell Colony in Peterborough, New Hampshire, as an ideal place to work out the idea during the summer months.

Having begun the preliminary sketches of his new work in May, 1925, in New York, Copland spent the months of July and August at the Colony, where he almost completed the suite.

Here he met Roy Harris, who had comparatively recently decided to become a composer. At Copland's suggestion, Harris was to go to Paris to study with Boulanger who, following the success of her first American pupil, was soon sought as a teacher by many other aspiring American composers. Among the artists of other fields whom Copland met that summer at the Colony were Louis Untermeyer and his wife, Jean Starr Untermeyer, Eleanor Wiley and William Rose Benét. Henry F. Gilbert from Boston was there, as well as Tennessee Anderson, the sculptress. The after-dinner discussions held by the composers were most often concerned with the welfare of American composers in general and with the problem of how to secure more performances of American music.

At the invitation of Clarence Adler, his former piano teacher, Copland went to Adler's summer camp, Karinoke, at Lake Placid for the month of September, where he completed *Music for the Theatre.* His former teacher built a "shack" especially for the composer, situated up the mountain and called "The Clouds." Of his creative procedure Adler has noted: "I have listened (at a distance, of course) to Copland in the throes of composition, and it is something to hear! He bangs and hammers at the piano, at the same time singing in shrill, dissonant tones."[10]

Music for the Theatre

Music for the Theatre received its first performance at a concert of the Boston Symphony Orchestra in Boston, November 20, 1925. It was conducted by Serge Koussevitzky, to whom the score is dedicated. Copland was paid for the performance, as he had been "tipped off" by the more experienced Koussevitzky to enclose a bill with the score and parts. Eight days later, with Koussevitzky and a small group from the Boston Symphony performing it, the work was heard at Town Hall, New York, in a concert of the League of Composers, who had commissioned it. Other composers whose works were performed at the League's concert were Tansman, Honegger, and Prokofieff.

Considered by some musicians as Copland's best work, *Music for the Theatre* is, to say the least, his most popular work of the French-Jazz Period. A suite in five parts for small orchestra, the composer had no play or literary idea in mind at the time of writing it. His choice of title implied a quality in the music suggestive of the theater. The suite has style and bears the stamp of individuality. Again employing cyclic implications, it is completely twentieth century in technical craft, containing both polytonal and polyrhythmic elements, and is completely national, American, in expression.

Written without key signature, characteristic of Copland's works during the ten-year period from 1925 to 1935 (beginning with "The House on the Hill"), *Music for the Theatre* contains the following structural, harmonic and rhythmic features:

I. Prologue (*molto moderato*, 2/4). The first theme, announced by a solo trumpet in prophetic mood, cadenza style, (reminiscent of a shofar [ram's horn] in the synagogue), has the flavor of the Lydian mode, with its characteristic augmented fourth. The strings enter, playing a nine bar introduction to the second theme, a descending diatonic idea composed of three tones on the motive "Three Blind Mice," a motive that appears frequently throughout Copland's music. The second theme, played by the oboe over the polytonally harmonized "Three Blind Mice" accompaniment, is soon heard (Example 4). Further evidence of Copland's economical use (or reworking) of the same material is noted in the open fifths of the bass line which, first used consistently throughout "An Immorality" as a persistent, nervous, rhythmic ostinato figure, in this version achieve a mood of calm, quiet, sustained repose.

Ex. 4

II. Dance *(allegro molto, 5/8 [2/8+3/8])*. Here, Copland frankly adopts the popular style of the jazz idiom in this brief, nervously rhythmical piece. Jazz polyrhythms are manipulated according to (1) the harmonic progression of a dominant seventh chord to its implied root in a 3-2 (5/8) application of the old 1-2-3-4 ragtime bass; and (2) by a modified canonic imitation of the same material in the melodic line above (Example 5).

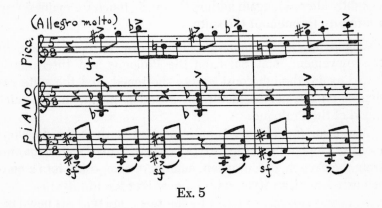

Ex. 5

Soon after, a literal "hot blues break" is heard, played by the E flat clarinet over a rhythmic bass (the "riff"), played in the piano, on a dominant ninth chord, whose inner voice moves up and down stepwise in a typical jazz-ostinato figure. An autobiographical glimpse of the composer is given in the "East Side,

West Side" motive,* which is used frequently as connecting material to the various sections of the Dance.

III. Interlude *(lento moderato,* 4/4). The Interlude is a real blues melody (containing a flatted seventh), repeated three times, each time with slight alterations. Shortly before the close of the Interlude the opening trumpet motive from the first movement is heard, played this time by the English horn. Copland thus continues the application of the cyclic principle of form in a purely jazz piece.

IV. Burlesque *(allegro vivo,* 3/8). According to the composer, Fannie Brice was the inspiration for this movement. A kind of jazz scherzo, this movement follows an A-B-A-B structural form. The A theme, first heard in the solo trumpet, is passed around throughout the orchestra by various solo wood winds and brass. The B theme, played by a muted trumpet (with the "wa-wa" mute, which establishes the blues mood), after several false starts, finally moves along in its slower tempo *(molto meno mosso,* 6/8 and 2/4). Near the end of this theme, the composer has cleverly "sneaked in" the trumpet motive from the Prologue (slightly altered), again adding the cyclic touch for maintaining continuity throughout the suite.

V. Epilogue *(molto moderato,* 4/4). No new themes occur in this movement; material from the Prologue and Interlude is heard again, though considerably shortened, and the suite cadences on the polyharmonies of B and E major, in the quiet mood of the Prologue.

Music for the Theatre is an important work in the development of Copland's musical style because it marks a separation from the French, or European, manner of composing into a consciously American style, with its new jazz idiom.

Koussevitzky was so taken by the score and with its new jazz content that he suggested to Copland that he must write a new work immediately—a piano concerto, no less—which the com-

* From "The Sidewalks of New York," composed by Charles B. Lawlor, Dublin-born composer who came to New York in 1887, and James W. Blake, New York-born author.

poser himself might perform with the Boston Symphony Orchestra.* Copland almost immediately began to search for suitable themes for the new work, and in January he began in earnest the actual composition of the concerto.

Eleven years later Nicolas Slonimsky wrote of the suite: "*Music for the Theatre* possesses a certain historical significance inasmuch as it gives expression of jazz music in a classical dance form for the first time."[11]

During December Copland appeared as lecturer in Rochester, presumably at the Eastman School, where, according to *Musical America*, he talked "entertainingly on the subject of jazz." He stated at that time that he did not believe American composers could create a type of music distinctly national without a literature of folk music as a background, and that he had found a solution for himself. What may be termed his "jazz aesthetic" is expressed in the following excerpt from his remarks:

> If we haven't a folksong foundation, we must invent one. I began by thinking—what is a folksong after all? And I came to the conclusion that in my case it was the songs I heard when I was a child—rather commonplace jazz tunes and music of the "Old Black Joe" variety. These, then, are my material, and I must accept them for what they are. If we have only these elements as essentially American, our music must make the best of it and do the work so well that something worth while will come from the effort.[12]

Stephen Foster-like songs plus the music of the early twentieth century popular jazz composers are, therefore, seen to provide the springboard for Copland's own jazz phase. In time, he was to discover other "essentially American" sources which were to have an even greater influence on his work than jazz, expanding his horizon and conception of musical "Americanisms."

* Regarding Koussevitsky's championship of Copland, Moses Smith has stated: "Although it is dangerous to ascribe a composer's successful development to a single set of external circumstances, it is safe to say that no influence was more responsible for Copland's present position in American music than Koussevitsky's championship." *Koussevitsky* (New York: Allen, Towne and Heath, 1947), p. 187.

Because of Copland's brilliant, almost instantaneous success as a composer, attained so soon after his return home from a period of study abroad, he began to be looked to as leader and spokesman for the younger American composers. Asserting this leadership was both natural and spontaneous to him. At the Salzburg Festival in 1923, Copland had determined, on his return home, to "do something" towards changing the patronizing attitude with which the American composer was generally regarded. As a first step in that direction he wrote the critique, "America's Young Men of Promise," which appeared in the November-December, 1925, issue of *Modern Music*, formerly the *League of Composers' Review*.

At the beginning of March, 1926, Copland, accompanied by Harold Clurman, went again to Europe for a six months' stay. Copland's immediate objective, upon invitation of the Société Musicale Indépendante, was to participate in the Société's concert of American music. In addition to revisiting Paris, the two Americans planned to attend the International Festival of Contemporary Composers at Zürich and to spend the months of June through September at Guéthary, Basses Pyrénées, in France, where Copland hoped to finish his piano concerto begun in January.

The first three months were spent in Paris, where the young Americans looked up most of their former associates and friends including, of course, Mlle Boulanger. Copland played his newest compositions for his former teacher and talked with her about the plan for the new piano concerto. It was at one of Boulanger's receptions that Copland met Roger Sessions, with whom he was to found (two years later) the Copland-Sessions Concerts, which functioned for several years in New York City.

In Paris Copland completed his two pieces for violin and piano, the "Nocturne" and "Ukelele Serenade."* They were first

* According to John Kirkpatrick, a string quartet of George Antheil's was scheduled on the American program of the Société Musicale Indépendante, and it was expected that the same musicians would play Copland's "Rondino." "But somehow," Kirkpatrick relates, "Antheil who was financing the quartet, got the idea that they must not be burdened with the rehearsals of any other music, whereupon Copland, nothing daunted, up and finished his two fiddle pieces and got Dushkin to play them." (*Op. cit., p. 6.*)

performed by Samuel Dushkin, violinist, and the composer at
the Société's concert of American music on May 5, 1926.[13] The
program also comprised Virgil Thomson's *Sonata d'Eglise*
(Choral, Tango, Fugue) for clarinet, trumpet, viola, horn, and
trombone; Herbert Elwell's *Nine Piano Pieces;* Copland's "As
It Fell upon a Day," which had been performed before the Société in 1924; Walter Piston's Piano *Sonata;* a *Quartet* by George
Antheil, and a Violin *Sonata* by Theodore Chanler.

A little three-part form, the rhythmic scheme of the piano
accompaniment to the "Nocturne" is derived from a slow application of the fox-trot rhythm thus: 𝅘𝅥𝅮𝅘𝅥𝅮𝅘𝅥𝅘𝅥 𝅘𝅥𝅮. The left hand, emphasizing beats <u>4</u>-<u>1</u>, conveys a tingle of tango rhythm to the
general "blues" aura. The B section, in slower tempo, is designated *meno mosso (grave)* and is of great depth. The first two
measures of this theme are later to become the material from
which Copland's most magnificent orchestral work of the French-
Jazz Period, the *Symphonic Ode,* is developed.

Following the slow blueslike "Nocturne," the "Ukelele Serenade" is in complete contrast, a highly jazz-rhythmed Allegro
vivo, extremely lusty and exciting. An interesting feature is the
second appearance of quarter tones in the music of Aaron Copland, used here to produce a blues effect (Example 6). For the

Ex. 6

notes to be "blued," the composer has given directions that appear in the upper-left-hand corner of the score and read thus:

Note ♭ means flat ¼ tone; ♯ means sharp ¼ tone. The title is evidently derived from Part II, which contains ukelele-sounding chords (arpeggiated triads in the right hand of the piano part), over which the violin sings a sustained melody.

The middle of June found Copland and Clurman in Zürich, Switzerland, where the fourth festival of the International Society for Contemporary Music convened during the week of June 18 to 23. Copland attended not only in the capacity of a musical auditor, but as a correspondent for *Modern Music*. He left the festival with the distinct impression that the music played was of secondary importance. The real value lay in the fact that an international meeting place had been provided where composers and musicians from all countries might come together.

Harold Clurman recalls the following incident that occurred in Munich: "One night Copland and I stopped in at the great Hofbräuhaus of Munich. As we entered a side entrance, the huge throng of beer-bloated, smoke-stewed, heavy-seated Germans frightened us so that we actually beat a hasty retreat."[14] Looking back on the experience, Clurman strongly suspects that "Munich and its famous beer-hall were then already in the grip of the rising Nazi movement." From Munich the two Americans went on to Guéthary where, for three months, they occupied the Villa Cendrillon, a house set on a high cliff above the sea. Here in this quiet Basque country, Copland began to work on the piano concerto.

Towards the end of the summer two little ideas that Copland discarded from the concerto found their way into little piano pieces which the composer called "Blues." These little pieces are entitled "Sentimental Melody" (originally "Blues No. 1") and "Blues No. 2," later called "Blues No. 4."

A two-page composition in 4/4 (C) marked *non allegro, legato*, "Sentimental Melody" (Slow Dance) is a one-part form repeated. Borrowing the dominant seventh final cadence from the Latin-American popular composers, Copland adds a diminished octave to enhance the blues character (Example 7). It was first performed in 1927 by the composer as a recording for Ampico.

Ex. 7

A three-page piano piece, "Blues No. 4" is the author's favorite blues piano composition and reveals the composer at his best in his first lusty use of literal jazz materials. Enclosed within the dimensions of a small three-part form, the piece's engaging features are these: the charming over-all polyharmonic tonality of F and A flat major; the compression into 3/4 meter of the ragtime elements of 1-2-3-4, while the syncopation, which occurs in both hands simultaneously, gives the flavor of the Charleston rhythm; the extra beat rest given in the repetition of Part I, which lends the effect of "hesitation," a rhythmic variation of early ragtime; a blues cadence, consisting of a triad containing the interval of a minor seventh. "Blues No. 4" had its first performance on May 7, 1942, by the pianist Hugo Balzo, in Montevideo.

Returning to New York in October with the concerto completed save for some pages of orchestration, Copland took a new and larger studio at 123 West Seventy-eighth Street. Working steadily, he completed the concerto in November and took it to Koussevitzky for approval. The conductor praised the new work and programed it for January 28, 1927, in Boston, with the composer as soloist.[15] The work is dedicated to Alma Wertheim, who had given financial assistance to the young composer during his first year back in America.

Concerto for Piano and Orchestra

Though played without interruption, the *Concerto* is really divided into two contrasting parts, which are linked thematically. The first is a slow, lyric movement; the second a fast, rhythmic one. Here again, following the same pattern as the small piano and violin and piano pieces, we have the two dominant moods of jazz: the slow blues and the snappy number, adapted, however, to the large symphonic frame. Still, one begins to sense the limitations of this style.

Following a short orchestral introduction, setting forth the vigorous first theme which is conceived on a line of broad universality, the piano enters quietly and improvises around this material for a short space; then the second theme, one of the loveliest melodies ever written in (or out of) the blues idiom, is sung by a flute and clarinet in unison over an accompaniment of muted strings. This simple, folklike theme is taken up by the piano in octaves in the right hand with a flowing accompaniment tastefully harmonized in the left hand (Example 8). The first measure calls to mind Gershwin's second "Prelude" for piano, published in 1927, which also makes use of the same blues melodic material. After a full development of the first theme in the piano, the second theme is heard again in triple canon in the strings, and, with the piano playing a figuration built out of the introductory material, it mounts to a sonorous climax.

Ex. 8

A few transitional measures lead directly into the second movement, which is in sonata form without recapitulation. The first theme, having the character of a "break," is announced immediately by the solo piano (Example 9). Ten measures in

Ex. 9

length, this first theme is one of the most uniquely contructed in all music literature. From the third measure on, the same notes are treated to a rhythmic expansion, difficult to find in any other composer's writings (even Stravinsky's) with such a virtuosic display of technique. This rhythmic expansion is rendered even more economical by the fact that underneath are used only the three original harmonies: F, G, and A flat. This cumulative rhythmic development (by expansion) was to become one of the individualities of the Copland style and is particularly brilliantly handled in the later *Piano Sonata*.

Following a full development of this material, the second theme, one of the most raucous, strident jazz themes ever invented, is introduced by a soprano saxophone, over a 4/4 polytonal ragtime accompaniment in the piano. The development, based entirely on these two jazz themes, contains a brief piano cadenza; unlike the classic and romantic concerto cadenzas, which present volleys of scale and arpeggio passages for virtuosic display, Copland's cadenza presents difficulties of a rhythmic nature, homophonic in texture, with the characteristic of an improvised "break." This is an excellent example of expressing an otherwise outmoded virtuosic device in terms of the twentieth century. Before the end, the massive theme of the first movement is heard *triple fortissimo* in the orchestra with crashing chords in the piano. This is followed by a brief coda containing fragments of themes from the first movement, ending with the introductory theme of the concerto in *grandiose* style, in the tonality of E minor. The coda adds cohesion (in the cyclic sense) to the entire work and brings the *Concerto* to a monumental close. Against a huge orchestration, which shows a great improvement over Copland's previous orchestral works, the piano proves itself a worthy protagonist.

On the occasion of the *première* of the *Concerto for Piano and Orchestra,* which took place on January 28, 1927, in Symphony Hall, Boston, Copland's father and mother made the trip up from Brooklyn to hear their son perform his work with the noted Boston Symphony.

The Boston *Transcript's* H. T. Parker called attention to his criticism with these headlines:

PIANO CONCERTO—COPLAND THE OGRE
PLEASURE, PLAUDITS, DERISION, WRATH
MR. KOUSSEVITZKY—TAKES A NEW WAY—
"That Terrible Concerto"

. . . neither ashamed of his own soil nor over-imitative of foreign example, [Copland] has tried to derive from jazz . . . such ways and means as could be used to other ends [than dance music]. It is furiously rhythmed: . . . harsh, vociferous, lurid, defiant. . . . Being such, it has transmuted jazz much beyond Mr. Gershwin's ruses and candors.[16]

Philip Hale, critic for the Boston *Herald*, wrote: "If this Concerto shows the present condition of Mr. Copland's musical mind, he is on the wrong track. . . . We found little to attract, little to admire, much to repel. . . . The [work] also shows a shocking lack of taste, or proportion." Recalling that the leading English reviewers when they first heard Schumann's *Symphony in B Flat* characterized it as belonging to the "Broken Crockery School," Hale stated that his objection to Copland's "broken crockery" is that it is "not of the first quality."[17]

The Boston *Post* was even more caustic. Quoting Copland to the effect that "you couldn't read a program into [the *Concerto*] if you tried," the critic reported that "with no effort at all the listener visualizes a jazz dance hall next door to a poultry yard. . . . It may be that [in time] we shall all agree that Copland's Piano Concerto and Gershwin's Rhapsody in Blue mark the highwater mark of American composition. Or it may be we shall not."[18]

Copland's parents were quite upset by the newspaper reviews, particularly that of the *Post*, and the injustices of the criticisms stirred the composer no less. He felt they had been unfair. Nevertheless, in a letter to Nicolas Slonimsky, written shortly after the *Concerto's* première, Copland thanked his friend, "Kolya," for the recent enclosure of all those "delightful write-ups" (newspaper reviews) and shrugged off the cruel barbs with a good-natured witticism: "After reading them," Copland continued, "I went to the mirror to see if I could recognize myself. . . . When the Concerto is played again ('O horrid thought!'), we must see if we can't get the police to raid the concert hall to give a little added interest to this 'horrible' experiment."[19]

A week later, on February 5, Copland again appeared as soloist in the *Piano Concerto* at the Boston Symphony's New York concert. According to H. T. Parker, the opinions of the New York press were mixed; but if the audiences in Boston had hissed and laughed, those in New York "listened intently, applauded warmly," while "no more laughter ensued than was to be expected."[20]

Fifteen years later, in 1941, Oscar Thompson stated that, in his opinion, Copland's *Piano Concerto* was the most impressive symphonic work in the jazz idiom by an American or European composer. "It is melodious, it is fluent and it has a driving force. That the composer . . . should subsequently have lost his faith in the idiom as a basis for art expression is significant, since no other serious composer had accomplished so much with it as he did in the Concerto."[21]

With the *Concerto for Piano and Orchestra* Copland felt that he had said all there was to say in the jazz idiom. He now began to look about him for other materials.

Experimentation and Recapitulation (1927–1929)

In contrast to the prolific jazz years, which produced nine works, this phase of Copland's work is notable for the smaller number of compositions written and also for their experimental nature. A searching, even groping, for a new direction is strongly sensed. His works comprise: "Song," in twelve-tone (or serial) technique; "Lento," a piece for string quartet, influenced by Stravinsky's "objectivity theory"; "Vocalise," an *étude* for voice and piano, Ravel-like in flavor, yet with a certain bareness of sound; the trio, *Vitebsk*, whose austerity and acid dissonance place it nearer the works of the Abstract Period than those of the French-Jazz; and finally, marking the climax, the tremendous *Symphonic Ode*, the second and higher peak of the entire French-Jazz period.

Preferring to write criticism (for which he was now paid) and to lecture rather than to teach in order to maintain himself, Copland, in the fall of 1927, accepted a position as lecturer at one of New York's leading educational institutions, the New School for Social Research. As a consequence, his critiques increase during this time, outnumbering by two his musical compositions. They are steadily becoming more important in a study of Copland's works, for they reveal his continued preoccupation with the newest compositional tendencies and his struggle to assimilate these tendencies into his own work.

In April, 1927, Copland arrived in Europe for a five-month sojourn which was to include two European festivals. In Paris, on May 30, in one of the most notable *premières* of the season, he heard Stravinsky conduct his opera-oratorio, *Oedipus Rex* (in concert form), at Diagilev's Ballet Russe. Stravinsky's newest style was to have an influence on young Copland, particularly in his "Lento" for string quartet, written a year later.

Here, too, he again met Roger Sessions, and the two young men developed definite plans to give programs of contemporary American music in New York, beginning in the spring of 1928.

The first of the European festivals which Copland attended was the 1927 International Festival of Contemporary Music at Frankfort, Germany, beginning June 30 and ending July 4. His suite, *Music for the Theatre*, along with Henry F. Gilbert's *The Dance in Place Congo* (a symphonic poem based on Creole rhythms and tunes), had been chosen to represent the United States.

In lieu of criticisms by the Frankfort press, Adolph Weissmann's review, as published in *Modern Music*, must suffice us here. Observing that the Europeans always look eagerly for new developments in American music, the critic deemed it a "pity" that Gilbert's "naive" *Dance* was chosen for the festival, for it "released a spirit of hilarity not always intended by the composer." On the other hand, Copland's *Music for the Theatre* produced quite a different effect. "The dependence on Stravinsky is obvious," Weissmann wrote, "but Copland nevertheless makes remarkable use of his jazz. It was so effectively treated, so varied, with such comprehension of its true objective, that the work ranks as a success in an unsuccessful festival."[22]

It was also during the month of July that Copland attended the Festival of Deutsche Kammermusik in Baden-Baden, Germany, as a correspondent for *Modern Music*. Among the works played at the two concerts of chamber music, Alban Berg's *Lyric Suite* found most favor. Unlike much of Berg's music (in twelve-tone technique), the *Suite* was comparatively easy to comprehend. Copland believed this to be due to its striking clarity of construction and noted that it was one of the best works for string quartet to appear in recent years.[23]

The Baden-Baden festival concluded, Copland went on to Königstein in Taunus (Germany), for the remainder of the summer (July-September), to compose. The British were still occupying the city and the American was conscious of the long rows of barracks and of many soldiers passing in the street. The young man visited frequently in the home of the Seligman family, wealthy German Jews, a branch of which resides in New York.

It was not a productive summer for the composer, or so he thought. The previous season he had composed numerous works in the jazz idiom, whose performances had brought him considerable fame. But after hearing these works presented Copland came to the conclusion that the "general spirit of jazz was much too limited to be used as the basis for a fully-rounded music. The rhythmic element, on the other hand," he wrote, "is important, I think, because it is typically American in quality, and yet may be used quite apart from a jazz context."[24] But how to go on? What should he write next?

At the German festivals (as well as at previous European festivals), Copland had heard some beautiful music composed in the twelve-tone technique, one of the twentieth century's most radical theoretical developments. If he were to work with twelve-tone, even if he did not become an exponent of the technique, perhaps the experience would solve his problem or show him the direction in which he should go. It surely would do no harm to try.

In the meantime, at the request of Fritz Reiner, he busied himself with rescoring the Scherzo movement from the *Symphony for Organ and Orchestra,* which Reiner wished to perform the following season. In addition, he began some preliminary sketches for a work to be drafted in large design, requiring a tremendous orchestra. It is also probable that, at this time, Copland was turning over in his mind the Jewish folksong that he heard the previous season at a performance of the play, *The Dybbuk.* It was later to form the material of the trio, *Vitebsk.*

It was during the month of August, 1927, that Copland wrote the "Song" for soprano voice and piano on a text by E. E. Cummings. Three pages in length, highly expressive in content, the "Song" reveals that new elements are projecting themselves into the composer's musical cerebrations; a new compositional direction is sought. Contrapuntal in technique (without any trace of jazz), this short work *(lento molto, 3/2)* employs the serial technique (a kind of "tone row") without, however, actually destroying all sense of tonality. The movements of the several lines form chords which somehow relate to harmonies.

The "row" (or series) seems to have been planned on this succession of notes: B-D-F-G-C-C sharp-A flat-F sharp-B flat-A natural-E-E flat.* The first three and one-half measures are quoted below, with numbers placed over the first entrances of each note (of the chromatic scale) to indicate in which order Copland might have selected the "row" (Example 10). Perhaps because of the song's experimental nature and interval difficulty, its first performance did not take place until October 11, 1935, when Ethel Luening, soprano, accompanied by the composer, performed it in an all Copland program at the New School for Social Research. Lacking the spontaneity and exuberance characteristic of the songs composed prior to this time, the "Song"

---

* In an interview on December 4, 1949, Copland stated that the choice in tone sequence outlined above "was something like that."

appears forced, contrived, and, in relation to the composer's total output, deserves recognition simply as an "atonal" experiment. Nevertheless, its material contains important "abstract" implications for works soon to follow in the composer's second style period.

Ex. 10

Returning to America early in September, Copland was again faced with the problem of earning a living. The two-year period of the Guggenheim fellowship was on the point of expiring; therefore, it was extremely urgent that he do something regarding his financial status.

Again Paul Rosenfeld, the critic, came to the composer's rescue by relinquishing his position as lecturer at the New School for Social Research and arranging for Copland to succeed him. At the New School, where he was to be associated for approximately a ten-year period (1927-1937), Copland lectured on modern music and arranged concerts of such music, for which he received a regular salary.

On Wednesday evening, December 28, 1927, the first concert of modern music, arranged by Aaron Copland, took place at the New School. The program, of considerable interest here, for it reflects Copland's "modern" leanings and musical taste during this time, comprised Ernst Křenek's *Concerto for Violin and Piano,* performed by Barbara Lull and Aaron Copland; Stravin-

sky's "Serenade for Piano," played by Carl Buchman; Hindemith's "Eight Songs" from *Das Marienleben,* performed by
Greta Torpadie and Aaron Copland; "Four Piano Compositions"
by Henry Cowell, performed by the composer; a group of pieces
for violin and piano including Ravel's "Berceuse," Von Webern's
"Four Pieces," Op. 7, and Aaron Copland's "Nocturne" and
"Ukelele Serenade," performed by Barbara Lull and the
composer.*

Alice Cogan, writer for the *Brooklyn Eagle,* has given us a
portrait of Copland during these years and a description of his
studio, which was then at 223 West Seventy-eighth Street in
Manhattan. Noting that his studio was hardly the movie version
of what a musician's living quarters should be, Miss Cogan described it as follows:

> A large room in an old-fashioned brownstone house in a quiet
> uptown street, simply, almost plainly, furnished. The grand
> piano between the two windows. A big easy chair in front of
> the fireplace. A small table and two or three smaller chairs. A
> bookcase filled with well-thumbed volumes. A smaller room
> adjoining the large one. In the closet, piles and piles of music
> scores. On the walls, two or three good prints. That is all.
> Nothing exotic, nothing sensational.
>
> Aaron Copland is like that, too. A quiet young man, fairly
> tall, well built though thin. His medium brown hair is combed
> back like a well-groomed college boy's. . . . He wears clothes
> of conservative grays and browns and is always faultlessly tai-
> lored. He looks like a young Englishman, well dressed, dignified,
> conservative, modest.[25]

After the eventful year of 1926-1927, as we have seen, except
for the short "Song" in atonal pattern, Copland maintained a
long silence of fourteen months. A matter of necessity, the re-
quirement that he produce a new work for performance at the
newly organized Copland-Sessions Concerts, set him composing
in early 1928 a "Lento Molto" for string quartet. This he planned
as a companion piece to the earlier "Rondino," composed in
Paris during his study years with Boulanger.

* From the official program.

In the "Lento Molto" *(tranquillo legato)*, Copland forsakes the "serial" technique of the "Song," with its contrapuntal texture, for a return to one employing a greater sense of tonality and a more homophonic texture, experimenting with motives built on major triads.

Undoubtedly influenced by Stravinsky's use of triads in his latest "objective" work, *Oedipus Rex*,* the short four-page work for string quartet is notable for its economy of means and expressive depths of spiritual calm and profundity. That is not to say that the "Lento" is without dissonance. It has that; but dissonance results, in this instance, from the impact of a single line moving against a triadic plane of sound.

There are two ideas in the "Lento," both based on triads: the first, presented by the upper three strings, is expressed by the movement, in mass, of the F sharp major triad into E major and back into F sharp major, in a lower register (pointillism),† (Example 11). Later the second idea, a diatonic melody outlining the tones of the A major triad, sung by the cello, makes its appearance.

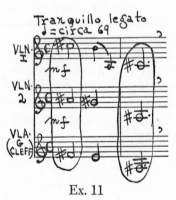

Ex. 11

Both of these ideas are developed individually by canonic imitation at the fifth. Working logically, the composer preserves

* In an article which appeared in *The Arts* in January, 1924, Stravinsky clearly states his theory of objectivity.

† A brief explanation of "pointillism" as applied to music will be found in Addendum, pp. 295–298.

almost always a classical balance in his structure. Though the device of canon appears in almost every work of Copland, it is pointed out here as a unifying element to the "Rondino," a work completely dissimilar in style and idiom, with which the "Lento" was subsequently published. Because of their pronounced dissimilarity of style and content, I have always had the impression that these two pieces are ill-matched.

As an aid to the cause of American music, Aaron Copland and Roger Sessions during this time organized a series of concerts, known as the Copland-Sessions Concerts (1928-1931), devoted principally to the performance of the music of the younger American composers. Due to the lack of space in a volume of this size we must be content with a brief summary of the accomplishments of these concerts, which are unique in the history of American music.

During their four-year existence, a total of eight programs was presented on Sunday evenings; two at the Edith Totten Theatre, two at the Little Theatre, two in Steinway Hall, and one each at the President and Broadhurst theaters.

These concerts introduced the music of seven young American composers in New York, with sixteen American composers receiving first performances of their works. An equal number of European composers (seven) was introduced to New York through the medium of these concerts, with eleven Europeans receiving first performances of their works. Of the forty-seven works performed, the Americans led with twenty-nine, while the Europeans were represented by a total of eighteen.*

Neither the International Composers' Guild, which performed contemporary European and a few American works between 1921 and 1927, nor the League of Composers, founded in 1923, could, in any way, up to the year 1931 approach this record of service to contemporary American composers.

Immediately after the Copland-Sessions concert of May 6,

---

* The joint venture of the two young Americans to further the interests of contemporary music was terminated for the reason that Roger Sessions felt he could not take adequate part in their direction from faraway Europe.

1928, Copland left for Santa Fé, New Mexico, to remain through the month of June. Here he rested, composed, and practiced for an appearance in July as soloist in his *Piano Concerto* at the Hollywood Bowl. In addition to working on the trio *Vitebsk* in Santa Fé, he wrote, at the request of the French publisher Leduc, a "Vocalise" for voice and piano.

Recalling that vocalises of an earlier age had provided the technical equipment for execution of the song literature, Professor Hettich of the Paris Conservatoire (editor of the vocalise series for Leduc) maintained that vocalises written by contemporary composers could provide the means by which young students might solve technical and interpretive problems of the newest music. Since 1907, he had edited ten volumes, consisting of one hundred *Vocalises-Études,* written by leading twentieth century composers, which are used as technical studies by the students of the Conservatoire. Fauré composed "Vocalise" No. 1, Volume I, and Copland, No. 71, Volume VIII.

Although for voice and piano, the Copland "Vocalise" ignores the pianistic aspects of the usual accompaniment and limits its texture to two lines (one for each hand), which freely imitate the vocal line. This two-line limitation of the piano accompaniment creates a certain bareness in sound, a characteristic of the works of the Abstract Period.

Other new tendencies found in the four-page work *(con moto)* may be briefly summarized as follows: the frequent change of meter; a 3/4 measure in the voice over a 4/4 measure in the piano; the modal flavor of the piano introduction that evokes an archaic mood; the polytonal, Ravel-like harmonies; and the treatment of the cadenza, in modern "cumulative" style. Possessing endearing qualities of grace and charm, the "Vocalise" follows in the felicitous French vein of the earlier "As It Fell upon a Day."

In July, Copland spent a week in Hollywood, where he appeared as soloist in his *Piano Concerto* at the Bowl on July 20, 1928, with Albert Coates as conductor. Directly after the concert, Copland went up to San Francisco to visit his friend Henry Cowell. There, on the following Monday evening, a reception was tendered him by the New Music Society of California, of which Cowell was president.

After his visit to the West Coast, Copland returned to the MacDowell Colony for two months, August and September, to engage in intensive work. Here he arranged the "Rondino" and "Lento Molto" for string orchestra and was busy completing the reorchestration of the organ symphony in a version without the organ. Making progress with the trio *(Vitebsk)*, he labored arduously on the new orchestral work, *Symphonic Ode*, which did not seem to proceed easily.

In September, the New York *Times* announced that, beginning October 1, Aaron Copland would present a course of twelve lectures on masterworks of modern music at the New School for Social Research. According to the *Times*, the classes would be open to laymen as well as to musicians and were designed "to engender appreciation of the modern school of music."[26] The lectures were to include the following subjects: (1) General Survey (Esthetics of Modern Music); (2) "Boris Godounoff" (Realism of Moussorgsky); (3) "Pelléas et Mélisande (Impressionism of Debussy); (4) "Das Lied von der Erde" (Post-Romanticism of Mahler); (5) "Daphnis et Chloe" (Post-Impressionism of Ravel); (6) "Pierrot Lunaire" (Expressionism of Schoenberg); (7) "Le Sacre du Printemps" (Dynamism of Stravinsky); (8) "Prometheus" (Mysticism of Scriabin); (9) "Creation du Monde" (Lyricism of Milhaud); (10) "Das Marienleben" (Neo-Classicism of Hindemith); (11) "Oedipus Rex" (Objectivism of Stravinsky); (12) Summary (Lesser Masterworks). The offering of so comprehensive a course of lectures in "modern" music as the above, in the hands of so authoritative a lecturer-musician as Copland, reflected not only the progressive spirit inherent in the founding of the New School, but also provided a further avenue for the influence Copland was to exert upon the music of his native city.

In May, 1928, *The Fontainebleau Alumni Bulletin* had published John Kirkpatrick's article, "On Copland's Music." A student at Fontainebleau during 1925, 1926, and 1927, Kirkpatrick, an American pianist and friend of Copland's, was also vitally interested in performing contemporary music. Author of the first article devoted to Copland's music as a whole, Kirkpatrick had written the composer to inquire what he had thought of his critical effort. Copland's reply, dated October 13, 1928, reached Kirkpatrick in Paris:

The article amused me as being the very first to treat my music *as a whole*. I was very grateful for the bibliography. There were three slips I noted: (1) the ballet doesn't end with Grohg dragging coffins off the stage! I'm not quite *that* gruesome!! Everyone disappears and Grohg simply walks off in a daze. (2) There is nothing "faulty" with the orchestration of the Organ Symphony. I rewrote it this summer for orchestra alone, but as a matter of fact, thought the purely orchestral parts of the original so good that I've kept them intact. (3) The third "slip" was the only one that worries me and I take it comes from your lack of experience as a journalist: the story I mean about Antheil and the Quartet [See footnote, pp. 88f-89 of this chapter]. It was true of course, but it's the kind of thing which is just as well left unsaid. God help me, if Antheil ever sees your article. Aside from these few points I thought you did yourself proud and gave me an excellent introduction to the world.

I was glad to know of all the copies of the Concerto. The score, I think, will be published next year.

You're right about the B flat-B sharp of the viola part of the Lento. I've just arranged both pieces for String Orchestra. I was always under the impression that N. B. [Nadia Boulanger] had a copy of the Rondino. Let me know if that isn't so.

Your suggestion for beginning the Concerto on a first beat was interesting but for some reason or other I actually hear it as a third beat with the trumpet imitation as the real first beat. Of course no one will ever believe this, but it's true none the less.

The only thing I finished this summer is a Vocalise for voice and piano, ordered by Alphonse Leduc for a collection and shortly to be published by him. But a big orchestral piece is on the way.

As you guess Cowell intended publishing "As it——." But as the only copy is in Mexico City and hard to get at, it may not come off this season. The Universal have announced *Tragadie*

um Suden for fall publication (ballet title of *Music for* ——)
[*the Theatre*].
What are your plans for the winter? I had hoped to have your
help at the New School this year! not to mention the C-S concerts. Write to me when you have time—news of yourself and
the Boulangerie. Greetings to you.

As always,

AARON*

December 14, 1928, found Copland in Boston to hear the
première of his *Two Pieces for String Orchestra* (an arrangement of the string quartet pieces, "Lento" and "Rondino"), performed by Koussevitzky and the Boston Symphony Orchestra.
The program also included works by Martinu, Prokofieff, and
Beethoven.

The following year, on February 3, 1929, Copland received
the first of what proved to be many performances of his music
in Mexico when *Music for the Theatre* was performed by the
Orquesta Sinfónica, Carlos Chávez conducting, in the final concert of the season. Maurice Muñóz, critic of *El Universal*, wrote
that Copland's work "requires, even demands, one's strictest attention, on account of its magnificent polyrhythms and harmonic construction."[27] The Mexico City performance was,
therefore, the third foreign performance of *Music for the Theatre*, the first having been by Koussevitzky, at the Paris Opera,
spring of 1926, and the second, at the Frankfort (Germany)
ISCM festival, July, 1927. Thus this novel work, because of its
individuality and freshness of inspiration, was the first of Copland's orchestral compositions to make its way into the contemporary orchestral repertoire.

Assistance to the growing movement of contemporary music
in the United States was noted in the report of the organization
of the Cos Cob Press, published in the New York *Times*, February 24, 1929. Through its president, Alma M. Wertheim, it was
announced that, regardless of their commercial value, this organization would publish orchestral and other works of native

* The Copland letters to John Kirkpatrick were made available to this study
by Mr. Kirkpatrick.

American composers. Edwin F. Kalmus, vice-president, would act as manager and distributor in this country and Europe. Orchestral works by Aaron Copland, Louis Gruenberg, and Emerson Whithorne had been accepted for publication and would be available in the fall. With the cooperation of publishing houses, conductors, and musical organizations in Europe, the Cos Cob Press hoped to open the field on that continent to the American composer.

This step was a boon to the American composer, for the established music publishing houses here then seldom, if ever, published the works of any of the younger "advanced" composers. Copland had been fortunate in finding French and German publishers for his smaller works but, for his larger works, like his colleagues he found the doors to the American publishing houses closed. In contrast to other music publishers, Cos Cob was "anxious to receive serious manuscripts in any musical form." Most of Copland's early symphonic scores, including such works as the *Dance Symphony, First Symphony, Music for the Theatre,* and *Concerto for Piano and Orchestra,* as well as the *Piano Variations* and trio *Vitebsk,* were, therefore, published during the next few years. Their publication added greatly to the composer's artistic stature, both at home and abroad.

At an earlier date, John Kirkpatrick had made a reduction to four hands of Copland's *Piano Concerto,* which the Cos Cob Press decided to publish. In view of the fact that Kirkpatrick, a long-time friend of his, was in Paris, Copland, perhaps unwisely, permitted the publication of this arrangement without benefit of a formal contract between the publishers and Kirkpatrick. A small "tempest in a teapot" soon developed, as recounted in the following letters sent from Briarcliff Manor, New York, the first dated March 10, 1929:

Dear John,
Funny, I was about to write to you when your letter came. The purpose was to tell you that the *Concerto* is being published by Alma Wertheim's new Cos Cob Press and your piano arrangement is being engraved at this very minute. (She is also printing score and parts.) I have made inquiries and the fee

you rightfully deserve is so miniscule (something like $20) that I thought you might forego it for the love of seeing your name in print on a piece of music. (Perhaps you would like to correct your own proofs?) Anyhow let's not ruin our friendship over business details!

The League introduced my newest piece on the 16th of last month. It is called *Vitebsk*—is for violin, piano, and cello and was marvelously performed by Gieseking and Messrs. Onnou & Maas of the Pro Arte Quartet.

Cowell is printing "As It ——" in the last number (July) of this year [New Music Edition.]

The Universal write that they are waiting to place the M. for T. [*Music for the Theatre*] as a ballet before issuing the score.

I've come out to Briarcliff Manor for the rest of the winter in order to finish the big orchestral piece. (Incidentally, the 10/16 piano piece is being incorporated into it.) It must be finished before I sail for Europe on May 14. So I'll be able to hear the piano progress you make myself.

If you run out of pieces to four-hand why not take a whack at my Organ Symphony. N. B. had my original score. . . .

I haven't seen a note of *Le Baiser de la Fée* [by Stravinsky] yet and your letter made me very curious.

Virgil [Thomson] has had much success over here.

Yours,

As ever,

AARON

In quick succession Copland received two letters from his friend who, evidently, had got his "Scotch ire" up regarding his part in the publication of the four-hand arrangement of the *Piano Concerto*. Realizing he had perhaps acted hastily, Copland undertook to set matters right by explaining to Kirkpatrick how the whole project developed. Dated April 9, also from Briarcliff Manor, Copland's second letter reads as follows:

Dear John,

I have your two letters. In view of the stand you take I thought it best to refer the whole matter to Mr. Edwin Kalmus who handles the business end of the Cos Cob Press, since in the last analysis, it has to do with you and him. I went in to see him yesterday—he was out—I explained your attitude to his wife— she promised to tell Kalmus and he is to write you a letter about terms, etc. (It seems they know you quite well).

You are absolutely right of course in saying that I had no "right" in arranging for publication without consulting you. But at first the Press only wished to publish score and parts, and only at the very last moment decided to do the arrangement also. They were in a great hurry to begin—there was no time to wait—I simply took it for granted that you would get what was coming to you. Of course if you were a complete stranger to me I shouldn't have done this—but taking a friend's liberty and not expecting you to be fleeced I said go ahead. My mind worked in this fashion: John will want his arrangement published—at best there isn't a large sum of money involved—apparently John doesn't depend on his arrangements for a source of income— ergo, the main thing is to have the arrangement published. It was because of this that I wrote you in the airy, nonbusiness-like tone I did.

Let me ask you to remember, first, that the Cos Cob Press is, as you say, a "philanthropic enterprise"—so go easy on them. They have a yearly budget and every penny you save them will go into the publishing of more American works. At best they can't sell many copies of the kind of stuff they print so that what Harms pays for a jazz arrangement that sells by the "millions" of copies has nothing to do with the matter. Secondly, please remember the very casual and friendly way you began making the arrangement.

Finally, the proofs are already finished and I have already corrected them—even before your letters came—so that I must throw myself on your good will and ask that no matter what happens you arrange the matter amicably.

As always,
AARON

The business arrangements were finally settled amicably and the temporary rift between the friends was soon smoothed away. In the meantime Kirkpatrick has earned the reputation of being one of the best interpreters of Copland's piano works.

At the close of the musical season in New York, which also marked the end of the second season for the Copland-Sessions Concerts, Copland left for Paris on May 14, 1929, to arrange a concert of contemporary American works. The concert, planned for June 17, would give the French artistic world an opportunity to hear a program representative of America's young "advanced" composers. The works of five composers were to be presented: Virgil Thomson, Roy Harris, Israel Citkowitz, Carlos Chávez,* and Aaron Copland, all of whom (with the exception of Chávez) had been, or were at the time, pupils of Boulanger.

The composers' chief aim in presenting the concert was to show the Paris art world that America, too, now had a young composers' movement, united in aims, whose technical and cultural background would compare favorably with the Russian Five or the French Six.

Boulanger assisted in planning and arranging the program and, of course, was present at the concert. Her attitude toward the American works was one of general approval.

Meanwhile, Serge Koussevitzky arrived in Paris to conduct five presentations of *Boris Godounow* before starting his summer vacation in the Pyrenees. The New York *Times,* with a Paris dateline of May 23, reported Koussevitzky had said that America had the most intense musical development of any country in the world and led in appreciation of good music. "A phenomenal musical renaissance is in progress in the United States," he continued. "Americans have the active temperament which [contrary to the opinions of many] has been the salvation of America's artistic development. They have stimulated orchestral advancement, just as they have created immense business enterprises. The American people have an inordinate genius for growth."[28]

Koussevitzky believed that Stravinsky was the most outstanding influence in modern music in America and named Aaron Copland, Roger Sessions, and John Alden Carpenter as Amer-

---

* In view of the fact that Chávez, although born in Mexico, was a member of the "advanced" young composers' group, he was generally regarded by them as an American. In any case, he is surely a North American composer.

ica's promising composers. He declared that American composers no longer found jazz a suitable medium.

The eminent conductor's enthusiastic statement regarding
music in America and praise of her younger men, coming as it
did approximately three weeks before the Paris concert of the
"five," focused the attention of the musicgoing public upon the
forthcoming event.

The concert of American works took place on Monday evening, June 17, in the Salle Chopin. Appearing as performers
were Mmes Marthe-Marthine, singer, and Ilona Kabos, pianist;
the Calvet String Quartet; MM. Aaron Copland and Virgil
Thomson.

The program included *Vitebsk* (Study on a Jewish Theme)
for violin, cello, and piano, by Aaron Copland; Three Songs:
"Strings in the earth and air," "When the shy star," "Bid adieu,
adieu" by Israel Citkowitz (text by James Joyce); *Sonata for
Piano* by Carlos Chávez; *Two Pieces for String Quartet:* "Lento
Molto" and "Rondino" by Aaron Copland; *Quelques Airs* by
Virgil Thomson, which included "Gregorian Waltz" (text by
Georges Huguet), "The Seine" (text by the Duchess of Rohan),
"The Cradle of Gertrude Stein" or "The Mystery of the Street
of Flowers" (eight poems of Georges Huguet set to music under
the title of *Lady Godiva's Waltzes),* "Susie Asado," and "Pré-
ciosilla" (texts of both songs by Gertrude Stein); *Sextette* for
string quartet, clarinet, and piano by Roy Harris.*

Did the young Americans receive a better press in Paris, the
cradle of modern music, than in New York? One might be in-
clined to think so. On the whole, the critic of the Paris-New York
Herald seemed more friendly to the works of the young Americans than did the French critics.

Writing in the first edition of the American paper, the critic
observed that great applause was bestowed on *Vitebsk,* a work
by Aaron Copland, which presented a very rational development of an interesting theme. He found the same composer's
"Rondino" quite charming and the songs of Citkowitz, notably
"When the shy star," rather successful. The songs of Virgil

* From the official program.

Thomson were termed "humorous after the manner of Erik Satie," while Roy Harris's *Sextette* contained "curious contrasts of classical sonorities with modern dissonances and strange effects of rhythms."[29]

The critic of the French newspaper, *Excelsior,* wrote that he would speak frankly of his disappointment on hearing the works of five young American composers: " 'Vitebsk,' by Mr. Copland, the 'Three Songs' of Mr. Citkowitz and the 'Piano Sonata' of Mr. Chávez sacrifice to intellectual communism, destroyer of all order, which they make a show of, in a sophisticated manner, in an elegant salon." Considering such an esthetic artistically dangerous, the critic continued:

> The opposite has been proposed by Mr. V. Thomson who, under a pretext of simplicity, writes distressing vocal platitudes in the spirit of the "School of Arcueil." Someone sings: "Have you wept before a motionless coach?" . . . Sad! Mid this chaos Copland's "Two Pieces for String Quartet" and Harris's "Sextette" almost seemed masterpieces.[30]

Pierre Leroi, critic of *Les Débats,* noted that however desirous one might be to discover new talents and to praise them as was fitting, one cannot but indicate a real discouragement on hearing the concert of works by young American composers:

> What is one to think of this jarring "Study on a Jewish Theme," of Mr. Copland . . . as well as of that crude "Sonata" by Chávez, in which it is impossible to discern the slightest theme and the most indefinite development? Some songs of . . . Citkowitz and Thomson manifested a distressing poverty, while the "Sextette" of Mr. Harris . . . denotes the most inexperienced hand in the world. Standing entirely alone, Copland's "Two Pieces for String Quartet" contained the only true musical elements of the entire evening. . . . Lento molto, reveals a distinctly lyrical character, and . . . Rondino . . . shows the unmistakable influence of Ravel.[31]

Praising the very devoted and talented interpreters, the critic stated, "not without sadness, that [the concert] was a huge success for all the composers."

As a result of this concert in the French capital, the Americans gave convincing proof of the existence in their own country of a healthy, vital movement within the ranks of its young composers toward a contemporary expression, French-American in viewpoint.

The most important fact of the concert, however, was that the young composers, particularly Copland, were received by an enthusiastic audience, which applauded heartily. It was evident, therefore, that whether the critics liked the concert or not, America had at last begun to concern itself seriously with a national musical culture, whose concerted effort in Paris won the acclaim of an international audience.

Soon after the Paris concert, Copland left for Gargenville in order to be near Boulanger for the remainder of the summer. Earlier, he had "got stuck" in the middle of the *Ode* and sensed that he needed his former teacher's criticism and counsel as to how to "get on" with the composition. There was an additional urgency—to complete the work in time for the Boston Symphony's fiftieth anniversary year, 1930.

Unable to find suitable living quarters in Gargenville, Copland, accompanied by Israel Citkowitz, took a house in the adjoining village, Juziers, Seine-et-Oise. Citkowitz was one of Copland's former pupils who, at Copland's suggestion, had become a pupil of Boulanger. The two young men spent a productive summer, from July through September, in the quiet, picturesque French village. Not only did Copland finish the sketch, or outline, of the *Ode,* but he also made great progress on its orchestration.

Symphonic Ode

Because of certain difficulties that required simplification, the *Ode* did not receive its first performance until 1932. With its massive formal layout and its Mahler-like orchestra, it is nearer the grandiose manner of the *First Symphony* Finale than to jazz, though this latter element is present in the second, or scherzo-like, section. In addition, Copland now had begun a process of

to a figuration of the opening theme, in diminution.* This rhythmic phrase (Example 13) is punctuated by the C octave, which soon expands into a polytonal punctuation (C major and B flat, scored for brass and tympani). That polytonal punctuation is immediately followed by sustained chords in open fifths and octaves. Both of these elements are developed through a new period of polyrhythmic designs, mosaic in effect, presenting frequent measure changes (2/4, 4/4, 3/8, 4/4), and leading up to the now famous (2/4 and 6/8) rhythm which the Boston Symphony Orchestra found impossible to play as notated. Recently, Copland recalled the incident as follows:

Ex. 13

Koussevitzky informed me that the orchestra had spent several hours' rehearsal on the *Ode* and still could not play it. He suggested that if I changed the 2/4 and 6/8 section to 5/4, the men could probably play it without any trouble. [In 1930, the change from 2/4 to 6/8 rhythm was not so familiar as it is today.] I laughed at the notion that this was a difficult rhythm and told Koussevitzky that there was nothing to it—the rhythm is an easy one to play. He immediately replied: "Come on up to Boston, take over the rehearsal yourself and you'll find out how 'easy' it is. After an hour's rehearsal, we can play about three bars," he jokingly concluded.

Since I was reluctant to make any change in the score, I went to Boston to attend the next rehearsal. Koussevitzky turned the orchestra over to me and left the hall. We went through the

* This idea appears even closer to the opening theme of the *Sextet* (see Chapter V, Example 5).

piece and I was convinced the rhythm was difficult for them. Thereupon I agreed to do as the conductor wished and changed the whole section to read 5/4 (Example 14).

Ex. 14

After a brilliant development of this new derivative, the music moves into the C section *(subito lento)*, which is a more lyrical expression of the Section A material. Here the notes appear for the first time as they are written in the original violin "Nocturne." The repetition of the B section is only approximate, with the composer going immediately into the 5/4 section. This, in turn, leads into Section D, which combines A and B to form a coda in the monumental mood of the opening.

Concerning the *Ode,* Copland recently commented: "I regard it as one of my most important works. I tried for something there; I tried hard; and I feel that I succeeded in what I attempted."

Regardless of any limitations in the score (its difficulty apparently being its chief limitation), the work's profound musical depth, expressed by means of a superior handling of musical materials, placed the composer, a young man just turned thirty, in the front rank of contemporary composers. Highly individual in respect to its melodic and polyrhythmic design, Jewish in respect to its grandeur and prophetic note, and French in its craftsmanship, the *Symphonic Ode* stands out as the most distinguished and compelling work of the first period.

V

Second Style Period (Abstract)
America, Europe, Africa, Mexico
(1929-1935)

THAT Copland is a man of his time, reflecting the spirit and mood of his age through his music, is no less true of the disillusion-filled depression years of the early thirties than it was of the careless, extravagant, jazzy, "bourgeois" twenties. Because of their "absolute" aesthetic conception, the works of the years 1929 to 1935 have been termed "esoteric" or "abstract." Presenting aspects of great tonal edifices, Paul Rosenfeld has stated that Copland's works of this time "resemble nothing so much as steel cranes, bridges and the frames of skyscrapers."[1]

The failure of the general music public, including most critics, musicians, and laymen, to regard the works of Copland's second period in their true light is undoubtedly due to two reasons: the scant performance of these works (due to their complexity and experimental nature), and a lack of understanding of their compositional techniques. It is to be hoped that the following pages will contribute to a better understanding of Copland's music of the second period, for these scores are among the composer's finest and are representative of his more "serious," expressive style.

Instrumental compositions only (no vocal scores were composed during these years) and few in number, the works of the Abstract Period comprise the following: the trio, *Vitebsk; Piano Variations; Short Symphony* (Sextet); and *Statements*. The composer's critical writings outnumber his musical works by two, there being a total of eight critiques published during these years on various subjects.

Copland's travels in Europe, Africa, the United States, and Mexico during this time reveal his growth as an international figure in contemporary music.

It was during the depression years that the young intellec-

tuals, who formerly had never given a second thought to politics, now became vitally interested in the economic plight of the country. Roosevelt's proclamation that we "need not be frustrated by our misfortunes but could be masters of our future" fired the imaginations and stirred the patriotic instincts of young artists in all fields. The first feeling of hopelessness was quickly supplanted by one of determination to attack the problem and marshal the vitality of our young creative minds toward a solution of our unfortunate predicament.

Harold Clurman, who shared student days with young Copland in Paris between 1921 and 1924, and whose experimental Group Theatre functioned between 1931 and 1941, has termed the thirties a period of "spiritual activity." "In the thirties," he wrote, "the demands of the spirit for the younger people could only be satisfied by action that in some way became social and political. Hence the appetite for meetings, collections, demonstrations, petitions, and parades on behalf of some cause in which a specific social issue was at stake."[2]

As noted in Chapter I, Copland's father and uncles were life-long members of the Democratic party. Copland, on the other hand, while never an enrolled member of any political party, has expressed himself as sympathetic toward the American-Liberal principles, principles which many of the creative artists living in and around New York adopted during the thirties and have retained to the present time. Recently Copland gave the following simple explanation of the basis for his choice between the liberal and conservative viewpoints:

> If one likes people, is sympathetic to them and concerned about their welfare in general, one's personal leaning is in the direction of the democratic or liberal viewpoint. If, on the other hand, a person is not gregarious, prefers to be alone, and concerns himself with the welfare of only a privileged few, his leanings are toward a more limited group—an aristocratic or conservative viewpoint.*

It is interesting to observe that the democratic or liberal po-

* Stated in an interview with Mr. Copland at the Town Hall Club, November 27, 1950.

litical viewpoint did not penetrate Copland's musical scores until the third style period, that of the American Folksong. Curiously, the abstract works are directed to a more limited group, not, however, aristocratic and conservative, but "radically" intellectual and "advanced" from the standpoint of the understanding of techniques involved and their small audience appeal. Thus there appears, as is usually the case in art, little evidence of a tangible carryover from an artist's ascribed political beliefs (in spite of what he may say) to the actual product of his creative imagination as expressed in definitive musical compositions.

Working at intervals during the summer of 1928 on the trio and the *Symphonic Ode,* Copland returned to New York in October to his lecture duties at the New School for Social Research. He now developed plans for the third season of the Copland-Sessions Concerts and, compositionally, completed the trio, which was to have its *première* early in the New Year.

Vitebsk

Although the trio, *Vitebsk,* belongs chronologically to the works composed before 1930, it is stylistically nearer the works composed after that time and, therefore, has been placed with the works of the Abstract Period. It stands in somewhat the same relation to the works of this period as does *Music for the Theatre* to the works of the Jazz Period. Further, in its reliance on a Jewish folksong for thematic material, it also contains the seed of yet another style to follow—the American Folksong Period.

As noted in Chapter I, with the exception of a setting of the Jewish folksong "Dance-Hora" and *Vitebsk,* subtitled "Study on a Jewish Theme," Copland has not turned to Hebrew sources for music materials. Representative of the more lyrical side of Copland's nature, the use of the long-lined melody does present different aspects of a composer who, up to this work, has seemed to prefer manipulating ideas of short three-, four- and five-note themes into large designs. The folksong, then, gives the work the quality of being long-breathed and lyrical in contrast to the nervous, short-breathed, gasping quality of some of the more rhythmic works.

The trio has, with Copland, a theatrical or dramatic origin. During the 1926-1927 season, he attended a performance of *The Dybbuk*, S. Anski's dramatic legend, presented by the Moscow Art Theatre in New York City's Neighborhood Playhouse, and was much taken with the Jewish folksong used throughout the play as background music. Upon inquiry, he learned that the folksong had no name but came from the village of Vitebsk, the birthplace of Anski. Sensing that the song's lyric and expressive qualities fitted it for extended musical development, Copland soon set to work on the trio. To that date (1929), this Jewish folksong is the first theme, not original with him, that Copland had used as the basis for a musical composition.

Scored for piano, violin, and cello, in one movement, with divisions of slow-fast-slow, an eloquent introduction *(lento molto marcato)*, with violin and cello playing in octaves, opens the work, enunciating a bold, incisive, declamatory style. Underneath, at intervals, the piano punctuates the two-tone motive (evolved from the main theme itself) with sharply accented

Ex. 1

chords in the polytonalities of C major and C minor, E minor and E major (Example 1).*

An interesting feature of the introduction is the use of quarter tones in the string parts which, as Berger has noted, suggest somewhat the portamento of oriental vocal style.[3] Following their use in *Vitebsk*, quarter tones have not again appeared in Copland's compositions to date (1955). It will be remembered that he first used them briefly near the end of the waltz movement of the *Dance Symphony* (*Grohg*) and again in the "Ukelele Serenade" for violin and piano in 1926 (cf. Chapters III and IV). All of these uses of quarter-tone technique are to give atmosphere rather than to be used as a fundamental harmonic basis. In the "Ukelele Serenade," by imitating the saxophone or clarinet in the "blueing" of a note, their use achieves a jazz spirit, while in *Vitebsk* their colorful interjection invokes a mood of intense, poignant, oriental wailing.

Following the dramatic quarter-tone-flavored introduction, the cello enters *(meno mosso-grave)*, singing the Jewish folk theme, full-voiced, *espressivo*, in the tonality of B minor (Example 2).

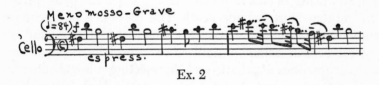

Ex. 2

Underneath the folksong, the piano continues its polytonal biting chords (sfz), interspersed with occasional imitations of figures from the melody. The second part of the folksong (refrain) is developed in stretto, so that all three voices are playing a contrapuntal weaving of the verse or refrain.

Section II *(subito allegro vivace)* is in the nature of a dance which expresses the same kind of sardonic mood and satirical, grotesque humor as Marc Chagall, the Jewish artist, portrays in his paintings of the rabbis. The music reflects the distortions

* Copland states that the rhythm ♪ ♩ is, to him, a jazz-conscious rhythm, expressive of "dá-da."

of the human spirit on being subjected to the degraded living conditions found in the ghettos; it expresses just the sort of thing the Russians ordered Shostakovitch not to do.

The piano introduces a dance rhythm in parallel fourths (taken from the introduction) which soon becomes the accompanying ostinato* for the sardonic dance, presented in the form of a fugato. The fugato† (or dance) theme, evolved from the "Vitebsk" theme, is so Hebraic or Slavic in flavor that it conveys the atmosphere of an authentic folk theme (Example 3).

Ex. 3

The jazz touch is present—a passage reminiscent of a "hot blues break," made out of the ostinato piano figure (in parallel fourths) heard in octaves in the strings, while the piano plays a "riff" of tone clusters underneath. This passage is not incongruous with the dance for it is readily seen that folk music and jazz possess certain common similarities, especially rhythmic and melodic qualities of a basic sort. In rejecting a literal reference to jazz, Copland reveals a refining of materials characteristic of the more austere works of this period.

The recapitulation is a fully realized statement of the Jewish folksong grandly orchestrated, featuring bell sounds in the piano part. A short coda, reminiscent of the folk theme, gradually descends in range and dynamics, bringing the rhapsodic work to a close.

Approximately eleven minutes in length, *Vitebsk* is undoubt-

---

* In his dance movements, Copland appears to rely almost entirely on the ostinato as a basic rhythm pattern; this has been apparent from the *Dance Symphony* onward.

† A fugato is a passage in fugal style which forms part of a primarily nonfugal composition.

edly one of our most skillful and perfect chamber music works. Its depth of emotion is at once apparent, for it projects two dominant aspects of the Hebrew spirit: aspirations and longings (expressed in the slow version of the folk theme); and the necessity to laugh sardonically at environment in order to endure it (expressed by the grotesque dance). Economy of means is viewed in the adaptation and development of the same music material to express two widely divergent characteristics of the Hebrew spirit. In spite of the fact that the work is based on a folk tune, the trio's harmonic basis and resulting "harsher" dissonances are achieved through polytonal (major and minor) blocks of sounds articulated simultaneously with heavy accents, stringent and acrid intervals of ninths and sevenths widely spaced and clashes of fragments of the theme propelled forward by means of linear imitation, giving, at times, the impression of playing in four keys at once (two in the piano).

The first performance of *Vitebsk* took place at a League of Composers' Concert, February 16, 1929, at which time Walter Gieseking was the pianist and Onnou and Maas, violinist and cellist, respectively. Noting that the work was "vociferously applauded" by the audience, W. J. Henderson stated that "the melody is distinctly Hebrew and Mr. Copland's treatment exhibited it first in a declamatory form and afterward in a sort of scherzando which was engagingly conceived."[4]

In October, 1929, shortly after Copland's return from a six month's stay in France (recounted in Chapter IV), with the collapse of the New York Stock Exchange, the world depression began.

The crash did not immediately affect the composer's economic existence. However, engagements for lecture concerts soon dwindled to almost nothing, the American people, for the time being, feeling they must relinquish all such "nonessentials." Because the musical works composed during these years were difficult to execute and to understand, Copland was not being performed; consequently, he was deprived of another source of income. Nor were commissions forthcoming, for even million-aires were retrenching. Instead, a new source of commissions began to trickle in from the theaters. In January, 1930, Copland took a place in the country at Bedford, New York, where he remained until July. For companionship he took along his friend Gerald Sykes, a writer of novels, short stories, and literary criticism who was engaged in writing a new work at the time.

Continuing his preoccupation with the economy of means in the handling of musical materials, that is, how to extract the very essence, both the musical and the expressive, from a motive or an idea, the composer removed himself to Bedford with the express purpose of utilizing those months to resolve an esthetic that long had confronted him: how far can one go with four notes? Characteristically, Copland had had the initial germ (or theme) in mind several years earlier. Except for brief trips to New York during February, March, and April for the Copland-Sessions Concerts, the composer remained completely isolated, working incessantly at the *Variations*.

In June, 1930, rather providentially, Copland received a portion of the RCA Victor Symphonic Award, a sum of $5,000. He began to make plans to go to Europe the following year (1931), where living was cheaper and where art and music even during depression times, unlike in America, were regarded as necessities of life.

Meanwhile, the young man gratefully accepted the invitation of Mrs. Elizabeth Ames, executive director of Yaddo, to spend the months of July through September (1930) as a guest on the estate of the late Mr. and Mrs. Spencer Trask.

On the beautiful, secluded estate, Copland began to visualize his dream of an American Festival of Contemporary Music, modeled after European festivals. He presented his idea to Mrs. Ames, who immediately expressed interest in the project and revealed a willingness to help. Together they began to develop plans for such a festival, designed to take place a year hence.

In a letter to John Kirkpatrick bearing the official letterhead of Yaddo and the date of July 27, 1930, Copland invited his friend to hear a performance of the *Concerto for Piano and Orchestra*. The concert would take place in New York's Lewisohn

Stadium under the baton of Albert Coates, with whom Copland had performed the work in the Hollywood Bowl two years earlier. Copland's letter continues:

The Stadium performance is to take place on the 9th of August, unless it rains—in which case it is postponed to the 10th. I'll expect to see you there. Why not come in for the morning rehearsal on the day of the concert?

I am spending the summer at Yaddo—the former estate of Spencer Trask, which is now a kind of Guest Home for creative artists. I'm hard at work on the "serious piano piece"—I think it will be called *Thematic Variations*—and hope to have it finished by October. The *Symphonic Ode* that I was working on last summer is finished and in Koussi's [Koussevitzky's] hands now. (He was to have played it last season, but found it so difficult rhythmically that he said he needed a whole summer to study it!)

Did you see the notice in the July *American Mercury* about your arrangement of the *Concerto*? . . .

The concert took place as planned on August 9 and marked Copland's first performance at the Stadium Concerts. Afterwards he returned to Yaddo, where he remained until the end of September. Again, on August 29, from Yaddo, Copland wrote to Kirkpatrick, giving him news of the activities of other American composers:

Dear John,

Roy [Harris] is in California—married to Hilda, who went out there in July. He plans to settle there permanently—in Baldwin Park just outside Los Angeles. (He's never taught in a girl's school!) . . . He wrote of projected performances of his Symphony at the Hollywood Bowl in August and at Rochester in Nov. I don't know whether he has started something new or not.

Roger's [Sessions] Sonata *is* finished. He's summering at Hadley, Mass.

You're right about *Thematic Variations*. I should like to call them like Bach did the *Goldberg Variations*—but thus far haven't been able to think up a good one.

Did I tell you that Teddy Chanler is devoting his next Musical Chronicle in the *Hound & Horn*—to appear in October—to my work? I read the article myself a few days ago (it's far from laudatory!) and think you'd be interested to see it when it comes out.

Regarding the European trip he was planning about eight months hence, Copland continued in the same letter:

I plan to go straight thru to Berlin but will probably visit in Paris for a space, particularly if Coates should do the *Concerto* in London in April. Keep me posted as to your whereabouts.

Returning to New York in October, 1930, Copland established a studio at the Hotel Montclair, Lexington Avenue at Forty-ninth Street. During the fall he completed the *Variations*, which were scheduled for a League of Composers' *première* early in the new year. As he was to perform the *Variations* himself, he was busy practicing throughout the fall months.

Piano Variations

One of the most controversial of Copland's works concerning which the public has some degree of information is the *Piano Variations* of 1930. With the possible exception of the *Piano Quartet* (1950), Copland in the *Variations* has come closer to the Schoenberg principles of the "serial" technique (use of the "tone row") without, however, completely relinquishing the principle of tonality. After twenty-five years, this complex composition, now regarded as one of the important works in contemporary piano literature, has made its way surely and steadily, propelled to a large extent by the composer's excellent performances of the work here and in Europe. Published in 1932, the *Piano Variations* have been more widely circulated in the concert hall, in the dance theater, and through phonograph recordings than have the other works of the Abstract Period.

That Stravinsky exerted a paramount influence on young Copland between 1923 and 1927 has already been shown. It was in

Paris in 1922 that Copland first heard Schoenberg's "atonal" *Pierrot Lunaire,* which evidently had some effect on his subconscious thought. His contact with Alban Berg's *Lyric Suite,* heard at the Baden-Baden Festival (July, 1927), seems to have interested him further in the "serial," or twelve-tone, technique, for he was groping in that direction in the "Song" composed later that summer in Königstein. An isolated experiment, he did not return to this technique until the *Piano Variations,* written three years later.

The entire ten-minute piano solo, based on a four-note motive or "motto," is announced at once: E-C-E flat-C sharp.* Consist-

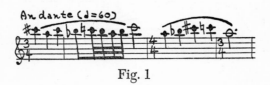

Fig. 1

ing of the theme with twenty variations and a coda, each variation is related to the following in the sense that it builds architecturally, solidly, one after the other. By comparing the theme of the *Variations* with the bassoon "Dance" theme from *Music for the Theatre,* a "blues" connotation of the *Variations'* theme is apparent in the shifting thirds between C major and minor, implying a polytonal melodic relationship.

Set forth in declamatory style, the short motive's final (fourth) note is punctuated by the polytonal harmonies of A major and A minor (or C major). The mood is bare, stark, and percussive. To determine the first appearance of all twelve tones in the composition, a number has been assigned to each. The theme itself makes use of but ten (both in melody and harmo-

---

* A striking similarity to the opening notes of Stravinsky's 1923 *Octuor* theme (Figure 1), is evident. Compare Figure 1 with Example 4. Stravinsky's work is based on a 33-note theme in the form of an "Air" with five variations. One of the most marked differences between the two works is that Stravinsky returns to the first variation of the theme after practically each variation.

In order to make the following analysis of the *Piano Variations* more meaningful, the author suggests that the "serious" reader have at hand the published music score.

nization), in the following succession: E-C-D#-C#-A-D♮-F#-G#-B-G♮ (Example 4).

Ex. 4

Architecturally falling into two large sections, Variations I through X rely almost completely on the steady quarter-note beat. The variations fall into uneven mosaiclike patterns of nine, eleven, ten, seven, eight, etc. bars which present the theme in various aspects, yet are always dependent on the more or less straightforward quarter-note fundamental rhythm.

Variation I presents the theme in its simplest form, a canon at the unison, and cadences on C sharp harmonized with B sharp.* Variation II presents the theme against itself: tones 1 and 2 in the melody harmonized with tones 3 and 4 in the lower voice. Tone 11 (B♭) makes its first appearance and is sounded four times, thus emphasizing it. Variation III presents the four tones against each other as in the preceding variation but with the range extending up and outward by means of pointillism. Variation IV features the theme harmonized in three voices, marking a further compression of the design. A development of

---

* In twelve-tone technic B sharp is identical with C natural, E flat with D sharp, etc.

the previous variation, Variation V intensifies the growing dramatic mood and brings to a close the first harmonic section of
the work. It has consisted of a central idea of four tones around
which seven other tones, at the composer's will, have related
themselves in varying aspects of polytonal relationships. C sharp
and C natural appear to be the tonic center, obliterating a sense
of tonality and establishing the work's pandiatonic character.

Variations VI and VII present the four tones transposed up a
minor third, establishing a new tonal basis. The "series" now
reads: G-E♭, -F♯-E♮, etc., although only tones 1-2-3-4-7-8 are
utilized. A feature of Variation VII is the introduction, for the
first time, of the twelfth tone. In the transposed version of the
series up a minor third, the twelfth tone automatically becomes
G sharp, a tone which appeared in the original relationship of
tones as number 8. The G sharp stands forth boldly in the welcome E major triad, a completely consonant cadence with which
Variation VII ends. The E major triad has been strengthened by
F major, which presents for the first time the tone F, the twelfth
tone of the original series.

Variation VIII shifts the relationship of the series still another third higher. We view the composer building gradually
on each degree of the E minor triad so that organically (or in-
ternally) the entire composition clings to a tonal frame. The
"series," now presenting a B-G-B♭-A♭, etc., relationship, features the theme concealed in an inner voice (left hand). Variation IX shifts the series back into the original relationship of the
beginning in the right hand, the E-C-E♭-C♯ version, etc. (in
pointillism), while the left hand slyly moves a chromatic step
up from the initial transposition, from G to G sharp, giving us
G♯-E-G♮-F, etc.

Variation X sets up still another relationship in which the tone
F comes into its own. The new series, unmixed with any other,
now reads F-D♭-E-D♮, etc. The theme, sounding grandly
(*fortissimo*) in three octaves, punctuated by the polytonal harmonies of B flat major and minor, is followed by the material
used in Variation IV. The repetition of the latter, occurring here

in its transposed form, suggests an application of the cyclic principle to the variation form and acts as a unifying element for the first half of the work.

Variation XI is in the nature of an interlude, improvisatory in character, quiet and tender in mood. Here the series slips up a half step, reading F#-D-F♮,-E♭, etc. This new tonal center prevails through Variations XII and XIII and presents the four-note motive in the form of two short scherzi.

Variation XIV returns the "series" to its original relationship, although its orthography now reads E-C-E♭-D♭, etc. This "series" is maintained through the succeeding five variations which reveal varied facets of rhythmic development. The motive appears in a cumulative rhythmic design worked out according to Stravinskian principles of changes in meter and later bears a blues aura in the allusions to restrained fox-trot and Charleston rhythms. Variation XVIII makes a temporary return to the scherzo mood, suggesting a scherzo-jazz-scherzo design of Variations XII through XVIII.

Variation XIX returns to the transposed version of Variation VIII, the B-G-B♭-A♭ "series." For four measures the theme is presented in quiet sustained chords, then moves forward rapidly to Variation XX. This treatment works the motive straightforward and retrograde at the same time and is characterized by leaps and bounds in an excitingly nervous rhythm. Through a kaleidoscope of rhythms the E major triad clangs out authoritatively and reaches a brilliant climax attained at the extremities of the instrument. The leaping and bounding continues in the low bass and leads into the coda, which returns to the original relationship of the E-C-D#-C# "series" presented in Variation IV. This is followed by a final statement of the theme in which all twelve tones appear in a grand orchestral-like fulfillment of what Variation III had implied.

The *Piano Variations* differs from the other works of this period and is unique because of its "sharper" dissonances; these are achieved through a combination of "serial" principles in conjunction with polytonal relationships. By means of the device of pointillism, tonal heights and depths are sculptured in terms of a texture that is sparse, transparent, economical, but sufficient.

While, within itself, the *Piano Variations* is significant and beautiful, it is even more remarkable in relation to the works that follow for, in writing it, Copland achieved a clarity of texture and a transparency of sound that were to become characteristic of his style from that time on. This newly won clarity and transparency were to be demonstrated in the orchestral works soon to follow.

With the composer himself at the piano, the *Piano Variations* was first performed at a League of Composers' concert, January 4, 1931, at the Art Center, 65 East Fifty-sixth Street. Copland played from a pencil copy at the time, the definitive version not being completely established until after the first performance.

The New York *Times* reported that the young American composer, "who started out in orthodox fashion not many years ago, has been attracted more and more to the 'stream of consciousness' school, and more than one passage yesterday recalled similar essays in words of Gertrude Stein. The auditors gave the variations courteous attention and some applause."[5]

The New York *Herald Tribune* noted: "Mr. Copland, always a composer of radical tendencies, has in these variations sardonically thumbed his nose at all of those esthetic attributes which have hitherto been considered essential to the creation of music." Observing that on the subject of modern music he did not wish to play the prophet, the critic hoped "some day to find enjoyment in such music as Mr. Copland's."[6]

In addition to the *Piano Variations*, the first part of 1931 brought forth several *premières* for Copland: two in the province of the theater, and one in the concert hall—a symphonic score. The theater works were a ballet, *Olympus Americanus* (February 3), based on the early "Passacaglia" for piano solo, and incidental music for Hans Chlumberg's play, *Miracle at Verdun* (March 16), both of which are discussed in Chapter VII, "Ballets—Music for Plays and Films."

The first performance of Copland's *Dance Symphony*, derived from the earlier ballet *Grogh* and winner of one fifth of the RCA

Victor Award made the previous year (1930),* took place on April 15, 1931, at the Academy of Music in Philadelphia. It was performed by Leopold Stokowski and the Philadelphia Orchestra in an Emergency Concert for the benefit of the unemployed musicians of Philadelphia. In addition to the Copland work, the program included three large works of Bach (in Stokowskian arrangements) and two by Wagner.

Regarding the Copland work, the *Inquirer* wrote: "The 'Jazz' or 'Dance' Symphony of Copland promptly proved popular and established itself as modern music of interest and individuality. It has substantial musical structure, with considerable diversity of material, and resourcefulness in treatment. . . . The work is original and unusual in effect and distinctly evocative in atmosphere."[7]

E. F. of the *Record* reported that some in the audience whispered, "It is too modern" while others, increasing their applause to drown the signals of disapproval, exclaimed "It is magnificent!" This critic described the *Dance Symphony* as a colorful ballet, rich in Oriental flavor. He quoted the composer as saying after the concert: "I am pleased with the reception. At least the audience was not indifferent." As a result of the concert the Musicians' Emergency Fund gained $7,000.[8]

In April, soon after the Philadelphia *première* of the *Dance Symphony*, Copland, accompanied by Paul Bowles, who was then studying with him, left for a rather lengthy stay abroad. Believing that he had not had sufficient contact with the contemporary German composers, Copland planned to spend at

---

* In 1929, upon the announcement of the RCA Victor Company of a prize competition of $25,000 for a new symphonic work, Copland set to work to try to complete his large orchestral composition to be called *Symphonic Ode*. About a month before the close of the competition, the young man realized that he could not possibly finish the *Ode* in time to submit it for the prize. Yet he was eager to be represented with a work in the first prize competition ever offered in America for a first performance via radio. Quickly seizing upon the early unperformed ballet *Grohg*, Copland extracted a suite of three dances, and, under the title *Dance Symphony*, sent it in to the contest. The judges, finding that no single work merited the entire $25,000 award divided that sum into five parts, giving $5,000 each to Copland, Louis Gruenberg, and Ernest Bloch, with $10,000 given to Robert Russell Bennett for two compositions. (Oscar Thompson. *Great Modern Composers* [New York: Dodd, Mead and Company, 1941], pp. 42-43.)

least six months in the German-speaking countries. The German opera, in particular, had become active in the performance of new works, notably Hindemith's *Neues vom Tage* and Kurt Weill's *Die Dreigroschenoper* (based on the plot of John Gay's old *Beggar's Opera*), *Aufstieg und Fall der Stadt Mahagonny*, and *Der Jasager*, the latter a school opera. These and other new works Copland was anxious to hear firsthand. During the latter part of the summer he planned a first visit to the Riviera.

Compositionally, before leaving New York, he had begun to write the *Short Symphony*, and brought some of this material along to work on.

Stopping first in Paris, he looked up old friends there. Invited to Gertrude Stein's country home at Bilignin (near Grenoble) for a week end, he was persuaded by Miss Stein to go to Morocco instead of the Riviera during the summer.

May and June found him in Berlin, where he organized and arranged a concert of American orchestral works scheduled to take place in December. While in that city, he resided in the home of Max Strub, violinist, situated in Charlottenburg, Uhland Strasse 3.

The ninth annual Festival of the International Society for Contemporary Music took place in Oxford and London between June 23 and 28. Copland attended, again in the capacity of critic for *Modern Music*.

Immediately afterwards, acting on Gertrude Stein's suggestion, Copland, accompanied by Paul Bowles, went on to Tangier, Morocco, for a three-month stay, July through September. There he rented a house and a piano, hoping to get on with the new symphony. However, the summer proved to be unproductive, perhaps because it was impossible to find a good piano. He made a brief journey into the interior, going as far as Fez, and came in contact with some of the folk music of this strange, exotic land. Yet Morocco, for him, did not prove to be the right atmosphere for composing.

In December of 1931, the concert of American orchestral compositions took place. Under the auspices of the Berlin group of the I.S.C.M. and with the support of the American section, the concert undertook to present a cross section of contemporary American effort. With Ernest Ansermet, conductor, the Berlin Symphony Orchestra performed four American works: a *First Symphony* each by Aaron Copland and Roger Sessions, Carl Ruggles's *Portals,* and Louis Gruenberg's *Jazz Suite.*

Copland's *First Symphony* (dating from 1924 in the organ version; from 1928 in the orchestral version without organ) thus received its first performance in the new version in Berlin.*

Nicolai Lopatnikoff, who covered the event for *Modern Music,* stated that, until recently, Europe had been quite unfamiliar with American music. "Negro music" and "jazz" (as well as Indian themes) were thought to typify the main characteristics of American music.

Lopatnikoff stated that Copland's *Symphony* justified the reputation which preceded him—that he was an imaginative and inventive musician whose emotional background was derived from the naturalistic elements of romantic music. Believing that, because of certain weaknesses in construction, the last movement was not quite up to the Scherzo, Lopatnikoff asserted that such objections were really minor beside the individual conception of the first movement, "whose sharpness and purity are validated by the emotional [and] personal elements of Copland's original art."[9] Lopatnikoff noted that Sessions' leaning toward the modern Central European school was obvious, in contrast to Copland's, whose style conceptions tended toward modern France. Ruggles, oldest of the four composers but probably the most dissonant of them, by his insistence on the non-repetition of tones, had worked out melodic and harmonic principles of his own which called to mind Schoenberg's "tone rows." Thus, with only one American work avowedly of "jazz" content, the Berlin musical public was given the opportunity of hearing contrasting facets of American contemporary trends of composition.

* This evidence contradicts Arthur Berger's statement that the work was first performed in its purely orchestral version on January 18, 1934, by Frederick Stock and the Chicago Symphony Orchestra. See his *Aaron Copland* (New York: Oxford University Press, 1953), p. 101.

Later in December, Copland returned to London to participate in a concert of American chamber music which he himself
had planned and organized during the month of June while attending the I.S.C.M. The concert took place on December 16,
1931, under the auspices of the London Contemporary Music
Center.

Henry Boys, English critic, who covered the event for *Modern
Music,* reported that the concert had the great misfortune to
take place on the same evening with a symphony concert devoted principally to modern British works. He noted, however,
that the few who attended were amply repaid, if not profoundly
moved, for the music gave the English audience a new
experience.

Copland himself opened the program by playing the short
"Sonatina" by the young Mexican, Carlos Chávez. According
to Boys, the composition, in spite of its simple, unsophisticated,
direct thought and diatonic contrapuntal texture, did not appeal
on first hearing.

Paul Bowles's *Sonata for Oboe and Clarinet,* though possessing a sure sense of style, lacked the workmanship to deal with
such a combination. It left the impression of immature and su-
perficial mode of thought.

More interesting than either the Chávez or Bowles works,
Boys found, was the *Piano Variations* of Aaron Copland, which
the composer performed. Noting the influence of Stravinsky's
Symphony for Wind Instruments and a passion for dissonance
only equaled by Bartók, Boys stated that so few concessions
were made to the audience in the presentation of the thought
that it would be surprising if a first hearing could make the work
intelligible. Irritated by its dissonant sound, one either suspected the composer of striving after originality for its own sake,
or else turned away from the work completely bewildered. If
true, this was a real defect for which Boys attributed one of
three reasons: "it might seem that the composer wrote only for
himself; he may not have completely assimilated his material;
or . . . it comes as a surprise to find that what one had supposed

to be designed in order to knock one down gives up its secret only when one allows it to persuade."[10]

Returning to New York City about Christmas time, Copland took a studio at 52 West Fifty-eighth Street. Soon after, the delayed *première* of his *Symphonic Ode* took place.

Commissioned by the Boston Symphony Orchestra for the celebration of its Fiftieth Anniversary (1930-1931), the *Symphonic Ode* did not receive its first performance until February 19, 1932, in Symphony Hall, Boston. Nine other composers had received commissions for the same purpose, including two other Americans, Howard Hanson and Edward Burlingame Hill, and seven Europeans: Hindemith, Honegger, Prokofieff, Respighi, Roussel, Stravinsky, and Ravel.[11] Eight of the commissioned works had been heard during the anniversary season; but because of the fact that Ravel did not complete his work in time, and because Koussevitzky wished to spend another summer in the study of Copland's difficult score, the works of these composers were not heard until the following year.

H. T. Parker of the Boston *Evening Transcript* wrote that the *Ode* was not music to be liked or disliked, for either word was too trivial for the work's matter or manner. With the exception of the transplanted Ernest Bloch, Parker stated that for the first time an American composer, of any generation, had written in the grand style and sustained himself unbrokenly through a whole spacious composition. Parker's review continued:

> There is no mistaking the power of the introductory and the final divisions. The one strives and ascends. The other calms and deepens. In the two Allegroes is the taut-strung vitality with which we live our urban lives, in this instance by imagined occasion excited and enriched. Into the slow division enters the severer beauty of our day and of this new music, which is the beauty of metal in motion.[12]

The critic of the *Christian Science Monitor* was convinced, despite the composer's denial, that the *Ode* had a literary idea, which he believed to be the following: "The first section represents the majesty of the ancient Hebrews, the second the pastimes of their descendants on Broadway, the third the melancholy strain in the race; in the fourth we are back on Broadway, but . . . as we pass to the fifth section [we are introduced by] a powerful crescendo to the August Prophets."[13]

The critic of the *Globe,* who signed himself "P.", noted that it was obviously futile to judge so complex a piece as the *Ode* at a first hearing. In his latest work Copland was too much the technician and too little the musician with an irresistible impulse to compose. "This composition," he continued, "despite some brilliant and moving pages, disappointed at least one of Mr. Copland's admirers. He must not let his musical sophistication, acquired in Paris, quench the innate originality and genuineness that have made his other works seem among the most promising yet written by this generation."[14]

The *Ode's* first New York performance took place the following month, on March 3. It was performed by Koussevitzky and the Boston group at Carnegie Hall at one of the Bostonians' regular New York subscription concerts.[15]

On April 2, Copland's earlier *Music for the Theatre* was heard in a radio-broadcast concert of the Philadelphia Orchestra under the direction of Stokowski,[16] while on the following day Martha Graham presented "Dithyrambic," a dance choreographed to Copland's *Piano Variations.*[17] Thus, through the media of the concert hall, radio, and dance recital, more Americans were becoming familiar with both the name and music of Aaron Copland.

The Yaddo Festivals of American Music came into being at Saratoga Springs, New York, on April 30, 1932. Unlike the Copland-Sessions Concerts (1928-1931), these concerts, as the title of the festivals indicates, were devoted solely to the presentation of American works.

Through the efforts and ideas of Aaron Copland and those of the executive director of Yaddo, Mrs. Elizabeth Ames, Memorial Hall was made available for the programs of the festival, an auditorium large enough to accommodate two hundred visitors, yet small enough to be well suited to the performance of chamber music. On one wall of the room were portraits of the two

Trask children, Christine and Junius, whose deaths late in the last century inspired their parents to convert the extensive estate into an abode for creative artists. It was these children who, calling shadows in a fish pond "yaddows," gave Yaddo its name.

Again, a brief summary must suffice us regarding Copland's second outstanding and more highly concentrated organizational effort in behalf of the composers of his native land.

During the first festival, comprised of three concerts of chamber music which took place during the week end of April 30 and May 1, 1932, eighteen American composers were heard in a total of thirty-five works. Copland, who appeared as accompanist and chamber music player during the festival, also substituted for George Antheil during the second concert, when Antheil suddenly fell ill. It was then that the *Piano Variations** really came into its own, with two superb performances of the work by the composer on succeeding days. Paul Rosenfeld, who was present, wrote that the *Variations* "fairly towered, starkly economical, maximally expressive, one hard, relentless moving object. One felt its author the composer of the coming decade."[18]

It was during the final program that Charles Ives's "Seven Songs" were sung by Herbert Linscott, accompanied by Aaron Copland, marking one of the early public performances of that composer's work. Rosenfeld stated that the songs of Ives revealed the presence of a great *lieder* writer among American composers.† Thus at Yaddo the younger men recognized the originality of their older colleague whose music continues to tower above that of all his American predecessors.

On Sunday morning a Conference for Critics and Composers was held with conspicuously few critics present, the first-line men from the New York and Boston daily papers apparently not being interested in hearing contemporary American creative effort. An Associated Press man misquoted Copland to the effect that "newspaper criticism is a menace, and we would be much

---

* Scheduled for performance by Copland at the third concert on May 1.

† Following Ives's death on May 19, 1954, Olin Downes wrote in the New York *Times* of May 30 his recollection that the first newspaper criticism of a major work of Ives appeared in the *Times* on January 30, 1927, following a concert of new works performed by the Pro-Musica Society on the previous night.

better off without it." This statement touched off fireworks that reverberated in the press for many days as angry critics, caught in the act of failing to assume the responsibility morally theirs toward American music, sought to find excuses and explanations to justify their absences from the Yaddo Festival.

The second Festival, also comprising three concerts, took place during the final week end of September, 1933, with more than two hundred music-minded persons in attendance. Eighteen composers were heard in a total of twenty-eight works, with Charles Ives again represented by the song "Where the Eagle Cannot See."

The second Festival featured a Sunday morning Conference for Interpretive Artists and Composers, of which Roger Sessions was Chairman. Obstacles in the way of widespread performance of American music which, regrettably, are as true today (1955) as they were twenty-two years ago, were cited as: the preponderance of music from abroad performed here, principally from the "classics," which cuts the public off from contemporary music; the influence of the larger music schools with their emphasis on the classic repertoire; the managerial point of view, which counsels a repertoire chosen to elicit the largest box office returns.

"The tone of the conference was mainly constructive," wrote F. D. Perkins, "with the composers laying little blame for the non-performance of American music, but discussing ways of bringing about its wider performance."[19]

A total of sixty-three works by thirty-six American composers was the significant achievement of Yaddo's first two seasons. In an attempt to found an American annual festival of contemporary music comparable to the best European festivals of a similar nature, Copland was struggling to focus the resources of the interpretive artists and the interest and concern of the critics and the relatively small enlightened public on our younger American composers.*

* It was not until 1936 that Yaddo presented another musical event, which, since that time, instead of "festival" has been called the "Music Period." A different committee, selected by the Corporation of Yaddo, presented Music Periods in 1936, 1937, 1940, 1946, 1949, and 1952.

Following the first Yaddo Festival, in 1932, Copland remained through the months of June and July at the Trask estate, where he made considerable progress on the *Short Symphony* and, we learn from a letter to John Kirkpatrick, began another orchestral work, subsequently to be called *Statements*.

It was Carlos Chávez who was responsible for Copland's first trip to Mexico. Since 1928, Chávez had founded and directed the Orquesta Sinfónica de México and also served as director of the National Conservatory of Mexico. He had often urged his North American friend to visit Mexico, but Copland, instead, had always preferred going to Europe. Recently, he had invited Copland to come to Mexico, where the symphony and conservatory might join forces in presenting an all-Copland concert. This latter suggestion proved irresistible and Copland decided to spend several months in Mexico, as his letter of June 22, 1932 (from Yaddo), to John Kirkpatrick indicates:

Dear John,

Thanks for the letter you sent. I'll be back in the city by the 15th and wish you could show me the arrangements then.

I had a letter recently which may concern you. The Mac-Dowell Colony are to run two concerts in N. Y. next winter celebrating its 25th anniversary. They want something of mine for the programs. I suggested you in the "Variations" (I'll be in Mexico then—I mean December). I've already corrected proofs on the V——. They should be out [published] soon.

My new work [*Short Symphony*] is being upset by the fact that I've started still a newer and am working on the two simultaneously. The newest piece [*Statements*] will have four or five short movements. I have one of these already—a slow movement for brass and flutes [later placed as the second or "Cryptic" movement] which pleases me very much. Of the other [*Short Symphony*], I have two of the three movements practically done.

Till soon
AARON

Though this was Copland's first visit south of the Rio Grande, he was already known to the Mexican concert public through orchestral performances of his works, for Chávez had already performed, with the Orquesta Sinfónica, *Music for the Theatre* (1928-1929) and the *First Symphony* (1929-1930).

In the four seasons (1928-1931), the Mexican Symphony Orchestra had presented forty-nine concerts, at which 196 symphonic works were performed. At least fifty-two of these were played for the first time in Mexico. The orchestra was unique in respect to its repertoire which, while it included some classics, placed its main emphasis on contemporary scores. Thus Chávez, like Copland, was an important influence in the development of music within his own country as well as a force in disseminating modern music in the world.

In late August, accompanied by his friend, Photographer Victor Kraft, Copland left New York by automobile for a five-month stay in the Republic of Mexico. He took along the unfinished *Short Symphony*, hoping to complete it, and the sketches of his newest orchestral work. In addition, he planned to write a short chamber work for the League of Composers' Tenth Anniversary concert, scheduled to take place in February. Because of the imminence of the all Copland concert, the two young men drove as fast as possible to San Antonio, Texas, where they placed the car in storage, after which they proceeded by train to Mexico City. (In those days there was no through road to the capital during the rainy season.)

The all-Copland concert, presented by the Conservatorio Nacional de México, was heard on September 2. It took place in the Teatro de Orientación under the sponsorship of the Secretary of Public Education, Department of Fine Arts. The program consisted of the following works: *Two Pieces for String Quartet*, performed by a quartet from the conservatory; *Piano Variations*, performed by Jesús Durón Ruiz; two pieces for chorus and piano, "The House on the Hill" and "An Immorality," performed by a chorus from the conservatory under the direction of Chávez. Following an intermission, during which Chávez talked informally on the music of Aaron Copland, the orchestra of the conservatory, conducted by Chávez, performed *Music for the Theatre.**

* From the official program.

Regarding the music of the concert, Salomon Kahan, critic of *El Grafico,* wrote: "Our illustrious guest [Copland] . . . already merits a place in the history of music . . . as an unassuming leader of musical reform in the United States, [and] as the creator of a musical synthesis in which dry dogmatism descends from its pedestal, and becomes more human. [Through Copland's talents] jazz remains purified, ennobled, elevated to symphonic dignity."[20]

The *Two Pieces for String Quartet* revealed almost a "classic taste" and approached a freshness which recalled Prokofieff's "happiest moments." The critic also praised the choral works, especially the "picaresque and captivating 'An Immorality.' " Kahan associated *Music for the Theatre,* especially the "Burlesque" movement, with the "fiesta of the rich in the paintings of Diego Rivera," terming it "profoundly satirical" and "enigmatic music *par excellence.*"

A second concert featuring works by Copland, under the auspices of the National Conservatory, took place on September 22, also in the Teatro de Orientación. The program, a mixture of classics and moderns, included works by Haydn and Revueltas; Copland's *Piano Variations;* three choral works by Chávez, de Lasso, and Copland ("An Immorality"); a "Passacaglia" for violin and viola by Handel; and Poulenc's chamber music work, *Rhapsodie Nègra.*

Praising Chávez for his excellent piano performance of Poulenc's *Rhapsodie Nègra,* the Mexican critic Kahan stated that "the profound impression which the great American composer, Aaron Copland, produced on us, as the interpreter of his *Piano Variations,* [convinces us that it is] an important work, destined to take its place in the front rank among the most representative works of modern composers."[21]

From Calle de Ramos Arizpe 24, Mexico, D.F., dated September 16, 1932, Copland wrote the following letter to John Kirkpatrick, then in Greenwich, Connecticut:

Dear John,

I've been carrying your letter of July around with me and here, finally, is an answer. I should have come out to Greenwich, but kept putting it off and off, until suddenly Chávez wired that his all-Copland program was to take place on September 2 so I left N.Y. precipitously and drove to San Antonio in eight days and got here on the morning of the concert. Perhaps you'd like to mail the arrangements to me here. If not, have patience and we'll look at them together in January when I return.

Thanks for showing the *Variations* to Martha Baird [pianist]. She sent me a *very* enthusiastic letter about them. I haven't heard from the MacDowell people.

Mexico is awfully nice. It's very quiet for such a big city and so one can work here. I hope to come home with a finished piece.

All good things

AARON

From the same address and dated September 29, Copland wrote the following letter to his mother in Brooklyn; it conveys some idea of the impressions of his first Mexican visit:

Dear Mother,

I received your letter today, the first one sent to my home address. Keep on sending letters here until further notice.

Last Sunday Chávez took me out to a town called Cuernavaca which is about 50 miles from here. Its a sort of week-end place like Atlantic City is for Americans. In order to get there you have to climb over an enormous mountain and in doing so get a marvelous view of Mexico City and the valley beyond. The town itself is very quiet and restful and extremely Mexican. So I am beginning to see a little of the country now.

Not that Mexico City is so noisy or so rushed. I have a phone here, but I must say it causes me no inconvenience, for people don't run after you here as they do in New York. This is fine for me because I can work so much better that way. My Spanish is improving. I can go into a restaurant now and order a whole meal in Spanish without any difficulty. It should be pretty good at the end of four months. In general, I lead a very quiet life here and it is quite like living in the country.

Tell Leon [his brother] not to worry about the car. We left it in an A. No. 1 garage in San Antonio and they agreed to take the battery out, and to jack the car up, and generally to take good care of it. I explained [to] them I wouldn't need it for four months. They charge $5.00 a month.

Talking about money, the Mexican peso has suddenly begun to improve in value, so that we don't get as many pesos for our dollar. So things cost a little more than they did four weeks ago. It's not serious yet—only a difference of about 10 cents on each dollar.

I get the Sunday *Times* each week. It gets here on Thursdays and costs 15 cents. Music still looks pretty slow. I also get the *New Republic* here so you see I'm well supplied with news of what's going on.

The concert last Thursday [September 22] went off very well. There weren't many critics because it was a repeat program. But here is one criticism at least [Kahan's]. Thats about all the news this week.

Love to all the folks
AARON

In a letter dated October 7 to John Kirkpatrick, Copland reveals a warm and lovely side of his nature (as well as an admirable quality of his race), in his desire to help a poor but talented Jewish boy in whose artistic potentiality he believed strongly:

Dear John:

Your remarks anent the published *Variations* amused me. You did find one mistake—the ties that are missing after Var. 20. But I can't agree about your strictures about the new A♭ in meas. 1 of Var. 19 or the E♭ in m. 19 of V. 20. The latter E♭ is necessary bcause there has been too much A♭. It comes as a surprise and therefore needs a reiteration in order to really establish it. Therefore to have it twice doesn't in this case "spoil the effect."

But that isn't why I'm writing you. I'm really writing to find out whether I can persuade you to give lessons to a young discovery of mine who is really very talented. Of course there's no question of money. He's a young Jewish boy (18) —— by name. I did my best to get him a scholarship chez Juilliard but he didn't even get as far as the examination stage because he lacked a high-school diploma. The fact is his family was so poor he had to go to work instead of to high school. Israel

[Citkowitz] is teaching him counterpoint gratis; I expect to teach him form and orchestration on my return and I'm hoping you will undertake his piano training. He already plays well, but without any comprehension of style, and without any steady technical equipment. But ask him to play the Scherzo from the Beethoven he has been studying and you'll see that he has a real gift. He's a very naive and simple boy—in a state of nature, as one might say, and I'm hoping it would interest you to teach him. . . .

I'm glad you've been playing yourself. After all, to be a pianist, one must play programs.

Always
AARON

About the *Ode*—I'd be very glad if you'd mail it to me here. Chávez has the new version, but insists that it ought to be published with the original rhythms. (He is giving it in November.) I need the other to do some comparing with him. Send it to Moneda 16 and mark it photostatic material, rather than music—please.

On November 18, Copland's *Symphonic Ode,* heard for the first time the previous February and March in Boston and in New York, was performed for the first time in Mexico City by Chávez and the Orquesta Sinfónica in the Teatre Hidalgo. Other works heard on the program included Debussy's *La Siesta de Un Fauno (Prélude à l'Après-midi d'un faune),* the Tcherepnine *Piano Concerto,* and Ibert's *Escales.* With the exception of the Debussy *Prélude,* all of the works were performed for the first time in Mexico City.*

After a two-month stay in Tlalpam, Copland returned to New York City in late December and moved into a new studio in Fifty-fifth Street. Chávez had made his five-month sojourn in Mexico an eventful one, performing as many of Copland's works as possible, and made propaganda in behalf of his North American friend through his various artistic connections. Thus Copland's first visit to the Southern Republic added to his world renown as a composer and proved to be the

* From the official program.

prelude to an important style influence that would affect his own artistic development during subsequent visits. This first visit was also to mark important hemispheric cultural implications when, years later, Copland was appointed by the United States government to make a "good-will" tour of the South American countries. During his Mexican stay he had made progress on both orchestral works and, in addition, had completed two short "Elegies" for violin and viola* scheduled for the April concert of the League of Composers.

A short note to John Kirkpatrick, dated February 19, 1933, offers further evidence of Copland's interest in the music of other composers and of his efforts to assist them in receiving performances of their scores:

Dear John,
 Thanks very much for the "Song" [of 1927]. It amused me to see it again.
 The Interpreters-Composers Party is coming off on Saturday next at Mrs. Wertheim's, 60 Washington Mews. Of course I want you to come. I'm playing a *Flute Sonata* of Paul Bowles; and I want to ask you to play (as the other attraction) the *Piano Sonata* of [Charles] Ives that [Jerome] Moross tells me you do so well. This isn't a "performance." You'd be playing it just so we could hear it.
 Please let's know about this soon.

Always,
AARON

From 100 West Fifty-fifth Street and dated May 29, 1933, Copland again wrote John Kirkpatrick, to ask for musical assistance in behalf of a younger composer:

Dear John,
 Paul Bowles is back from Europe and has been asked to have some of his music played over Station WEVD on Sunday June 18 at 8 p.m. I'm writing to ask if you won't help by playing his

---

* It is just possible that Handel's "Passacaglia" for violin and viola, performed on the Mexico City September 22 concert of classics and moderns, suggested the choice of instrumentation for Copland's "Elegies." These pieces are currently withdrawn for revision.

Sonatina for Piano which I can recommend as a highly amusing and successful piece. It's simple to play technically, except for a spot here and there in the last movement (which shows the influence of Gottschalk b'gora!)

If you can do it and will do it—as I hope you will (because I'd like it to be in your repertoire as there will undoubtedly be more opportunity for playing it places), please send him a wire *immediately* . . . and he will send you the music right off.

Always alles gutes

AARON

From June 9 to 15, 1933, the Eleventh Festival of the I.S.C.M. took place in Amsterdam. No American works were heard until the final concert (June 15), when Aaron Copland's *Piano Variations* and three songs by Ruth Crawford,* on poems by Carl Sandburg, were presented.

Herbert Antcliffe, who reviewed the festival for the New York *Herald Tribune,* reported that both American works "created a good impression for their technical qualities and for the piquancy of their ideas. The clarity and simplicity of the *Variations,* well played by Victor Babin, were supplemented by some original ideas of combining sustained sounds with staccato chords that were effective," he wrote.[22]

Copland remained in New York that season, 1933, for a period of six months—from January through June—during which time he acutely experienced the pinch of the Depression, as did many of our creative artists in various fields. On the invitation of Harold Clurman, director of the Group Theatre, to spend the summer at Green Mansions (approximately fifteen miles north of Lake George), where the Group Theatre had its summer headquarters, Copland at once accepted. From July through September he lived at nearby Friend's Lake with some theatrical friends who were performing at Green Mansions. Copland found it a pleasant place to work and his close proximity to activities in the theater was to prove invaluable to him in the subsequent

* Ruth Crawford (Seeger), 1901-1953, was the first woman to receive a Guggenheim Fellowship Award.

writing of ballets, operas, and incidental music to plays and films.

From various cards and letters written to John Kirkpatrick we learn that Copland was occupied during this time with arranging the programs for the second Yaddo Festival of Contemporary American Music, to take place at the end of September.

Compositionally, we learn (from the same source) that the newest orchestral work *Statements* was progressing, for in a letter dated September 6, Copland informed Kirkpatrick that "the five-part piece is coming along gradually. I'm writing all five movements at once. See you at Yaddo if not before." In addition, at Friend's Lake, Copland completed the *Short Symphony*, on which he had been at work since 1931.

Short Symphony (Sextet)

Completed in 1933, and dedicated to Carlos Chávez, the *Short Symphony* received its first performance in Mexico City on November 23, 1934, by the Sinfónica de México under the direction of Chávez. Because of its difficulties for both performers and listeners, the *Short Symphony* remained unheard at home in this form until Stokowski performed it in an NBC *première* on January 9, 1944.*

In 1937 Copland arranged the *Short Symphony* into a *Sextet*, scored for string quartet, clarinet, and piano, which is the version most often heard around New York and the one referred to in this study. A fifteen-minute work, the *Sextet* version received its first performance in Town Hall, New York City, on February 26, 1939.

By way of reaction against the economical *Piano Variations*, built entirely out of a four-note motive, in the *Sextet* Copland used at least six themes. It was in 1924, in his *Symphony*

---

* Although Mitropoulos announced the first North American concert performance of the *Short Symphony* for November 1953, because of the difficulty of the work and because of an inadequate amount of rehearsal time he substituted, instead, the more familiar *Appalachian Spring*. Consequently, the *Short Symphony* remains to this day unperformed in a North American concert hall.

for Organ and Orchestra, that the composer first attempted the symphonic form which, in that work, resulted in a prelude-scherzo-finale (the latter movement in sonata form with cyclic implications) structural design. The *Symphonic Ode* of 1927-1929 bears the rough outline of a symphony in one movement, built out of a two-measure phrase. To the French, jazz, and Jewish elements present in the *Ode,* there was added in the *Sextet* the composer's assimilation of the principles of "serial" technique (in terms of polytonal relationships) as they appear in the *Piano Variations.*

The first movement of the *Sextet,* marked *Allegro vivace,* opens with a five-note motive, in declamatory style, with the polytonal relationships of D major, D minor, and G major (Example 5). In place of the polytonal solid-sounding chord which punctuated the statement of the *Variations'* theme (see Example 4 in this chapter), Copland uses a device which may be designated an extension in the form of a short trill, or an ornamental flourish, in the piano part. For six pages this theme is developed, revealing many unusual and beautiful derivatives of the initial motive. Then comes the second theme, bearing syncopated, jazz implications. The second theme receives a shorter development than the first and is soon interrupted by derivatives from the former. There is a strong feeling of recapitulation, with the declamatory theme presented in a new tonality with varied harmonic treatments accorded its several derivatives.

Ex. 5

Just before the second theme is heard again there occurs one of those unfortunate lapses of style occasionally found in the scores of even the greatest of masters. In this instance the style

lapse is caused by a poor choice of harmony (Example 6). In-
truding upon a passage that is predominantly polytonal, this
second inversion of a dominant-seventh chord is completely at
variance with the distinguished harmonic language of the rest
of the movement. This out-of-style (in this instance) dominant
seventh occurs in a sequential passage not only once but twice!

Ex. 6

The slow movement, marked *Lento* and later *Più mosso,* one
of Copland's most beautiful and expressive slow movements,
follows an A-B-B-A song-form design. The A theme denotes
Copland's fondness for the descending form of the scale used
very plainly (Example 7). The mood here, in contrast to the vitality and high spirits of the first movement, is introspective and
almost immobile. After a high point has been reached, the first
theme melts into the B section, tonality of F major. This theme
is remarkable for its graceful, flowing melody in the clarinet,
which somehow conveys a restrained dance character through
its simple rhythmic and harmonic setting.

Ex. 7

The Finale, marked "precise and rhythmic" is remarkable for
its development according to cyclic principles and for its percussive, "pepped-up," at times deliriously rhythmed textures.
In characteristic Copland scherzo mood, the whole movement

grows out of two ideas* that are immediately presented (Example 8). A dazzling rhythmic development ensues with various

Ex. 8

themes from this and the earlier movements presented in terms of Stravinskian metrical changes, jazz polyrhythms (including a striking adaptation of the Charleston), and, for the first time in any of Copland's work to that date, Mexican polyrhythms (Example 9). Each instrument appears to follow its own independent linear existence, tossing about the various themes of the entire work, fitting them together like pieces of a mosaic. A coda, derived from a lyrical version of the declamatory theme (from the first movement), leads into a final forthright statement of that theme, followed by a quick cadence in F.

Ex. 9

Notable gains realized in the *Sextet* over the earlier *First Symphony* and *Ode* may be designated as the following: a greater ease and flexibility in the handling of the symphonic form; a more thorough assimilation and cohesion of the music materials;

---

* Reduced to its simplest orthography, idea 1 is none other than our old friend, the D flat major triad (or C sharp major) in $\frac{6}{4}$ position; idea 2, the G and A major triads.

a rejection of literal jazz materials and the use, instead, of their distilled essence; a pristine transparency and skill in the handling of the orchestration; the development of a more personal and more clearly defined style on the part of the composer who, maturing as a man and as an artist, consequently has deeper thoughts and emotions to express.

Following the Second Festival of Contemporary American Music at Yaddo, which Copland again directed, he returned to New York in October, 1933, to resume his lectures at the New School for Social Research. He also continued to be active in the arrangement of programs for the League of Composers, on the board of which he served, for many years, as a member. Some idea of his function in League affairs is indicated in his letter of November 22, 1933, to John Kirkpatrick:

> I waited before answering your note for the weekly League meeting. Mrs. [Claire] Reis says its alright about the expenses, but in return she wants me to ask you to play the Nabokoff "Le Coeur de Don Quichotte" which you heard him do. It will be perfectly all right to use the notes at the performance. Nabokoff was being persuaded to play it himself, but got out from under, which leaves us high and dry. There isn't so much time so answer immediately and I'll mail you the notes immediately.
>
> About Roger's [Sessions] song. The copy I gave you, it appears, belongs to Ada [MacLeish], so please save it for her until you see her. Roger would like to give you a few pointers about performance of the song in another week or so. He's always in New York on Tuesdays (sometimes on Wednesdays). Perhaps you might arrange a time, when you are ready, directly with him. . . . Ada is often in Farmington, Connecticut. Would it be easier to rehearse with her there? Just as you like.

Accepting the invitation of his cousin, Leo Harris, to occupy his bungalow situated on Lake Bemidji, Minnesota (approximately 140 miles west and slightly north of Duluth), for the summer, Copland spent the months of July through September of 1934 in that northwest scenic spot. It was here that Ruth Page, American dancer, wrote to him regarding a commission for a new ballet that was destined to be a forerunner of several important works the composer has written in that form.

In October Copland went to Chicago with the virtually completed ballet score and, with Miss Page and company, settled down to two months' intensive rehearsals, reshaping the score and choreography in preparation for the initial performance of the new work. The *première* of the new ballet (subsequently called *Hear Ye! Hear Ye!*), on November 30, his second in that form but the first to receive a stage presentation, is discussed in Chapter VII.

With his friend Chávez conducting the Orquesta Sinfónica de México, Copland's *Short Symphony* received its first performance in Mexico City on November 23, 1934. Busy in Chicago with the final rehearsals of *Hear Ye! Hear Ye!*, the first performance of which took place one week later, Copland was unable to go down for the performance. Unfortunately no reviews from the Mexican press regarding the reception of the new work are available. Instead, we have a letter from Chávez to Copland, dated December 1, 1934, in which the conductor expressed his high regard for the *Short Symphony* as a work of art.

Affirming that the November 23 concert was the best of the entire season, Chávez wrote his friend that the *Short Symphony* was placed between Stravinsky's *Suite* and his (Chávez's) ballet, *H.P.* Furthermore, the audience was warm and enthusiastic, something that seldom happened with either his or Copland's works, the conductor noted. "The dialectic of this music *[Short Symphony]*," he continued, "the way each . . . note comes out from the other as the *only* natural and logically possible one, is simply unprecedented in the whole history of music." Upon receiving the score of the *Short Symphony*, Chávez told Copland that he was filled with these thoughts: ". . . here is my music, the music of my time, of my taste, of my culture."[23] And how proud he was to see his name as the dedicatee on the title page of the score!

Copland returned to New York in December, 1934, immediately after the *première* performance of his ballet in Chicago. With two world *premières* behind him, that of the *Short sym-*

phony and *Hear Ye! Hear Ye!,* he planned to complete the orchestration of the symphonic work, *Statements.*

During the spring semester, February through June, Copland taught classes in Composition at Harvard University, substituting for Walter Piston, who was on leave of absence.

Unable to make much progress on *Statements* while engrossed with his classes at Harvard University, Copland returned to the MacDowell Colony where he had previously spent two summers, for the summer of 1935. Amid the peace and quiet of the New England countryside, he completed the orchestral work upon which he had been engaged since 1933. Though not performed in its entirety until 1942, *Statements* belongs to Copland's Abstract Period and must be considered stylistically in relation to the other works of that period.

Statements

Statements was commissioned by the League of Composers for performance by the Minneapolis Symphony Orchestra and its conductor, Eugene Ormandy. On January 9, 1936, the last two movements only, "Jingo" and "Prophetic," were performed for the first time by the Minneapolis group. It was not, however, until January 7, 1942, that the full version received its premiere, by the New York Philharmonic Orchestra under the direction of Mitropoulos. An eighteen-and-a-half minute suite, *Statements* is dedicated to Mary Senior Churchill, a long-time friend of Copland's and a patron of the arts.

Regarding the title, the composer has given the following explanation: "The title of 'statement' was chosen to indicate a short, terse orchestral movement of a well-defined character, lasting about three minutes. The separate movements were given suggestive titles as an aid to the public in understanding what the composer had in mind when writing these pieces."[*] These titles

* From *Program Notes of City Center of Music and Drama,* New York, edited by Howard Shanet, October 19, 1947.

are: "Militant," "Cryptic," "Dogmatic," "Subjective," "Jingo," and "Prophetic."

1. The "Militant" statement, scored for full orchestra, is based on a single theme, five measures in length. Copland's characteristic harmonic imprint is clearly discernible in the wavering from minor to major thirds—E♭,C,E♮. A single-lined, forthright statement, tinged with a Lydian flavor (emphasizing the tritone), the theme is punctuated with an E flat dissonant brass chord set in jazz rhythm, modified Charleston (Example 10).

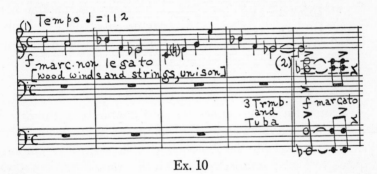

Ex. 10

(Note the polytonal implications of the melody.) The entire movement grows out of these two elements. Its texture is polyphonic and while there are tonal impressions, the movement has no central key location.

2. The "Cryptic" statement, orchestrated for brass and flute alone with an occasional use of bass clarinet and bassoon, at once sets forth three ideas which are treated as mosaic designs with implications of the "serial" technique. These ideas, projected in a linear style, make up the entire material of the movement. Expressive and personal in mood, unusual orchestral timbres eloquently whisper or proclaim the composer's "secret" musical thoughts.

3. The "Dogmatic" statement, scored for full orchestra is, in reality, a short scherzo movement. A three-measure phrase, the first theme, in the progression from F to D minor, has a Proko-

fieff harmonic flavor. The theme of the *Piano Variations* forms the material for the brief second part in which the texture of the theme itself, by the device of pointillism, is dramatically declaimed in its orchestral setting, distributed between the timbres of horn and trumpet (Example 11). The "Dogmatic" statement is remarkable for the way it fuses tonal, atonal, and polytonal harmonic elements expressed in terms of the composer's individuality.

Ex. 11

4. Scored for strings alone, without double bass, the first of the "Elegies" for violin and viola (composed in Mexico in 1932) was incorporated into the "Subjective" statement. The composer appears to have been occupied with this simple tonal progression (Example 12). The "Subjective" statement follows the structure of a little three-part form.

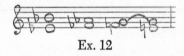

Ex. 12

5. The "Jingo" statement, the most humorous of the set of six, utilizing the full orchestra, follows the rondo form. Using characteristically short themes, the rondo design falls into the following more or less easily discernible patterns: a-b-a-c-b-d-c-b-d-a-e-a-a. A quotation of the familiar Irish folklike tune, "The Sidewalks of New York,"* is intermittently heard as the d

---

* "The Sidewalks of New York" became popular because of its use during Al Smith's presidential campaign. Because everybody knew it then, it has become a folk tune. As we have seen, Copland also quoted a fragment of this theme in the "Dance" movement of *Music for the Theatre.* This theme also appears in Mozart's *Clarinet Quintet.*

section. Copland has "borrowed" this three-quarter waltz-tempo melody, set it in the rhythm of two *(alla breve)*, and given it a kind of hurdy-gurdy or carousel harmonization which, in this version, musically "pokes fun" at Tammany Hall. Besides being entertaining, the choice of this folklike theme is significant, for it begins to point rather directly to Copland's next style development, the Folksong Period, for which the trio, *Vitebsk*, had already provided a hint.

6. The final statement, "Prophetic," scored for full orchestra, is rhapsodic in form, by turns expressive and dramatic. Following a rather slow, introductorylike first section, the main theme is heard, a choralelike melody sung by the solo trumpet. The first section returns, shortened, as does a portion of the chorale theme. Not extremely dissonant, the texture combines linear motion with splashes of trials, expressing heroic concepts. The movement ends ominously with a solo tam-tam stroke, triple *pianissimo*.

Under the caption "Copland at His Best . . . ," Virgil Thomson reviewed the first complete performance of *Statements*, seven years after the work's completion. Terming the six "shortish" pieces "succinct and stylish music," Thomson stated that they are clearly written and "very very personal." He found "Jingo" the most amusing, "Cryptic" the most individual, while "Militant" seemed less inspired than the others. Continuing, he wrote:

"Dogmatic" and "Prophetic" are excellent, though I found them less true than the "Cryptic" statement, which is not cryptic at all, but an utterly honest and personal transcript of romantic feeling. The whole group is a manly bouquet, fresh . . . sweet . . . sincere . . . frank and straightforward. These highly personal pieces show Copland at his best, and that means being one of the most direct of living music writers and one of the most amiable of men.[24]

Thomson thought the work was admirably played, Mitropoulos's "dry" interpretation suiting Copland's musical style "to a T."

Noting that the composer of *Statements* possessed an original mind, Howard Taubman observed that there were some fine effects in the second movement and that the fifth was a "delectable" scherzo with a "fascinating" rhythmic scheme. "In the fourth and sixth," he continued, "Mr. Copland let himself become more spacious and lyrical, and the mood became him. Making allowances for the strict confines of the form, he has imposed himself and except for an occasional heaviness of theme and treatment, the 'statements' add up to a distinctively personal music."[25]

An analysis of the four large works of the Abstract Period— the trio *Vitebsk, Piano Variations, Sextet (Short Symphony)*, and *Statements*—has revealed a complete synthesis of the already existing style ingredients (French-Stravinsky-Jazz-Jewish elements) with the new element, that of the "twelve-tone" or "serial" technique bound up with polytonal relationships expressed in terms of the composer's personal identity. With the exception of the *Piano Variations*, the music of this period has received few performances and even today, 1955, remains virtually unknown by the general public. It is difficult for audiences to grasp because of its polytonal, "serial," implied dissonances, and because of its "abstract" or "absolute" conception. Upon repeated hearings and study of the scores themselves, the music surrenders its serious and complex language. Only time can tell whether or not these more "serious" works of Copland will outlive the more "popular" works of the Folksong Period which follows.

Third Style Period (American Folksong)
Introduction to Chapters VI, VII, VIII
(1934-1955)

CHAPTERS VI, VII, and VIII herald the advent of a new style which, because of its reliance for material on folk-music sources and the simplicity of its musical language, may be designated as that of the American Folksong, thereby marking Aaron Copland's third style period. Extending from 1934 to the present year, 1955, the third period has produced far and away the composer's most fruitful and prolific work.

A change of aesthetic direction, remarkably healthy, of which some indication had been hinted, is clearly apparent in the work of this period. In 1933, at the second Yaddo Festival, Roger Sessions and others sounded a warning to the effect that the American composer (collectively) "must end his isolation and get in touch with current musical activities in general, especially in the phase of musical education which concerns the public as a whole."[1] Almost paralleling Hindemith's 1927 utterance,[2] Copland, during the early thirties, stated his dissatisfaction with our composers' efforts (including his own) to fulfill the needs of the American public, pointing out that the composers were in danger of working in a vacuum. "Moreover," he said, "an entirely new public for music had grown up around the radio and phonograph. It made no sense . . . to continue writing as if they did not exist. [It seemed] worth the effort to see if I couldn't say what I had to say in the simplest possible terms."[3] It is, therefore, in the light of the above statement that we must approach the works of the new "folksong style."

The most striking fact about the work of the third period is its functional nature: music written for varied purposes and performed by special groups of performers. Thus we view Copland again taking another point of aesthetic departure from modern European developments, that of *Gebrauchsmusik,* or music for use.

John Tasker Howard has stated that *Gebrauchsmusik,* which originated in Germany around 1927, is closely allied with neoclassicism, in that it also tends to simplify music. Receiving its impetus from Paul Hindemith, the *Gebrauchsmusik* movement has taken two directions. The first has been "developing music for amateurs to perform: operettas and cantatas for school children; instrumental pieces for school and college orchestras; and works in which the audience participates by singing some of the choruses and songs." The second, music "for performance by professionals, but intended for a wider audience," includes incidental music for plays and films; for radio; light operas having a popular appeal; and music which has "political and social significance in a changing world."[4]

Written for a variety of social situations and numbering approximately forty scores, for the sake of convenience and simplification, I have arranged the compositions of Copland's third style Period (American Folksong) under two large divisions: "*Gebrauchsmusik* American Style," and "Patriotic and Absolute Works."

The first large division, "*Gebrauchsmusik* American Style," contains the following functional categories: (1) Music for American Youth—devoted to those scores written (or practical) for performance by high school or college groups; (2) Exotic Travel Souvenirs—works based on the folk music of foreign countries; (3) Radio commissions—compositions expressly commissioned for radio performance; and (4) Theater works—consisting of ballets, music for plays and films, opera.

With these various categorical divisions, naturally a number of scores will fit more than one classification, just as there are a few scores that appear as "misfits," isolated, and not belonging to any one of the four groupings; these latter, for convenience's sake, are placed in the categories nearest their particular musical function.

Chapter VI is devoted to the first three categories: Music for American Youth; Exotic Travel Souvenirs; and Radio Commissions; while Chapter VII is concerned solely with the Theater Works.

The second large division, "Patriotic and Absolute Works," comprises such works as *Lincoln Portrait, Preamble for a Solemn Occasion, Third Symphony,* and the *Quartet for Piano and Strings.* In a sense, the Patriotic Works are *Gebrauchsmusik;* but their seriousness of purpose and tone stamps these works as superior qualitatively to the first large division and therefore justifies their consideration along with the Absolute Works, in Chapter VIII.

VI

Third Style Period (American Folksong) Gebrauchsmusik American Style: Music for American Youth—Exotic Travel Souvenirs— Radio Commissions (1935-1944)

INTRODUCING the music of Aaron Copland's third style period, that of the American Folksong, Chapter VI embraces three categorical classifications of *Gebrauchsmusik* American style: music for American youth, exotic travel souvenirs, and radio commissions.

Music for American Youth

Few (if any) American composers have written works of such excellent quality and understanding of the musical capacities of American youth as has Aaron Copland. Small in quantity but large in selectivity of material and its adaptation for school purposes, these works are eminently useful, for they were all created in specific school situations.

The composer's ability to transform an abstract writing style of the utmost difficulty into its exact opposite, one of extreme simplicity, is a paradox to be explained only by the knowledge that the composer at last realized for what purpose he was writing.

Copland was soon to have an opportunity to put his new aesthetic approach, to compose in the "simplest possible terms," to practice. In the middle thirties, upon the invitation of Lazare Saminsky and Isadore Freed to write two children's piano pieces for an educational piano series they were editing for Carl Fischer,* Copland wrote "Sunday Afternoon Music" and "The Young Pioneers." These two- and three-page piano solos were written in August, 1935, at the MacDowell Colony, Peterborough, New Hampshire. According to the editors the purpose of the series was to enlarge the musical horizon of the youth of our day, to enrich its knowledge and to attune its ear to the new musical life.

Copland's two piano pieces offer admirable contrast: the first is slow and lyric, the second, fast and rhythmic, with the slow piece the more conventional of the two. In the form of an extended, repeated period, "Sunday Afternoon Music" is built on the expansion of a single harmonic (mildly dissonant) progression. It is readily played by students who have studied piano two and a half or three years.

"The Young Pioneers" refers not to our early American ancestors but to our youngest generation, those brave enough to venture the mysteries of twentieth century harmonic, rhythmic, and dissonant discoveries. The entire piece is built out of a one-measure motive, made up of only two tones, and is easily played by a young student who has had three to three and a half years of piano study.

In Peterborough, Copland also wrote the two-part chorus

---

* Among other composers who contributed to the series are Cowell, Freed, Hanson, Jacobi, Josten, Kramer, Moore, Saminsky, Sessions, Shepherd, Taylor, Thomson, Wagenaar, and Whithorne.

entitled "What Do We Plant?" on a text by Henry Abbey. Asked by the Henry Street Music School (New York) to provide a short, simple work for its Girls' Glee Club, Copland obliged with a composition of approximately two minutes and twenty seconds duration, in a setting for soprano and alto voices with piano accompaniment. Such devices as unison singing, a harmonization relying on thirds and sixths with an occasional fifth or octave, counterpoint (including imitation), combined with a "catchy" melodic line, all serve to make the work attractive to American youth.

A *Play-Opera for High School*

Copland's largest work composed for school use is his play-opera, *The Second Hurricane*. In the fall of 1935, Grace Spofford, Director of the Music School of the Henry Street Settlement, suggested to the composer that he write a stage work for young people to sing and which Henry Street might produce. Earlier the Music School had performed such works as Kurt Weill's *Der Jasager* (The Man Who Always Said Yes) and Hindemith's *Wir Bauen Eine Stadt* (Let's Build a City). In spite of these excellent examples of European *Gebrauchsmusik*, Miss Spofford continued to look for a stage work created by American artists for American youth that would typify our ideals and aspirations.

Edwin Denby, having been persuaded to write the libretto, began work in the fall of 1935 on what he called a "play-opera for school performance." Within a few weeks he presented Miss Spofford and the composer with the finished libretto of *The Second Hurricane*.

Although Copland began composing the musical score in January, 1936, since he was still busy with the orchestration of *El Salón México,* he did not make much headway with the opera until summer. The first of June he left by boat for Tlaxcala, Mexico, where he spent the first of two summers. Denby joined him there later, the quaint village offering a congenial working atmosphere for the two collaborators. Between June and September Copland wrote most of the musical score. The principal problem seemed to him to be one of style. "I wished to be simple to the point of ordinariness," he stated. "This was comparatively easy in relation to the more colloquial passages of the libretto where the music approaches musical operetta, but in the more dramatic moments it was rather difficult to make the distinction between grand opera and high school opera."[5]

Realizing that heroic deeds fraught with danger have a fascination for high-school youth, Denby gave his libretto a modern American setting and his characters the opportunity to measure their collective strength against one of nature's calamities, a hurricane followed by a flood. The characters involved in the drama are the principal of a high school, six student volunteers, an aviator, and a chorus of parents and children.

In view of the fact that it is impractical to quote at length from the 112-page score, certain idioms which project "Americanisms" are cited: the easy flowing, mildly syncopated first chorus, reflecting our happy-go-lucky, careless temperament; "Gyp's Song," with its tender, nostalgic, folklike mood and blues connotation, "Jeff's Song" (the little Negro boy), a vocal version of the "snappy number," and the Negro spiritual-like choral text and setting (with its minor seventh) of the *a cappella* section in "Two Willow Hill" (Example 1), all manifestations of Copland's earlier jazz style. However, for the very first time, a significant new "Americanism" finds its way into *The Second Hurricane,* one that the composer had not used heretofore, yet which was to establish the authenticity of his "Folksong Style" —the interjection of a bit of early Americana in the form of the

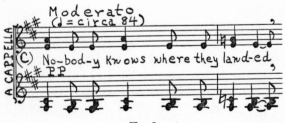

Ex. 1

revolutionary song, "The Capture of Burgoyne" (Example 2).*

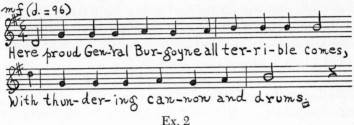

Ex. 2

Out of this very first quotation of a North American folksong which, as we shall see, received its impetus from Copland's recent exposure to and manipulations of Mexican folk materials in *El Salón México,* was born the three (survived) ballets, several of the film scores, *Lincoln Portrait,* and other orchestral works, including his latest, the opera *The Tender Land.*

Following the *première of The Second Hurricane* on April 21, 1937, Virgil Thomson found the work "vigorous and noble," the libretto "fresh" and "permeated with a great sweetness," and asserted that linguistically Denby's libretto was the finest English libretto to appear in some years. "Unfortunately," he continued, "the show peters out before the end, the plot falling to pieces at the very moment when our anxiety is greatest about the fate of the characters."[6]

Perkins, of the New York *Herald Tribune,* believed that the chief success of the ninety-minute work was its scholastic suitability for a purpose which it served notably. He thought that the work should prove an appropriate vehicle for schools throughout the country, wishing to present musico-dramatic performances with home talent, without going to great expense for settings and properties.[7]

The Second Hurricane stands, therefore, as one of the first examples (if not the first) of American *Gebrauchsmusik* in play-opera form actually to employ "Americanisms." Of its com-

* The published version of *The Second Hurricane* attributes the source of both melody and words from "Old American Songs" issued by Brown University from the Harris collection of *American Poetry and Plays* (see p. 98f of piano-vocal score).

poser, who taught in Henry Street Music School for four years (1935-1939) and was acquainted at first hand with the musical capacity and skills of youth, Miss Spofford wrote: "He gave to his work that conviction and devotion which a great man often gives to a task in simple surroundings."[8]

Strictly speaking, Copland has written only one work (to date) designed especially for performance by high-school orchestra—*An Outdoor Overture*. However, one of his shorter orchestral pieces, based on an American folk tune and commissioned for radio performance, *John Henry*, is well within the capabilities of the high-school orchestra and deserves consideration here.

Following the successful *première* of Copland's high-school play-opera, which Alexander Richter, Director of Music at New York's High School of Music and Art, had witnessed, Mr. Richter made up his mind that Copland was just the composer to write a work for his school orchestra. Furthermore, the High School of Music and Art was about to undertake a long-term campaign with the slogan 'American Music for American Youth" and Mr. Richter proposed to Copland that his work should sound the "opening gun" of the campaign. Richter suggested that the composer write a single-movement work, between five and ten minutes' duration, in the form of an overture or rhapsody. The composition should be optimistic in tone and make a definite appeal to the adolescent youth of this country.

Copland was so taken with the idea that he interrupted the orchestration of his ballet, *Billy the Kid*, to write the work Richter wanted for his students. He began work on the new composition October 18, 1938, and completed the preliminary sketch two and a half weeks later, on November 5, finishing the orchestration the following week. When the composer played his piano sketch for Richter, the conductor pointed out its open-air quality; together they settled on the title: *An Outdoor Overture*.

Falling into a Slow-Fast-Slow-Fast structural design, the *Overture* sets forth two brisk marchlike themes and a long solo for trumpet, featuring the descending B flat major scale, in two octaves, the rendition of which, if well done, is calculated to bring joy to a young trumpeter's heart and win the composer his eternal gratitude.

Dedicated to the High School of Music and Art, the work received its first performances in the school auditorium on December 16 and 17, 1938, under the direction of Mr. Richter.

In the summer of 1939, the Columbia Broadcasting System's "School of the Air Series" commissioned Aaron Copland and a number of other American composers (of whom the author was one) to write three- and four-minute orchestral works based on American folk tunes. This cultural radio series, developed by Alan Lomax,* had a twofold aim: the composer would receive both a fee and a performance of his work, which would be heard over a wide area of the country; the interest of the general public might be more easily captured by a short (rather than a long) work based on an American folk tune. Copland's work, approximately three and a half minutes in length, is entitled *John Henry* and is based on the railroad ballad of that title, the original of which has at least 500 verses. This work is, therefore, another type of the "music for use" variety.

Scored for chamber orchestra and completed on February 25, 1940, *John Henry* received its first performance by Howard Barlow and the Columbia Broadcasting Symphony on March 5, 1940.

Remaining faithful to the intention of the original folksong, the composer has written a simple though effective radio piece, entirely practical for performance by the high-school orchestra. This is proved by the recent performance of *John Henry* by the Toledo (Ohio) Youth Orchestra, conducted by Cecile Vashaw, in its April, 1952, concert, a final rehearsal of which the author attended. Certain "Coplandesque" features, greatly relished by the youthful players, are these: (1) the second arrangement of the folk tune, set in close harmony for trumpet, horn, and trombone; (2) the third setting, utilizing an ostinato figure in the

* The composers' commissions were based on tunes taken from the Lomax collection, *American Ballads and Folksongs* (New York: The Macmillan Co., 1934).

bass and polytonal harmonies above, in which later appears the composer's characteristic imprint of major and minor thirds sounded simultaneously and suggestive of a train or boat whistle; (3) the American (syncopated) polyrhythms; (4) realistic effects obtained by anvil strokes in the percussion, suggestive of John Henry's mighty hammer; (5) a sixteenth-note rhythm (ponticello) in the strings reinforced by sandpaper scraped in the same rhythm which, together, invoke the sound of a train or of machinery in motion.*

In addition to the chorus "What Do We Plant?" and the play-opera *The Second Hurricane,* both of which were specifically written for performance by school choral groups, Copland has composed four other choral numbers of which at least three are excellent examples of American *Gebrauchsmusik.*

In commemoration of the New York Schola Cantorum's first conductor, Kurt Schindler, Aaron Copland and a number of other North and South American composers were commissioned to set melodies from Schindler's collection, *Folk Music and Poetry of Spain and Portugal,* for the Schola's spring concert. Copland's contribution was the short *a cappella* chorus "Las Agachadas" (The Shakedown Song), and was first performed on March 25, 1942, in Town Hall, with Hugh Ross conducting the Schola Cantorum.

Basing his composition on Melody No. 202 in the Schindler collection, Copland arranged the Spanish song for solo group and eight-part mixed chorus. Setting the voices in a characteristic folk way, he has preserved the spirit of the dance-song by assigning a guitarlike accompaniment to a mixed chorus, which vocally "strums" a simple I, IV, V, I chordal dance accompaniment to neutral syllables. Because of the extended bass range, the chorus is more easily performed by senior than junior high-school groups.

---

* In addition to *John Henry,* the Toledo Youth Orchestra, on the above-mentioned program, performed two pieces from Copland's *Rodeo* concert suite, "Saturday Night Waltz" and "Hoe-Down," in a highly creditable manner, demonstrating that other of the composer's *Gebrauchsmusik* scores are suitable to school needs and capabilities.

Two choruses from the film score *North Star* (composed in Hollywood, in 1943) * are published: one from the peaceful first part of the film, "Younger Generation," sung by the children; and one from the second or war portion, "Song of the Guerrillas," sung by a male chorus with piano (or orchestral) accompaniment.

"Younger Generation" appears in a simple and practical arrangement for S.A.T.B., by Frederick Fay Swift. In the key of F major, the composer has captured the quality of a "modern" folksong in "patter" style. It is suitable for performance by junior high-school groups.

"Song of the Guerrillas," for male chorus, in the dark tonality of B flat minor, has, in the beginning, that brooding atmosphere so characteristic of the Russian folksong; it calls to mind both the composer's national origin and a folk strain. Because of the extended ranges for both tenors and basses, the vigor and masculine virility required by the text and music, this chorus can be heard to best advantage when performed by a college or amateur men's glee club.

Based on the poem by Genevieve Taggard, "Lark," Copland's final short choral-piece which, because of its serious tone, hardly fits the classification *Gebrauchsmusik,* is set for a four-part chorus of mixed voices, *a cappella,* and baritone solo. Falling roughly within a three-part form, the work calls to mind the earlier two choruses (1925) written for women's voices, "The House On The Hill" and "An Immorality," one projecting a modal flavor and the other a jazz idiom. The distilled essence of these two mixtures now appears in a single composition, with the result that "Lark" presents the aspect of a much more subtle and seriously conceived work than the two earlier choruses. While "Lark" is possible for superior high-school *a cappella* choirs, it is better suited for performance by college choral groups because of the harmonic idiom and baritone solo.

Composed in 1938, at the MacDowell Colony, "Lark" did not receive its first performance until April 13, 1943, when it was

---

* *cf*. Chap. VII, "Music for Plays and Films" section.

performed by Robert Shaw's Collegiate Chorale at the Museum of Modern Art in New York.

Of its first performance, Howard Taubman, of the New York *Times,* wrote: "Mr. Copland's setting of . . . Genevieve Taggard's 'Lark' has a memorable blend of strength and refinement. The composer companions the poet, adding lift to the affirmation in the words and surrounding them with a vision that is gracious and light and exulting."[9]

In 1940, the H. W. Gray Music Publishing Company conceived the idea of inviting a number of American composers to write short works for the organ. Its first volume, published in 1941, included organ works written by Aaron Copland, Frederick Jacobi, Douglas Moore, Walter Piston, Roger Sessions, Leo Sowerby, and Bernard Wagenaar.

Completed on August 20, 1940, at Tanglewood (his first season there), the "Episode" is Copland's second work for organ, the first having been the large *Symphony for Organ and Orchestra,* composed in 1924. The spacious opening fifths of the "Episode" convey something of the pastoral mood in the beginning of *Billy the Kid.* A short four-page work, presented in a little three-part form, the first part expands the polytonal harmonies of D and B flat major; the second part, a folklike theme with the contour of a *cantus firmus,* is set over a marchlike ostinato figure derived from the original motive. The polytonal harmonies return and the piece closes in the mood of the opening. An attractive concert piece, the work is suitable for performance by college-level organ students who would be interested, presumably, in its modern idiom. "Episode" was first performed by William Strickland, organist, March 9, 1941.

Substituting for Walter Piston, who was in Europe, Copland taught the Composition classes at Harvard University during the spring semester, February to June, 1935. July and August he spent at the MacDowell Colony, where he wrote the two children's piano pieces and the junior high-school chorus, returning to New York in September. Opening a studio at 1 University

Place, Copland resumed his lectures at the New School for Social Research, his eighth season there.

Late in September, 1935, a press release by the publicity secretary of the New School announced Copland's plans for a series of five one-man concerts devoted to American composers, to take place on alternate Friday evenings beginning October 11. The release cited these concerts as a precedent in America, for, it claimed, this was the first time in this country that a series of programs had been prepared, each devoted to the work of a single American composer.

The composers presented in the series, chosen as outstanding representatives of contemporary American music, included Aaron Copland, Roy Harris, Walter Piston, Roger Sessions, and Virgil Thomson. The programs surveyed the production of these composers during the previous ten years (1925-1935), including chamber music, piano works, songs, and two-piano arrangements of orchestral scores.

Lack of space prevents the listing of works of all the composers performed in the series, but the all-Copland program of October 11, 1935, is typical of the concerts offered: *Piano Variations* (1930), performed by John Kirkpatrick; "As It Fell upon a Day," for soprano, flute, and clarinet (1923), performed respectively by Ethel and Otto Luening with Robert McBride; *Symphonic Ode* for orchestra (1927-1929) [arranged for two pianos by John Kirkpatrick], performed by Messrs. Kirkpatrick and Copland. Following the intermission were three songs: "Old Poem" (1920), "Song" (1927),* and "Vocalise" (1928),* performed by Mrs. Luening and Mr. Copland; *Vitebsk* (trio, 1929), performed by I. Karman, C. Stern, and Mr. Copland; *El Salón México* for orchestra (1935)* [arranged for two pianos by John Kirkpatrick], performed by Kirkpatrick and the composer.

Thus is briefly mentioned a third large effort, under the aegis of Aaron Copland, in bringing the music of five of our leading composers to the attention of the American public and, during the process, of educating it, to some degree, in the techniques

---

* The official program announced these works as first performances.

and purposes projected by these composers over a period of ten years. This unusual series of concerts, which deserves to be artistically ranked with the Copland-Sessions Concerts and the Yaddo Festivals, proved of real musical value, for it attracted interested audiences which looked on the composers' efforts with seriousness and, to some extent, with understanding.

Following a second visit to Mexico in the summer of 1936 (his first was in 1932), Copland performed his *Piano Concerto* with Chávez and the Orquesta Sinfónica. (This was his first summer in Tlaxcala, where he and Denby composed *The Second Hurricane.*)

Returning to New York in September, the composer took an apartment at the Hotel Empire, which was to remain his residence for several years. At the same time, he took a studio at 115 West Sixty-third Street, where he could work day or night without being disturbed. Herbert Kubly has described this studio as a "poorly heated, barren loft on the top floor of a nondescript building in midtown Manhattan." But the loft, like Copland's music, was arid and sunny, and the composer maintained this "rugless hideaway" for ten years (1936-1946). "Among the high walls of his loft, the plank floors and the disorderly heaps of score paper," wrote Kubly, "Aaron Copland finds the lonely melancholy he likes."[10]

Exotic Travel Souvenirs

Donald Fuller has pointed out that exoticism is "the use of somebody else's folk music than your own"[11] as differentiated from indigenous music, the use of folksongs native to a composer's own country. The classification, "Exotic Travel Souvenirs," therefore, well suits both compositions, *El Salón México* and *Danzón Cubano.*

El Salón México

It was during his first visit to Mexico, in the fall of 1932, that Copland conceived the idea of writing a work based on Mexican themes, although it was a year later before he began to shape these "musical souvenirs" into an orchestral form. From the very beginning the idea was connected in his mind with a popular dance hall in Mexico City called Salón México, from whence the work derived its title. Although a two-piano version of *El Salón México* was performed in the October 11, 1935, series of one-man programs held at the New School for Social Research, as we have noted, its orchestral version was not completed until 1936.

El Salón México bears an extremely important relationship to the other works of this period, for with it Copland "hit on," or discovered, the simple, folklike, easily understood musical language that was to form the style basis of the entire third period. The work therefore stands in virtually the same chronological order to the works of the third style period as does *Music for the Theatre* to those of the Jazz Period, or *Vitebsk* to the Abstract Period. However, it must be remembered that it was not until the appearance of *Billy the Kid*, in 1938, that the American Folksong Style as such became crystalized and definitive. Let us then look for the indications in *El Salón México* out of which the simple, folksong style was born.

Almost all of the Mexican themes appearing in the work were derived from either Frances Toor's *Cancionero Méxicano* or from Ruben M. Campos's erudite work *El Folk-lore y la Musica Méxicana*. The most direct quotations of complete melodies are those of "El Mosco" (No. 84 in the book by Campos), which is presented twice, immediately after the introductory measures (in which may be found fragments of "El Palo Verde" and of "La Jesusita"), and "El Malacate" (No. 79 in the Campos volume).

Following an introduction of an improvisatory character, *El Salón México* divides easily into two large harmonic parts, the progression from G major, through closely related tonalities, to E major; then from E major, through many distantly related harmonies, back to G major. Expressively, the work represents a series of moods or impressions which appear somewhat in this order: the lyrically sentimental, the garish, the lusty, the improvisatory, the humorous, and the frenetic—the latter, with its whipped-up rhythmic verve (Copland style).

Yet these kaliedoscopic impressions are revealed through the simplest of means. The harmonies are either triads or appropriate (to the folk tunes) polytonal combinations.

The means by which the frenetic rhythmic sections accelerate the excitement of the dance tunes are typical Copland devices. These include frequent changes of meter, from 8/8 to 5/8 to 8/8 to 3/4, as applied to bits of Mexican tunes that flit about in the orchestra, at times producing a "hopped-up" atmosphere. A device which breaks the conventionality of the two-measure folk phrase, extending it to three measures, and lending a touch of delightful vulgarity at the same time, is seen in the 3/8 measures of rhythmic accent (Example 3).

Ex. 3

El Salón México received its first performance in Mexico, in 1937, with the composer present. Its *premiére* is described in later pages of this chapter in connection with other of Copland's activities in Mexico at that time.

A second "Exotic Travel Souvenir" is the *Danzón Cubano*, for two pianos, written six years later, in the fall of 1942, in Oakland, New Jersey. A six-minute piece, it was composed for the League of Composers' twentieth anniversary celebration, which took place in New York's Town Hall on December 9, 1942. In addition to serving as commentator for the program, Copland performed his "birthday piece" with Leonard Bernstein.

In a free adaptation of the rondo form, Copland chose for his material four terse Cuban themes of a pronounced rhythmic character, three of which have a Spanish (or Cuban) origin and the fourth, a Negroid flavor with a "dark blues" cast. Catchy and easily recognizable, the themes are subjected to a cascade of Cuban polyrhythms, simply harmonized, which features the syncopated beat, the typical Cuban rhythm (♫♩♫♩) , and the displaced accent (Copland style). Exhibiting a purely entertainment content appropriate to a "birthday-piece," *Danzón Cubano* makes an engaging companion piece to the two-piano version of *El Salón México*. Both are "musical souvenirs" of Copland's Latin-American visits and combine to make more attractive the all too meager literature for two pianos.

Radio Commissions

To the present date, 1955, Copland's "Radio Commissions" total four: *Music for Radio; John Henry; Letter from Home;* and *Preamble for a Solemn Occasion*. Only two of these will be discussed here, *Music for Radio* and *Letter from Home,* the author believing that the functional nature of *John Henry* (for school use) and *Preamble* (for patriotic purposes) justifies the transfer of those works to other categories.

Recognizing the radio industry's "inevitable" responsibility toward American composers (who were credited with having gained increasing and deserved respect in recent years), Davidson Taylor, director of "serious" music for Columbia Broadcasting System, stated that radio found itself, in 1936, "in a position to offer the composer not only money, an orchestra and an assured audience, but also certain new musical materials in the form of instrumental effects made possible through the microphone—effects which are entirely useless in the concert hall."[12]

It was primarily the latter fact that caused CBS, in the fall of that year, to commission six leading American composers, Aaron Copland, Louis Gruenberg, Howard Hanson, Roy Harris, Walter Piston, and William Grant Still, to write works that would utilize radio as a specific medium. The musical specifications for the commissions were the following: the compositions must be completed by June 1, 1937; they must not exceed forty minutes in length; the instrumentation must be for large orchestra, including three saxophones.

According to the composer, *Music for Radio* was completed in Mexico in 1937. A week before its first performance, CBS, in a press release, announced that the third musical work in its series of Columbia Composers' Commissions had a program, or scenario, that not even its composer, Aaron Copland, ventured to interpret. The composer, therefore, was "putting it up to the audience," in a contest, to name and define the composition which would be given its world *première* on July 25, 1937, by Howard Barlow's orchestra on the CBS Sunday afternoon program, "Everybody's Music." For the time being the composer was calling his work *Music for Radio*. "However," continued the press release, "the listener who sends in a permanent title which is most successful in telling Mr. Copland what his music is, will receive an autographed copy of the original score." [13]

Music for Radio (Saga of the Prairie),* in one extended movement, is cast in a free sectional form with the following large over-all design: A-B-A-C-D-B-A-E-C-B-A-B-D. It was undoubtedly the D section, with its folklike theme presented in the manner of a cowboy song, and the general nostalgic character of the piece that suggested the winning subtitle, "Saga of the Prairie," to Miss Ruth Leonhardt of Grosse Pointe, Michigan.

Special effects for radio which the composer has noted in his score may be briefly mentioned as follows: As the trombone player uses a solo tone mute in the free or improvisatory section, the trumpet player is instructed to play his answering motive with "Felt hat over bell." The flute solo is designated to be played "at the microphone"; the player has eight bars of rest in which he may move to the microphone and comfortably adjust his embouchure. In a four-measure rhythmic phrase (vamp), with brass using "straight" mutes, the bassoon player is directed to play his off-beat notes with a "slap tongue," giving a jazz effect; Saxophones 1 and 2 are also instructed to "slap tongue." Cup

* The winning subtitle.

mutes and Harmon mutes, which belong more to jazz than symphonic instrumentation, are frequently asked for in the trumpets.
At the end, with high woodwinds, soft brass, and strings sustaining, the final note, middle C, is sounded very softly, on the vibra-
phone, uttering a timbre we have since almost exclusively associated with radio.

On October 17, 1944, at the Ritz Theatre, New York, Paul
Whiteman, Musical Director of the Blue Network and its Radio
Orchestra, gave the first performance of Copland's short work,
Letter from Home, written the previous spring. The work was
one of several commissioned by the American Broadcasting Com-
pany, in both serious and popular fields, for which a Creative
Music Fund had been set up to aid composers.

Composed in a simple folklike, song-form style, the *Letter*
evokes moods by turns pastoral, jaunty, and nostalgic. Although
the themes are the composer's own, they are treated in the simple style made so familiar in *Billy the Kid, John Henry,* and
Rodeo. A very relaxed, easygoing work, there occurs a curiously
incongruous mixture of the chromatic-harmony style with the
diatonic in several of the short bridges or episodes. An overuse
of the main theme, which becomes sentimental and banal
through more than a half-dozen references, the *Letter* has
scarcely more significance than background music for movies
and, as such, must be designated as one of the composer's weaker
orchestral scores.

Copland spent the month of May (1937) in Hollywood, in
quest of a studio assignment to compose music for films. George
Antheil, film editor for *Modern Music,* has noted that many excellent composers came out to Hollywood for the same purpose
and returned East again for "scarcely any of them have gotten
jobs." In Antheil's words, Hollywood music was at that time a
"closed corporation." [14] As we shall see in Chapter VII, it was
not to be long before Hollywood came to New York to seek out
Aaron Copland, who, since, has made a significant contribution
to film music scarcely equaled by any other American composer.

Nevertheless, the summer of 1937 was to prove an eventful
summer for the composer. Early in June he left Hollywood for a

four-month stay in Mexico, again principally at Tlaxcala, to attend the first Festival of Pan American Chamber Music and to be present for the world *première* of the orchestral version of his *El Salón México*. Both events were to take place in the capital.

Sponsored by Elizabeth Sprague Coolidge, the Festival took place at Mexico City between July 13 and 24, 1937, in the Palacio de Bellas Artes. Under the direction of Carlos Chávez, compositions from the Americas were presented in six concerts. In addition to two composers from Brazil, Jacobo Ficher (Russian-born, who was the Coolidge prize winner), Francisco Casabona, and Silvestre Revueltas of Mexico, whose works were performed during the Festival, North American composers whose compositions were also heard included Roy Harris, Edward Burlingame Hill, Walter Piston, and Aaron Copland. Copland was represented by his *Music for the Theatre*.[15]

After the Festival, Copland returned to the little house in Tlaxcala he had occupied the previous summer. He had brought along a sizable amount of work to accomplish during these months, including his *Short Symphony*, for which he planned a version for sextet, utilizing piano, clarinet, and string quartet.

On August 27 (1937), Chávez performed the orchestral version of *El Salón México*, for the first time anywhere, with the Orquesta Sinfónica. From nearby Tlaxcala, Copland attended the final rehearsals of his score, offering suggestions where needed to both his friend and the orchestra.

The *Excelcior* critic, G. Baqueiro Foster, stated that the success of the seventh concert of the 1937 series given by the Symphony Orchestra of Mexico was due not only to the variety of the numbers performed, but also to the emotional nature of the repertoire. In addition to Copland's new work, selections from Bach and Beethoven were performed under the able direction of Chávez.

It was known beforehand that Copland's *El Salón México* would give a "surprise," said Foster, and the work was received with the same sympathy as Mexican audiences have received the best work of Revueltas. Noting that Copland had made a synthesis of what is strongest and most characteristic of the folk music in Mexico in melody, rhythm, and harmony, Foster stated that with the discernment of a great modern musician, Copland "makes it into a symphony, enlarging those elements in which strangeness, not for a single moment, takes away one whit of the freshness and beauty of the Mexican song." He asserted that Copland's is Mexican music made as only Mexican composers ought to make it, "embodying the very elements of our folk song in the purest and most perfect form." [16]

A second concert on August 30, presenting works of Beethoven, Bach, Copland, and Stravinsky, was labeled by the critic of *El Universal* as "A Fine Concert for Working Men." In an unsigned review, regarding *El Salón México* the critic wrote: "For the first time—or for one of the first times—we have heard a folklore composition without European influence. Copland shows us the path to follow as regards the investigation of musical folklore. The critics of art are unanimous in saying that the music is technically flawless." [17]

Leaving Mexico by ship, Copland returned to New York about October 1, after making a brief boat stop at Havana. He again took up residence at the Empire Hotel, reopened his studio in West Sixty-third Street, and resumed his lectures at the New School for Social Research.

On December 19, 1937, forty-eight representative composers assembled at the Beethoven Association in New York City for the express purpose of finding ways and means to protect the economic rights of American composers of serious music. On the above-mentioned date, a Proclamation* was drawn up by a Temporary Executive Board of the newly formed organization, called the American Composers' Alliance. With Aaron Copland, Chairman, the Executive Board consisted of Marion Bauer, Douglas Moore, Elie Siegmeister, Quincy Porter, Roy Harris, Wallingford Riegger, Virgil Thomson, Goddard Lieberson, Roger Sessions, and Bernard Wagenaar.

Lacking an organization to protect performances of their copyrighted music, the serious composers, by banding together, hoped

---

* The Proclamation was published in *Modern Music,* January-February, 1938, pp. 92-95.

to better their economic condition by demanding and insuring the collection of fees for performances of their works. Copland headed the Alliance from 1937 to 1944, serving without remuneration of any kind, during which latter time the American Society of Composers, Authors and Publishers began to collect fees for serious music performance.

Although he worked arduously for the new organization he had helped found and served its interests faithfully, for economic reasons beyond his control* Copland chose to quit the American Composers' Alliance for its more representative rival, the American Society of Composers, Authors and Publishers, familiarly known as ASCAP.

Upon a request by Whittlesey House to publish fifteen lectures he had presented at the New School for Social Research during the winters of 1936 and 1937, Copland spent three months, March through May, 1938, in Princeton, New Jersey, as the guest of Roy Harris, where he prepared the book's manuscript. Under the title, *What to Listen for in Music*, the volume of lectures was published in 1939.

Having absented himself from Europe for seven years, upon the completion of his first book, Copland went to London and Paris for the months of June and July, 1938. Because of the economic and political uncertainties that had prevailed in the European countries during the early and middle thirties, Copland had, in the meantime, to his artistic advantage, come into contact with the fresher, more virile Mexican contemporary movement.

Nevertheless, he had an intense curiosity to know what, if any, new music was being written in Europe during those chaotic years and who the younger, experimental composers were. He also wished to hear the European *première* of *El Salón México*, scheduled for performance during the current Festival of the International Society for Contemporary Music in London.

Of the music performed at the Festival, excerpts from Hinde-

---

* Performing rights of works in the Boosey and Hawkes Catalogue are vested in ASCAP, in the United States. Because of this collecting arrangement Copland, perhaps wisely, chose to become a composer-member of ASCAP.

mith's opera, *Mathis der Maler,* made the most impression on Copland and it appeared on the final program along with *El Salón México.* Of the latter work, its composer recently said to the author: "In London, the audience reacted in quite an excited way to *El Salón México;* I felt that that performance was the first time the work was received in the way I had originally expected. It went over 'with a bang,' as a composer desires with a piece of that type."

Shortly before Copland left New York, Lincoln Kirstein, director of the newly formed Ballet Caravan, approached him with a commission (and a book of cowboy songs) to write a new ballet—a "Western," no less—based on the career of the notorious Billy the Kid. At the close of the London I.S.C.M. Festival, Copland left for Paris where, with Eugene Loring's scenario for a guide, he composed the music for the ballet.

Following *Billy the Kid's* theater triumph in Chicago in October, 1938, the spring of 1939 brought forth several first performances in both Paris and New York, including such scores as *El Salón México, An Outdoor Overture,* and *Billy the Kid.* Thus, internationally as well as at home, the composer's fame and reputation were steadily increasing.

Having examined in some detail the various examples of *Gebrauchsmusik* scores composed during these years in which, in *El Salón México,* is discovered the seed of the third style period, let us turn to Chapter VII and view how its North American manifestation was to become crystallized in the ballets and other works for the theater.

VII

Third Style Period (American Folksong) Gebrauchsmusik American Style— Theater Works: Ballets—Music for Plays and Films—Opera

(1931-1955)

DEVOTED entirely to the Theatre Works, Chapter VII discusses the final category of Copland's *Gebrauchsmusik American Style*: ballets, music for plays and films, opera.

Ballets

Taking up the ballets first, we note that they are four in number and date from 1934 to 1944. We point out that it was in the ballet form that Copland first reached the pinnacle of greatness and unhesitatingly declare that, in these stage works, Copland is without peer in the American dance theater. Not only has he attained personal greatness, the attribute of a creative artist who has developed his own art communication, but for his nation and country, by means of the ballet form, Aaron Copland has expressed the strength, power, and conviction of our American traditions, marking them with a definitiveness of contemporary musical language never before achieved by an American composer. In so doing, he has laid the cornerstone of an American national art, established a recognizably American musical idiom.

Just as Stravinsky, in the first years of this century, evoked folk and primitive-historical origins of the Russian people and translated them into a contemporary language evidenced in such works as *The Firebird, Petrouchka,* and *The Rite of Spring,* so we find a parallel in the ballets of Aaron Copland, who, perhaps objectively, has achieved comparable results with American sources. Copland has captured the primitive Negro "jazz spirit" in the political travesty *Hear Ye! Hear Ye!*, the virility and hardy spirit of the West in his cowboy ballets, and the religious and mystical quality of our Pennsylvania ancestors in the Shaker ballet.

Donald Fuller has pointed out that in the mid-thirties, when Copland began his use of folk material drawn from various geographical sources, most composers then generally regarded folksongs as outmoded material for musical compositions. Acknowledging Copland's example as a foremost instigator of the revived folk trend, Fuller stated that many "still feel [Copland] has discovered a true serious American folk style for general use by all American composers."[1]

Full credit for this achievement is not due to Copland's efforts alone, for such dancers as Helen Tamiris, Ruth Page, Eugene Loring, Agnes de Mille, Martha Graham, and others had been struggling toward such a nationalistic expression for years. It was when these dancers found their composer, Aaron Copland, that a definitive American dance repertory was born.

It is my purpose in this portion of the chapter, therefore, to consider at some length the four ballets, in their chronological order, and to mention briefly the smaller contributions that led to their creation.

One of the first indications that an American composer of ballets might be in our midst was given by Helen Tamiris, who, in 1931, made a choreographic adaptation of Copland's piano piece "Passacaglia" (written in 1922, in Paris) which she called *Olympus Americanus*. It was divided into six parts: "Basking in the Sun," "Dance on an Ancient Theme (Priapic Ritual)," "Tempo," "Dance to Hermes and Aphrodite," "The Races," and "Triumphant." Tamiris stated that the ballet was an attempt "to weld the contemporary spirit with the classic" and that its themes "mark the accents of life in ancient Greece and in our twentieth century."*

---

* From the official program.

Making her last appearance of the season at the Guild Theatre, New York, on April 3, 1932, Martha Graham danced Lehman Engel's new "Ceremonials," and "Dithyrambic," a dance choreographed to Aaron Copland's *Piano Variations.* Although "Dithyrambic" had been seen four times that season, John Martin stated that it was actually the outstanding item of the program. Admitting that it was a difficult composition for an audience to grasp, nevertheless, according to Martin, it never failed to evoke an enormous response. "At every re-seeing one is impressed more deeply with the magnitude of this composition, not to speak of its masterly performance, and with the strange, hard beauty of the music . . . to which it is danced."[2]

Hear Ye! Hear Ye!

The circumstances surrounding the creation of the ballet *Hear Ye! Hear Ye!* are as follows. In 1933, Copland's *Music for the Theatre* was performed at the Coolidge Festival in the Library of Congress, Washington, D.C. Ruth Page, the dancer, was present and, hearing the suite for the first time, was impressed with the theatrical and rhythmic qualities of the work. In 1934, as a result of the reorganization of the Chicago Grand Opera, Miss Page became its *première danseuse* and *maîtresse de ballet.* Desiring to produce a new American ballet during her 1934-1935 Chicago season, she wrote to Copland at Lake Bemidji, Minnesota, where he was spending the summer of 1934, regarding a collaboration. In August, upon his acceptance of the commission, Copland joined Miss Page in Chicago, where the scenario for the ballet, subsequently called *Hear Ye! Hear Ye!,* was sketched out.

Cecil Michener Smith, writing in *Modern Music,* noted that a sudden spurt of interest in the art of the dance led the Chicago Grand Opera Company to present, on November 30, 1934, a "quadruple-header" ballet program under the direction of the "indefatigable" Ruth Page. In addition to two works from her standard repertoire, the world *premières* were given of *Hear Ye! Hear Ye!* by Aaron Copland and *Gold Standard* by Jacques

Ibert. Both were conducted by Rudolph Ganz and danced by Miss Page and Company.

The ballet (scenario by Miss Page) is a satirical treatment of an American court of justice attempting to find the murderer of a night-club dancer, in which the music is largely a running commentary upon the action. Professor Smith* tells us that two bits of material are projected which might be termed leading motives: first, a "motive of accusation," appearing each time a new suspect is accused of the crime; second, "a playful, polytonal episode which gives the interludes of the debating attorneys a character reminiscent of the 'promenade' in Moussorgsky's *Pictures from an Exhibition*."

The score contains an adagio dance, succeeded by a chorus girls' routine for which Copland wrote characteristic jazz; a parody of the Mendelssohn "Wedding March," which Smith termed the wittiest scene of the ballet; while at both the beginning and end of the work a parody of the "Star Spangled Banner," representing a distortion of American justice, forms the theme of the ballet. "Certainly the music is thoroughly representative of the American scene," Smith wrote, "and makes no obsequious bows toward any foreign authority."[3]

Composed at the peak of the Abstract Period and following the difficult *Piano Variations*, *Short Symphony*, and *Statements*, *Hear Ye! Hear Ye!* bears no resemblance to these works nor does it possess any of the folksong style characteristics. Rather, it is a "throwback," a hybrid, descending from the earlier "jazz" style.

Billy the Kid

It was not until four years later that Copland wrote his second ballet, *Billy the Kid*, which, as we have noted, was composed during July and August, 1938, in Paris† and Peterborough, New

---

* Professor Smith was at the time a member of the music faculty of the University of Chicago.

† In this connection it is perhaps well to recall that Copland's first ballet effort, the unproduced *Grohg*, was also written in Paris (1922-1925).

Hampshire. Following such *Gebrauchsmusik* American Style works as the children's piano pieces, *El Salón México, The Second Hurricane,* and *Music for Radio, Billy the Kid,* by virtue of its scenario, choreographical treatment, and dependence on cowboy songs for its musical materials sustains, for the first time in the theater, an authentic American pioneer tradition.

As in the instance of *Hear Ye! Hear Ye!,* the world *première* of *Billy the Kid* took place in Chicago in October 1938, featuring Eugene Loring, who created the choreography and danced the title role, with the Ballet Caravan. The first New York performance, by the same company, took place on May 24, 1939, at the Martin Beck Theatre.

Terming *Billy the Kid* a "perfectly delightful piece of work," John Martin wrote that the new ballet "falls inescapably into that category which, in spite of the implications of the term, must be called significant." Stating that the new work opened up new possibilities of theater dancing, Martin appeared convinced that in Loring the American dance had a young creative talent of genuine importance. Of the music he wrote: "Aaron Copland has furnished an admirable score, warm and human, and with not a wasted note about it anywhere."[4]

From the ballet music the composer has arranged a concert suite (incorporating about two thirds of the original score) on which the following discussion is based:

I. Prelude, "The Open Prairie" *(lento maestoso),* presents a single pastoral theme, six measures in length. Harmonized in open fifths, both the harmonization and wood-wind setting convey the wide expanse and nostalgic loneliness of the open prairie. For the most part the short movement relies on a swaying, ostinato bass using the tones C and G in this rhythm, $\frac{3}{4}$ ♩ ♩. ♩., suggestive of impending tragedy.

II. "Street Scene in a Frontier Town" *(moderato),* projects a rollicking mood with its opening theme, the folk tune "Great Grandad," indicated to be played by a "tin whistle only in stage performance." Freely adapting folk melodies to the rondo form, the movement presents the following over-all sectional design:

A-B-B-A-A-B-C-D-C-B-A. Section C is short and contains a quotation from "The Old Chisholm Trail," while D presents two soli trombones in a brief reference to "Git Along Little Dogies." The third appearance of section A ("Great Grandad") reveals Copland's lively treatment of the old 4/4 (Um-pah, um-pah) bass as a meter of three beats against four (Example 1). The cowboy songs have polyrhythmic and polyharmonic settings and imply more by suggestion than would have been realized in a literal quotation. A bridge of eight measures connects this movement with the "Mexican Dance (*Jarabe*)" in 5/8 meter.

Ex. 1

III. Although the action and music of the ballet are continuous, there is a definite feeling that the Mexican Dance* introduces a third part. Thus this section presents two main themes: A, the Mexican theme in 5/8 meter; and B, the cowboy song "Good-by, Old Paint," in 3/4 meter. An interesting feature of this section is the appearance of a cowboy rhythm used as an introductory "vamp," in 7/8 meter, to "Good-by, Old Paint" (Example 2).

Ex. 2

---

* Lukas Foss, who arranged excerpts from *Billy the Kid* for piano (a work useful to both musician and layman), has given the title of "Mexican Dance and Finale" to the ⅝ rhythmic section.

IV. "Nocturnal Card Game" begins with a bridge of six measures, dramatic and ominous in tone, and leads into a short reprise of the "Open Prairie" motive. This is followed by an eloquent setting of "Oh, Bury Me Not on the Lone Prairie (The Dying Cowboy)." Muted strings grow restless—four times the composer indicates "a trifle hurried"—and at the Allegro, the chase is on, with the posse in hot pursuit of Billy. Low-pitched percussive instruments interspersed with rat-a-tat (double-tonguing) of muted trumpets, indicative of fast pistol shots, and occasional shrieks from the high strings make this approximately three-minute section a colorful and exciting western gun battle. Billy is captured and placed in jail.

V. With the desperado safely behind bars, the townspeople turn their thoughts toward a "Celebration," marked allegro, which follows a modified rondo form with its garish dance-hall saloon tunes. In the opening theme, through the harmonization of the bass tones in C sharp major and the off-beat accompanying chords in C major, the grotesquely humorous effect of a player-piano sadly out of tune is realized.

VI. Epilogue. The "Open Prairie" theme returns, this time in darker, purple hues with trombones and timpani punctuating a slow ostinato which accompanies the mourning of the Mexican girl over the dead Billy. From C minor, the mood brightens into the G major tonality where an idealized version of the opening theme is heard, *fortissimo,* over E major harmonies, polytonally. The tragedy is finished; the new dawn breaks through hopefully as the theme moves with a full lyrical sweep toward the final cadence in E major.

Rodeo

Following the sensational success of *Billy the Kid* in both stage and concert versions, the Ballet Russe de Monte Carlo, in the spring of 1942, commissioned Copland, in collaboration with

Agnes de Mille, choreographer, to write a second cowboy ballet—*Rodeo*. In the meantime the composer had written incidental music to several plays and film scores, including *Of Mice and Men* and *Our Town*, and produced such "serious" works as the *Piano Sonata* and *Lincoln Portrait*.

Returning to Stockbridge, Massachusetts, in May, 1942, for his third summer of teaching at Tanglewood, Copland began work on the new ballet, which he completed in four months, May to September.

From nearby Oakland, New Jersey, where he was to reside for the next several months, Copland attended the *première* of *Rodeo* (originally subtitled "The Courting at Burnt Ranch"), which took place on October 16, 1942, at the Metropolitan Opera House, starring Miss de Mille, with Franz Allers conducting.

Noting that the success story of the season was the Monte Carlo's "all-American" *Rodeo*, Edwin Denby wrote that the audience was enthusiastic about the "cowgirl-gets-her-cowboy" story. "Somehow the flavor of American domestic manners is especially clear in that peculiar desert landscape," he wrote; "and that is its fascination. The dance, the music, the décor . . . are each drawn to that same local fact with affection; and so they have a mysterious unity of a touching kind."[5]

John Martin stated that comparisons with Eugene Loring's *Billy the Kid* were inevitable because of the subject matter and because Copland had composed the scores for both works. However, he was of the opinion that, fundamentally, the two ballets are utterly unlike. Terming *Rodeo* a notably original work, Martin said that Copland had written an "enchanting" score.[6]

Following its New York stage success, the composer, during the fall and winter of 1942, extracted *Four Dance Episodes* from the ballet to form an orchestral suite for the concert hall. A suite of American dance forms, presenting moods by turns gay, nostalgic, lyric, and zestfully exuberant, the *Episodes* are unique for their definitiveness of American polyrhythms.

I. "Buckaroo Holiday," the most artful of the suite, opens with a gay, lighthearted introduction consisting of two ideas:

a syncopated version of the old familiar C major scale, in Copland's favorite descending form, which is punctuated by jazz polyrhythms having a Charleston origin. Motives, or derivatives, from the two folksongs, "Sis Joe" and "If he'd be a Buckaroo by his trade,"* which form the main material for this movement, are tossed about through the orchestra along with a simple hymnlike refrain having a "blues" harmonic connotation. As an introduction to the main statement of "Sis Joe," the composer makes use of a twenty-three-measure polyrhythmic "vamp," derived from the old ragtime bass (Example 3). The interjection of silent bars midway of the "Buckaroo" tune adds humor and the element of surprise to a characteristic setting.

Ex. 3

II. The contrasting "Corral Nocturne" is simple and expressive, employing no actual folk material. In song-form design, the melodic material, based on a triadic figure repeated in sequences, though vague and indistinct, is pleasing and restful. One phrase, sung by oboe and bassoon, recalls the "Be it ever so humble (Home Sweet Home)" phrase from "The Story of Our Town."

III. An introduction with the aspect of a string orchestra tuning up establishes the proper atmosphere for the lovely folk-

* John A. and Alan Lomax's *Our Singing Country* was the composer's source for both tunes.

song that forms the thematic material for "Saturday Night Waltz." What a composer's find! Although the waltz form is generally associated with a European origin, Copland has given this exquisite American folksong an American cadence with his gentle use of syncopated American rhythms in 3/4 meter (Example 4).

Ex. 4

IV. The final movement, the fast "Hoe-down," presents the square-dance tunes "Bonyparte" (in A and B sections, with a more or less literal treatment) and approximately five bars of "McLeod's Reel"* in a rondo form. As in "Buckaroo Holiday," the polyrhythmic "vamps" (derived from jazz and rural American sources and, consequently, completely American in idiom) add humor, lightness, and zest.

One of Copland's most accessible and easily understood orchestral works, the *Rodeo* suite is simple and direct both in design and language, really Americana at its best. In it, the composer does not permit the basic limitations of the folksongs to restrict him, but, on the contrary, he shapes and manipulates these materials into the general design of his formal structure. In this lies the difference between composing and arranging.

* Both square-dance tunes appear in Ira Ford's *Traditional Music of America*.

Appalachian Spring

During the two-year interval between *Rodeo* and *Appalachian Spring*, among other works, Copland had composed *Danzón Cubano* (for two pianos), another film score, *North Star*, and the "serious" *Sonata for Violin and Piano*.

Appalachian Spring was composed in 1943-1944, as a ballet for Martha Graham, on a commission from the Elizabeth Sprague Coolidge Foundation. Copland began it in June, 1943, in Hollywood (where he was engaged in writing the musical score for *North Star*), but did not complete it until the following June, in Cambridge, Massachusetts where, during the second semester, he filled the post of Horatio Appleton Lamb Lecturer at Harvard.

During the time of the stage rehearsals for the ballet's *première*, Copland was in Tepoztlan, Mexico, where he had gone to write his *Third Symphony*. He returned to Washington, D.C., however, in time for its first performance, which took place on October 30, 1944, in the new Coolidge Auditorium in the Library of Congress.*

Performed by Martha Graham and company with Louis Horst conducting a chamber orchestra of thirteen instruments, the principal roles were danced by Miss Graham, Eric Hawkins, Merce Cunningham, and May O'Donnell. Two other ballets, Milhaud's *Imagined Wing* and Hindemith's *Herodiade*, completed the evening's entertainment.

According to S. L. M. Barlow, Copland's *Appalachian Spring* was the real exhilaration of the evening. "Here were the tart herbs of plain American speech, the pasture, without the flowers of elocution," he wrote; ". . . the clean rhythms . . . the irony and the homespun tenderness that, in a fine peroration, reached a sustained exaltation." Terming the work one of Copland's most lovable scores, limpid, sparkling, and rhythmically diversified,

* It was originally planned for the 1943 Coolidge Festival, but Copland's delay in completing the musical score required the work's postponement until the 1944 Festival.

Barlow stated that *Appalachian Spring* was "more solidly built, more solidly engineered, than some of [Copland's] other ballets."[7]

Copland has stated that the title, *Appalachian Spring*, was chosen by Miss Graham, who borrowed it from the heading of one of Hart Crane's poems, though the ballet has no connection with the poem.

Widely acclaimed both in Washington and New York, *Appalachian Spring* in 1945 received the Pulitzer Prize for Music and also the award of the Music Critics' Circle of New York as the outstanding theatrical work of the 1944-1945 season.

In the spring of 1945, the composer arranged an orchestral suite from *Appalachian Spring* for concert use which has become an important addition to the contemporary orchestral repertory. It is divided into eight sections and played without interruption, the instrumentation making use of wood winds, horns, trumpets and trombones in twos, piano, harp, percussion, and strings. The suite was given its first concert performance on October 4, 1945, by the New York Philharmonic Orchestra under the direction of Artur Rodzinski.

Although the ballet suite has the flavor of Shaker hymns and dance songs, there is only one one direct quotation, the Shaker hymn, "Simple Gifts," which the composer "discovered" in Edward D. Andrews's collection of Shaker folklore entitled *The Gift to Be Simple*. However, many of the themes and motives which Copland used in his orchestral score reveal certain Shaker characteristics: the repeated tone; melodies made from major arpeggios; tunes containing ascending and descending scale passages, and other folk idioms. In view of the fact that these above-mentioned folk characteristics were already properties of Copland's own musical style, such an indigenous subject was both a natural and a happy vehicle for his distinguished gifts.

The ballet has its origin in a pioneer spring celebration of a newly built Pennsylvania (Quaker) farmhouse in the early 1800's. Section I (very slowly), built up out of an extension of the A major triad, serves to introduce the various characters of the ballet: the bride and her young farmer husband; an older neighbor; a revivalist and his flock. A hymnlike theme, or *cantus firmus*, growing out of a figuration of the A major triad, emerges from time to time to cast a halo of simple, religious piety over the entire scene (Example 5).

Ex. 5

Section II (allegro), introduced by a fast A major triad, establishes a sentiment both elated and religious in a folklike theme of two measures which forms the material for this part.

Section III (moderato), bringing the bride and groom to the fore in a tender and ardent scene, recalls the opening material in deeper, richer harmonies. This leads into Section IV, the unison dance of the revivalist and his flock, the music suggesting the folksy atmosphere of square dances and country fiddlers (Example 6).

Ex. 6

Section V, the solo dance of the bride, is marked "still faster." It relies for its material principally on a derivative of the fast A major theme (introduced in Section II), the bride expressing a joyful premonition of motherhood. Section VI returns to the slow introductory mood, evoking a calm, pastoral atmosphere.

Section VII, employing five variations on the Shaker hymn, "Simple Gifts," forms a musical background to which the bride and her husband enact scenes of daily activity. Used literally, the folk hymn, in the key of A flat, is introduced by a clarinet, simply and effectively harmonized. By the skillful use of the devices of augmentation, canon, and counterpoint, Copland has composed a work more contrapuntal in texture than any of his previous works, and in these variations he has struck, for the first time, the note of an American baroque.

According to Manfred Bukofzer, the baroque style, which reached its final peak in Bach and Handel, places its emphasis on the constructive element in music, maintaining a relentless consistency of patterns through the whole movement of a composition; and in this, Bukofzer stated, lies its strongest appeal to the modern composer.[8]

Bukofzer's statement accurately describes the contrapuntal treatment Copland has accorded the Shaker hymn, and, with the third variation utilizing brass and strings, the composer has even caught the baroque instrumental sound (Example 7). Vari-

Ex. 7

ation 4 presents the hymn in broad chorale style, and, with a grand peroration, Variation 5 concludes the Shaker hymn in a majestic and fervent mood.

Section VIII portrays the bride taking her place among her

new neighbors, who soon depart for their own homes, leaving the couple to anticipate the wonder and beginning of their life in the new farmhouse.

In addition to his four ballets, we find American dancers demanding and utilizing other Copland music not primarily conceived for the dance theater. To list a few: in California, Edwin Lester's group adapted *El Salón México* for choreographic purposes; while in New York, in 1947, Doris Humphrey introduced to Broadway her "Day on Earth," set to Copland's "serious" *Piano Sonata* of 1939–1941. In 1951–1952, Jerome Robbins, inspired by Copland's *Concerto for Clarinet and String Orchestra,* created a ballet called *The Pied Piper,* presented by the New York City Ballet Company, which has brought the *Clarinet Concerto* a popularity it had not found in the concert hall. On February 24, 1954, the Toledo (Ohio) Ballet presented the first performance of a dance version of *The Red Pony,* Marie Bollinger Vogt, choreographer, as a feature of one of the regular subscription concerts of the Toledo Orchestral Association, Wolfgang Stresemann, conductor. Composed originally as a musical background for the film of the same name, the ballet version was based on the children's suite extracted from the film score for concert use, discussed later in this chapter.

With these several examples of Copland's "serious" works as well as the *Gebrauchsmusik* scores adapted as choreographical vehicles, we must inevitably conclude that, given a descriptive "program" or, preferably, a dance interpretation, the general public will accept, without question, Copland's most dissonant works. To acknowledge that Aaron Copland is "great" in the dance theater and "our greatest composer of the ballet thus far" is simply to re-echo what our leading dancers have known for years.

Incidental Music to plays

Early in 1931, Copland was commissioned to write the incidental music for the Theatre Guild's production of Hans Chlumberg's play *Miracle at Verdun*. Approximately fifteen minutes in length and scored for small orchestra, the music was recorded on a phonograph record and played during the stage perform- ance, amplified by loud speakers. The music is, by turns, pic- turesque and martial, providing a background for a company of resurrected soldiers of all nations, marching. The popular soldiers' song *"Morgenrot"* appears frequently in the musical background.

There was a lapse of eight years before Copland found an- other opportunity to write music for the stage. Then, in 1939 and 1940, in rapid succession he wrote six dramatic scores. Two of these were incidental music for plays, one for a puppet show, and three for film.

In January of 1939, Copland received a commission from the Mercury Theatre to write the incidental music to its production of *The Five Kings*. This was a composite of several Shakespear- ean plays by Orson Welles, who directed the play. According to the composer, the music consisted of "typical brief 'cues,' trumpet alarums, and 'battle music,' etc.—whatever was neces- sary. I remember using one or two tunes from the period, French and English, I believe. It is scored for the usual four instruments (standard theater group), one of which was a Hammond organ, for percussion sounds." After opening in Boston, February 27, 1939, the play closed without reaching Broadway.

Soon after, Harold Clurman engaged Copland to compose the incidental music to Irwin Shaw's experimental play *Quiet City*. A Group Theatre production, featuring Frances Farmer and others, the play opened in New York on April 16, 1939. Re- garding the production Clurman has noted: "We presented [*Quiet City*] on two Sunday evenings to an audience as uncon- vinced as the company was unsure. We decided not to subject the production to further scrutiny. All that remained of our hard work was a lovely score by Aaron Copland, which is not infre- quently heard nowadays at orchestral concerts."[9]

One of the New York World's Fair (1939) scientific exhibi- tions in the Hall of Pharmacy featured a marionette show, "From Sorcery to Science." With music commissioned by the exhibitors from Aaron Copland, the play was performed by Remo Bufano's giant puppets.

According to the composer the musical score, consisting of four or five episodes each of two or three minutes' duration, was written in five days. On the sixth day it was recorded on phonograph records, which were played mechanically during each show. Scored for an orchestra of thirty-five, the work's general character was that of highly developed background music for the radio.

Music for Films

In *Toward a New Music,* Carlos Chávez stated that the movies are the medium of expression of our epoch. As an organization for spreading ideas and feelings, he believes that their power is unequaled, comparable only to the Church in its best times.[10]

Copland himself has stated that history has shown that composers have shaped their music according to musical needs created by historical events. In the wake of the discovery of the radio, the phonograph, and the sound film (all of which he believed comparable in importance to the invention of the printing press), an entirely new listening public has been developed, though not a concertgoing public. It was with the full realization of the potentialities of the sound film, bearing both artistic and political implications, that Copland approached the new medium. Proof of his belief in the challenge of the sound film to the contemporary composer is offered in the following terse statement: "The cultural level of music is certain to be raised if better music is written for films."[11]

Many will recall that it was in August, 1926, that Warner Brothers Pictures, with the Vitaphone Corporation, presented the first complete synchronized musical score to accompany the film *Don Juan,* starring John Barrymore. The musical accompaniment was conducted by Henry Hadley and performed by the New York Philharmonic Symphony. With the first talking picture, *The Jazz Singer,* in 1927, starring Al Jolson, the screen became theater.

Documentary Films

Twelve years later, in 1939, Aaron Copland wrote his first film score to accompany the documentary film *The City*, for presentation at the New York World's Fair. Following an outline by Pare Lorenz, two cameramen spent six months during 1938–1939 recording delightful and unpleasant scenes in small towns and cities in various sections of the United States. These thousands of feet of film (for which nobody consciously posed) were worked into a dramatic sequence by Henwar Rodakiewicz and Oscar Serlin. Copland then added the musical score to the completed film.

Copland's second documentary film score was not composed until 1945, when he wrote the musical score for *The Cummington Story*, produced by the Overseas Unit of the United States Office of War Information. An intimate portrait of life in a rural New England town, the film makes a strong plea against intolerance.

Films Produced in Hollywood

To date Copland has composed music to five films that were produced in Hollywood, one of which, *The Heiress*, received an Academy Award (1950) for the excellence of its musical score.

Copland has stated that he believes Virgil Thomson has offered the best explanation of the purpose of music in the films, an aesthetic Copland consciously adopted in composing musical scores for that medium. "It is [Thomson's] conception that the score of a motion-picture supplies a sort of human warmth to the black-and-white, two dimensional figures on the screen, giving them a communicable sympathy that they otherwise would not have, bridging the gap between the screen and the audience." [12]

Theodore Strauss has given us a portrait of the composer as he appeared to Hollywood in 1939 on his first picture assignment, to write a musical score to accompany John Steinbeck's *Of Mice and Men*. Not totally unknown to the film capital, for he had performed his *Piano Concerto* in the Hollywood Bowl approximately ten years earlier, Copland· was now approaching his fortieth birthday. Strauss stated that he had not found Copland the "enfant terrible" he had been reported to be, but "one senses a mathematical intelligence in the features—the thick-lensed glasses perched on a sharply pointed nose, the high receding forehead . . . a boyish sort of man who likes to laugh and does." Describing Copland's eyes as "quizzical," Strauss said that the composer looks upon the world "with that perpetual sense of wonder that only children and poets are supposed to have." [13]

Copland's primary purpose in writing the music for *Of Mice and Men* was to compose music that would suggest the film's background, life on a California ranch. To do this he occasionally employed music of a folksonglike character, simple tunes that Steinbeck's itinerant farm hands (with whom the drama is concerned) might have whistled. "The temper of the music varied," he wrote, ". . . with every scene, but always I tried to keep away from the overlush harmonies that are so common on the screen and usually defeat their own purpose by overemphasis." [14] The film score *Of Mice and Men* received its New York *première* on February 16, 1940, at the Roxy Theatre.

Music for Movies

Completed in 1942, and dedicated to Darius Milhaud, Copland's *Music for Movies* literally lives up to its title, for it is a concert suite fashioned from several of the composer's film scores. The suite contains two excerpts from *The City*, "New England Countryside" and "Sunday Traffic," respectively the first and third movements; two excerpts from *Of Mice and Men*, "Barley Wagons" and "Threshing Machines," respectively the second and fifth movements; and a single excerpt from *Our Town* entitled "Story of Grovers Corners," which forms the fourth movement.

Scored for chamber orchestra, using one each of wood winds and brasses (two trumpets, however), with an occasional use of percussion and harp (or piano), *Music for Movies* at once reflects Copland's new aesthetic of a simple and more direct ap-

Hall on June 13, 1940, with Frank Craven, William Holden, Martha Scott, Fay Bainter, and others in the principal roles. Bosley Crowther, the New York *Times* film critic, hesitating to employ superlatives, reported that *Our Town* "captures on film the simple beauties and truths of humble folk as very few pictures ever do; it is rich and ennobling in its plain philosophy—and it gives one a passionate desire to enjoy the fullness of life even in these good old days of today." Praising Lesser for his courage in producing a picture in this fashion, Crowther stated that "the score of Aaron Copland's offers a subtle tonal response to the vagrant moods." [15]

Two days later Crowther again praised the screen version of the play, noting that *Our Town* is a "startlingly vivid example of the great potentialities of this medium, when it is intelligently used." [16]

Our Town

In addition to the excerpt that appears as the fourth movement in *Music for Movies,* Copland has made an orchestral concert version of *Our Town,* in one extended movement, of nine minutes' duration, and scored it for large orchestra. In 1944, he arranged three excerpts from the film score for piano solo. These are entitled: (1) "Story of Our Town"; (2) "Conversation at the Soda Fountain"; (3) "The Resting-place on the Hill." Not difficult technically, the little suite is one of the infrequent instances in which original background music for a Hollywood film has been made generally available.

Though the music lacks the dramatic quality usually associated with Copland's theater or film scores, its pastoral tone and subjective quality are striking. The one dramatic moment of the play, the death of Emily, in the film has become softened into a misty, ephemeral, dream sequence. Hence the one opportunity for dramatic writing that the composer might have had was, for the movie, reduced to "background" music.

A pastoral, hymnlike atmosphere is immediately established in the opening of both the orchestral piece and the piano suite, called in the latter work, "Story of Our Town." (This is the same material as that entitled "Grovers Corners" in *Music for Movies* (see Example 10). In stressing the humble quality of the townspeople, Copland has, twice, subtly woven a condensation of the two final phrases of John Howard Payne's "Home Sweet Home" ("Be it ever so humble, There's no place like home") into the latter phrases of this short movement, each time with a varied harmonization. Although the first harmonization is equally attractive, exuding a mild polytonal flavor, the second setting, which conveys a sense of calm and well-being to the film's background, is presented here (Example 11).

Ex. 11

The second movement of the piano suite, called "Conversasation at the Soda Fountain," has been wisely omitted from the orchestral version. Melodically inconsequential music, this sequence merely provides a conversational background to the scene in the drugstore where Emily and George first discover they are "made for each other."

The third movement, entitled "The Resting-place on the Hill," suggests in its opening phrases the impression of heights and spaciousness. This blends into a hymnlike, pianissimo section, indicative of the atmosphere of the quiet church graveyard, then moves into the sequence where Emily dreams that she dies and joins those on the hill. Both the hymn and dream sections are in a 3/4 meter and the latter, without recalling the actual material, suggests the mood of "Dance of a Young Girl," from Copland's earlier *Dance Symphony.* (The orchestral movement contains most of the above music, in a different sequence from the piano suite, while other more melodic sections of the film score have been substituted for the "Conversation at the Soda Fountain" episode.)

Of infinite sweetness and gentleness, the music from *Our Town* is one of Copland's smaller but tasteful works. Because of its inherent simplicity and tunefulness, the music is easily performed (in both versions) by amateur pianists or symphonic groups.

Between *Our Town* and *North Star* there was an interval of three years, during which time Copland completed the impressive *Piano Sonata, Lincoln Portrait, Sonata for Violin and Piano,* the ballet *Rodeo,* and various smaller compositions. Most of these works were commissions, indicating that the composer was writing the kind of music for which there was a need, on the part of serious musicians and the general public.

Copland's third Hollywood assignment was to write a musical score to accompany the film *North Star,* produced by Samuel Goldwyn for RKO Pictures. *North Star* was based on a story by Lillian Hellman, and Lewis Milestone was again the director. Since the assignment was unusually large, Copland remained in Hollywood from February to September, 1943, working on the musical score.*

North Star provided the composer unusual scope for, in addition to the usual background music, he had to supply songs, choruses, and dances; there was opportunity to express many varieties of moods in writing music to accompany war, love, and comedy scenes. Its chief problem was that of style: "Since the picture takes place in Russia, there was ... the problem as to how 'Russian' the music ought to be," the composer wrote. "It was something of the same problem Shostakovitch would have had if he had been asked to supply a score for a movie set in the United States." Several sequences take as their starting point actual folk material, but in only three instances was direct use made of Soviet material. In the composer's opinion, the most effective of these is the "Song of the Fatherland," analogous to our own

* Frederick Sternfeld, "Copland as a Film Composer," *The Musical Quarterly,* April, 1951, pp. 161-175, has given the erroneous date of 1942 instead of 1943 as the date of the musical score for *North Star.*

"My Country 'Tis of Thee." Since the American actors did not attempt to speak with a Russian accent, in general, the composer adopted a style that would suggest, without overemphasizing, the Russian element.

North Star received its world *première* simultaneously at two theaters in New York City, the Victoria and Palace, on November 4, 1943.

Bosley Crowther termed the film a heroic picture whose force was weakened by the fact that the producer and director had mixed theatrical forms too freely. "There are music (by Aaron Copland) and rollicking gaiety of the sort familiar to light-hearted peasants in musical comedies set in mythical foreign lands. When the people of the village gather for a sociable evening al fresco, it might even be a scene from 'Oklahoma.' " The critic found that when the bombs suddenly began to fall and the style of the film changed to "vehement reality," the contrast was "too prodigious." He concluded, however, that *North Star* "has so much in it that is moving and triumphant that its sometimes departures from reality may be generally overlooked."[17]

Between *North Star* (1943) and Copland's next two Hollywood assignments, *The Red Pony* and *The Heiress* (both in 1948), five years had elapsed. Meanwhile, the composer had also written the musical score for the documentary film, *The Cummington Story* (1945), mentioned earlier in this chapter. Now forty-eight years old, Copland had attained his mature growth and was producing large works which reflected a complete amalgamation of all material into a clearly defined personal style. The musical scores for *The Red Pony* and *The Heiress* are to be considered, therefore, as products of the composer's mature thought.

Based on John Steinbeck's tale of *The Red Pony*, the musical score for the film was composed from February to April, 1948, on the studio lot of Republic Pictures, in the San Fernando Valley.

Suite from The Red Pony

For his first year as conductor of the reorganized Houston Symphony Society (1948–1949), Efram Kurtz asked Copland to write a work for his opening concert. The composer suggested, instead, a suite from the movie *The Red Pony,* which Kurtz accepted. The suite was completed in August, 1948, at Richmond, Massachusetts, and received its *première* performance in Houston, at the City Auditorium, on October 30 of the same year.

Stating that the composer was present to hear "what he must have known in advance was a hit," Hubert Roussel, music critic of the Houston *Post,* was of the opinion that *The Red Pony* concert suite "is by no means Mr. Copland's magnum opus, but it is clear, joyous, ingenious and irresistibly spirited music. By turns tender and bombastic in a light and whimsical manner, well studded with humorous dissonance, it made everybody feel good."[18]

Completely descriptive, the concert suite from *The Red Pony* bears the imprint of Copland's "concert" style, with, however, a difference in philosophical content. Using his own themes, tonal vocabulary, and techniques, the composer has defined his work as a "children's suite" for the reason that much of the music is meant to reflect a child's world. In shaping the suite, which is scored for large orchestra, the composer recast much of the musical material so that, although all the music was present in the film, its continuity has been reorganized for concert purposes.

I. "Morning on the Ranch," idyllic in mood, employs motives suggestive of nature's gradual stirrings at daybreak and the beginning of the daily chores. The following folklike theme suggests the atmosphere of simple life in the American West (Example 12).

Ex. 12

II. "The Gift" is music taken from the episode when, one evening after supper, Jody's father takes him down to the barn to surprise the boy with the gift of a red pony. With the opening chords and ethereal quality of the orchestration, Copland has caught the wonder and delight of the small boy in this most magnificent of gifts.

III. Although Jody is usually occupied with school, homework, and ranch chores, he frequently exercises his imagination with fanciful daydreams. On the long walk to school Jody has one of his most exciting adventures, picturing himself with Billy Buck (the cowhand) at the head of an array of knights dressed in shining armor; on another occasion he is the ringmaster at the circus. Copland has combined these two imaginary episodes into "Dream March and Circus Music." In a characteristic polytonal orchestration, Copland has announced the march theme (beginning slowly) with a solo trumpet, pianissimo, in C, with the march rhythm played by the tuba, in D (Example 13).

Ex. 13

IV. In "Walk to the Bunkhouse," Copland has described Jody's and Billy Buck's rhythmic gait in terms of cowboy polyrhythms of the type he had used previously in such scores as *Billy the Kid, Rodeo,* and the final movement of the *Violin Sonata.* It is a modification of the old 4/4 (um-pah) rhythm, viewed here as a combination of 3/4 and 2/4 measure. Above the rhythm the composer has written a cowboylike melody for solo trumpet. Over the trumpet melody is a simple counterpoint in the violins that indicates the spaciousness of the outdoors; it follows the general outline of basic triadic harmonies. Although

introduced separately, these polyrhythms appear together toward the end of the movement (Example 14).

Ex. 14

V. "Grandfather's Story" begins in a quiet narrative mood,
expressing a yearning for the past glories of "westering." As the
old man recollects the hardships and victories of the pioneers,
the only harsh dissonances of the entire work enter the score.

VI. "Happy Ending" returns to the material of the first movement, presenting a gayer, an almost fanfarelike, mood. The folklike melody of the beginning is again heard, this time with bold-
ness and conviction.

Just as German music has portrayed its child's world in terms
of Schumann's *Scenes from Childhood* and French music has
described its particular national character through Debussy's
Children's Corner, so American music has its counterpart in
Copland's *The Red Pony* suite, which, in a comparable art form,
has elevated to a high degree the yearnings and aspirations of
American children. In this sense the work is an American small
"classic."

It was George Antheil, probably with the longest Hollywood
tenure of our native-born serious composers, who stated in an
interview that opera and film music are very closely related, for
both belong in the same category of theater music. "They are

far less separated from each other," he affirmed, "than they are from another large category—music for the concert hall."[19]

In defense of this view Antheil was asked, why has not the main title of a film score generally taken on the function of the operatic overture? "It really ought to," he replied; "it should be the one place in a film score where strictly musical form dominates." Noting that he, himself, had recently written a "real" overture for the film *We Were Strangers,* which had proved unacceptable to the "front office," Antheil said he was obliged to rewrite it. "By now," he continued, "everybody knows [that] . . . Copland's title music for *The Heiress* was deleted from his score and replaced by an orchestral version of a little French song that is sung in the film. Copland felt obliged to write a letter to the press disclaiming responsibility for that part of the score."[20]

Seven months after the completion of *The Red Pony* film score, Copland returned to Hollywood during the months of November and December, 1948, to fulfill his fifth assignment, to compose the musical score for the film *The Heiress.*[*] Based on Henry James's novel *Washington Square, The Heiress* (an adaptation by Ruth and Augustus Goetz) had enjoyed a successful Broadway run with Wendy Hiller in the title role. The Goetzes also wrote the adaptation for Paramount Pictures which was produced and directed by William Wyler.

A visit to Tanglewood in July, 1951, provided the author with an opportunity to study the film score (in manuscript) at first hand and to discuss its music with the composer.[†]

In the writing of the musical score it was Copland's problem to compose a period piece of 1850 that would sound as if it was being played in New York in 1950. To achieve this he chose typical musical selections representative of the period of the play, such as mazurkas, polkas, Gossec's familiar "Gavotte," bal-

---

[*] The manuscript of the musical score bears the dates (in Copland's autograph) Nov. 8–Dec. 28, 1948.

[†] There is no concert version of the musical score to *The Heiress,* nor does the composer contemplate making one, for the music, eloquent in the film, as we shall see, scarcely lends itself to suite form.

let music of the nineteenth century including E. Ketterer's "Waltz No. 2" and "Queen of the Flowers," to create an authentic background of the period. In addition, the composer himself wrote original music in the style of the 1850's, a "Mazurka No. 2," "Garden Waltz," and "Polka No. 2," the latter having the flavor of a Bohemian polka.

Perhaps the most important feature of the musical score lies in the fact that Copland assigned to each of the principal characters a musical motive, an adaptation of the operatic leitmotiv principle. Unlike many of his Hollywood colleagues, Copland did much more than merely label his characters with a recognizable motive. As the characters themselves develop, the musical motive undergoes development, harmonically, melodically, sometimes contrapuntally, and always rhythmically. Thus this often "foreground" music assists materially and psychologically in the dramatic conflicts that ensue.

Since it is impractical to trace the development of each leitmotiv through the film score, several examples, chiefly from the music surrounding the heroine, will suffice to show how the composer adapted this principle to film purposes.

Although Paramount studio officials saw fit to delete the overturelike title music which Copland had written for *The Heiress,* an act that destroyed both the dramatic continuity of the mood and structure of the film score, the author believes that, because this music provides the germ of the leitmotiv idea, it must be restored here in order to understand the composer's intent and method of work.

The Heiress

The first three measures of the original title music at once suggest the film's dramatic and tragic mood by the immediate introduction of both the doctor's and Catherine's musical characterizations (Example 15). The inner conflict of the former is stressed through the device of imitation, while the romantic intensity of Catherine is outlined by the sweeping descending diatonic scale; her defiance and strength are revealed in the development of the motive in measures 4, 5, and 6.

Ex. 15

A happier, more carefree Catherine is reflected in the sequence entitled "The Cherry Red Dress," when she is seen tripping down the stairs (Example 16). Here the composer has developed Catherine's motive by means of diminution, extensions, and sequential repetitions, resulting in a totally different mood and giving it the quality of "background" rather than "foreground" music.

Ex. 16

For the episode "Morris Suggests Love," Copland has used an eighteenth century Italian love song, "Plaisir d'Amour," composed by Giovanni Martini. In order to provide a nineteenth century quality, Copland, by means of augmentation, has retarded the love song from its original 6/8 meter (*allegretto grazioso*) tempo to a 3/4 meter accompanied with the direction, "slowly and expressively" (Example 17).

Ex. 17

The hour of the elopement has arrived. After waiting long past the hour when Morris is to appear, Catherine dashes out of the house at the sound of an approaching carriage, only to see it disappear down the street. In this episode Copland has artfully combined the fast sound of the carriage wheels with the now sardonic refrain (to Catherine's ears) of the last two tones of the love song sounded simultaneously in a cacophonous discord.

During the preceding episode the composer has very subtly directed the Catherine theme toward a very familiar one. In the episode "A Defeated Catherine," the familiar theme is suddenly recognized as the theme from Copland's *Piano Variations* of 1930! What is it doing in *The Heiress?*

When asked this question, the composer at once explained that he "had had that particular variation on hand a long time and, although it seemed out of character with the other Variations, it seemed to fit here." Frugal composer! He had saved those twelve measures for eighteen years, waiting for the right opportunity to present itself for their use.

Another familiar bit of material is recalled as a rhythmic figure from the trio, *Vitebsk*, the thirty-second note followed by the double-dotted eighth which appears in the introductory bars of the trio (cf Chapter V, Example 1). We therefore view the composer returning to abstract materials (derived from a jazz source) to express complex human emotions.

Starring Olivia de Haviland, the film version of *The Heiress* opened in Radio City Music Hall, New York, on October 6, 1949. Enthusiastically received by both audience and press it was, therefore, not surprising to read in the New York *Times* of March 24, 1950 (front page), that *The Heiress* was the recipient of the 1949 Hollywood Academy Award, bestowed in 1950. To Aaron Copland went the award for the "Best Scoring of a Dramatic or Comedy Picture."

The man upon whom had already been bestowed the Pulitzer Prize and the award of the Music Critics' Circle of New York (both in 1945) for his ballet *Appalachian Spring*, the Boston

Symphony's "Merit Award" (1947) for his *Third Symphony* became, in 1950, the recipient of the highest award presented by the film capital of the world.* Coming to Hollywood in 1939, as a little-known composer whose "modern" tendencies were looked upon with misgivings, after a ten-year period of experiment, study and work in the new medium he won the coveted Academy Award. He had already become a recognized master of the stage and the concert hall when the film provided him a larger audience than the other two mediums combined. Thus the scope of the composer's influence was steadily extending, not only over North and South America but to Europe as well. In proof of the latter statement, mention is made of the fact that in the Spring of 1951, both *The Red Pony* and *The Heiress* were exhibited at a film festival in Trieste and at a conference on movie music in Florence.

Opera

Following the "leitmotif" characterization development of *The Heiress*, it was not only inevitable but also a matter of natural evolution that Copland's next work for stage should prove to be an opera.

Between the composer's first and second operas eighteen years had elapsed, for *The Second Hurricane*, designed for high school performance (as noted in Chapter VI), was composed in 1936 and received its first performance in 1937. Vastly differing in respect to stylistic idiom employed, Copland's second opera, *The Tender Land*, 1952-1954, as it was first performed bears some outward similarities to *The Second Hurricane:* both works were in two acts, were of a comparable time duration, were and are simple and direct in their musical language, are manifestations of folk expression (Negro-folk and jazz in the first opera, Middle Western-pastoral or landscape in the second). Nevertheless, dramatically, the composer again stumbled into

---

* Among additional honors conferred upon Copland, mention must be made of his election to membership in The National Institute of Arts and Letters, New York, in 1942; to The American Academy of Arts and Sciences, Boston, in 1951; and to The American Academy of Arts and Letters, New York, in 1954.

the same pitfall in his second work for the singing stage, for he again chose a libretto not stageworthy.

The Tender Land

Commissioned by Richard Rodgers and Oscar Hammerstein, 2d, for the thirtieth anniversary of the League of Composers, *The Tender Land*, with libretto by Horace Everett, received its world *première* on April 1, 1954, by the New York City Opera Company, Thomas Schippers, conductor, New York City Center of Music and Drama. Paired with Menotti's *Amahl and the Night Visitors*, critics one and all praised Copland's new work for its fine musical qualities and condemned the weak libretto for its utter failure in character delineation, particularly in respect to the women of the drama.

Following the *première*, Copland, ever the objective artist, took to heart the criticisms and, with the help of his talented collaborator, began to rework the opera in terms of strengthening the book.

Critics immediately noted an improvement in the version presented at Tanglewood, August 2 and 3, 1954, which, due to lack of time, contained only the extended first act revision and not the third act. Again, following these performances, Copland took the opera back to his studio desk and, by the end of 1954 (or early 1955), *The Tender Land* had reached its final form— an opera in three acts, of approximately two hours' duration, which now fills an entire evening. The first performance in the final, perfected version will take place on May 20 and 21, 1955, at Oberlin Conservatory. The following remarks refer to the final version and take note of the extensive revisions which, upon an adequate stage presentation will, in my opinion, unquestionably stamp *The Tender Land* as one of our most significant American operas.

Inasmuch as the problem of the libretto is the problem of every opera composer in America save perhaps the Italian American composer Menotti (who by nature and national background is endowed to write his own), it will serve a useful purpose here to see how Everett and Copland successfully solved their problem.

The beginning bars, consisting of soft, widely spaced chords, from which emerges a simple folklike tune evocative of *Billy the Kid* and *Appalachian Spring*, serve to open the curtain upon a breathtaking American Gothic farm scene conceived in the spirit of a Grant Wood Middle Western landscape. The simple aura of simple folk, remindful of the quality of the music from *Our Town*, pervades the atmosphere surrounding the main characters of the drama, Ma Moss, Laurie and Beth Moss (her daughters), Grandpa Moss, the Splinters and Jenks families. The two drifters, Martin and Top, also have their counterpart in the two itinerant farm hands, George and Lennie, from Steinbeck's *Of Mice and Men*, for the film version of which Copland earlier had composed music.

In the first act, librettist and composer have added a scene between Laurie and Ma Moss, stressing the fact that the young girl has lingered along the way home from school on a summer's day, pausing to dream and to wonder what the future holds for her beyond tomorrow's high-school graduation. This scene points up the pride, sympathy, and understanding that the mother holds for the young girl at the threshold of womanhood. Ma Moss also introduces the conflict (not clearly present in the original version) between parental authority, represented by Grandpa Moss, and the impatience of youth to make its own decisions and choices. This also serves to delay the appearance of the two drifters, Martin and Top, so that their entrance seems both prepared and natural (not arbitrary, as in the first version). Act I, therefore, moves steadily by means of several arias and concerted numbers for Ma Moss, Laurie, Martin, and others, interspersed with typical Coplandesque polyrhythms and dissonant-sounding chords to point up the dramatic action, on to the brilliant finale in the form of a quintet sung by the principals, "The Promise of Living," the finest concerted piece of the entire opera.*

---

* The end of Act I bears the completion date, 9/22/'53, in the composer's autograph.

Act II captures the square-dance mood of *Rodeo* with effective
dancing and singing by the chorus, celebrating Laurie's eve of
high-school graduation. Borrowing a leaf from *The Second Hurricane*, Top's rendition of the Southern Appalachian "Courtin'
Song" *authenticates the American folk idiom employed in the
score and adds to the scene's rustic gaiety (Example 18). The
plot to get Grandpa Moss drunk so that Martin may court Laurie

Ex. 18

without parental interference boomerangs into an actual love
match, high-lighted by a duet between the enamored pair. Here
Copland has introduced a two-note motive of infinite tenderness
and longing into the orchestration, which Martin soon sings as
"Laurie, Laurie, Is there someone in there that's called Laurie,
Laurie?" (Example 19).

Ex. 19

* Note in composer's score: "Melody and words adapted from Cecil Sharp's
English Folk Songs From The Southern Appalachians."

Ma Moss's suspicion that the two drifters are in reality the strangers who recently seduced several young girls of neighboring farms arouses Grandpa's instinct to protect his young. Another insert (approximately three pages) interrupts the tender and passionate duet between Laurie and Martin to develop the increasing dramatic tension between age and respectability (typified by Grandpa) and the youthful, awakened Laurie, who tries to explain that she has done nothing wrong, that she has merely "grown up"! Although Ma Moss's suspicion is proved unfounded, Grandpa breaks up the party and orders the strangers away at daybreak. Act II ends with a hasty "Good night" by the departing guests, with the two boys returning to the shed for the night.*

Act III (formerly Act II, Scene 11) shows Martin, unable to sleep, walking about the yard. Laurie, also wide-awake, sees him and rushes out of the house to join him. Here the composer and the librettist have inserted twelve pages which, missing in the first version, build up the love story and make entirely believable and convincing the fact that Laurie is now prepared to cast aside her graduation plans in order to fulfill the larger purpose of life, to go away with Martin. In this ecstatic love scene Copland has written some of the most emotional music of his entire career. The bitter-sweet polytonal harmonies, enhanced by the composer's skillful use of dissonance, color the various moods, fanciful thoughts, and poetic aspirations of the lovers. The opera moves on to its inevitable conclusion, with Laurie following after Martin, and Ma Moss understanding at last that her daughter, too, must discover the world in terms of an ever-widening horizon.

Thus, with the bolstering up of the libretto, which, in turn, gave the composer greater opportunities for character delineation and dramatic conflict, Copland's new opera must be regarded as a milestone if not a masterpiece in the American theater, for *The Tender Land* is sincere, indigenous, gay, lusty,

---

* The end of Act II bears the completion date, March 12, 1954, in the composer's autograph.

at times powerfully beautiful, poignantly nostalgic, and emotionally moving. Although all of these inherent human qualities have been reflected successfully and frequently in our literature, painting, and dance theater, I venture to assert that in spite of several earlier distinguished operatic attempts to capture the American scene (i.e., Hanson's *Merry Mount,* Thomson's *Mother of Us All,* Moore's *Giants in the Earth,* all of which suffered more or less from "book trouble"), not until *The Tender Land* were these above-mentioned qualities crystallized and projected successfully into a "serious" American opera form.* In my opinion, what *Oklahoma!* contributed to the revitalization of the Broadway musical comedy, *The Tender Land* has achieved in the American opera theater, without, however, Copland's having had at the start a plot of the quality of *Green Grow the Lilacs* on which to embroider a musical fabric. I believe that in his refusal to "give up" until a satisfactory libretto was finally attained is further proof that he has shown us once again how to move ahead, this time toward achieving a native "serious" opera all our own, and not rely on European operatic traditions.

Taking leave of the ballet and theater works, in which Copland is unquestionably great, with the new opera marking the very pinnacle of his theater works, let us proceed to Chapter VIII, the patriotic and absolute works, for they provide the severest test of a composer's genius.

---

* Although some may lament the omission of Gershwin's *Porgy and Bess* from the above list of American works, I am of the opinion that time has shown that *Porgy and Bess*, although based on an excellent libretto, because of its "lighter" musical idiom, belongs in the category of a Broadway show rather than opera. Gershwin's effort should, therefore, I think, be compared with the accomplishments of other masters of Broadway musicals such as Jerome Kern, Cole Porter, Richard Rodgers, and Leonard Bernstein (*Wonderful Town*) rather than with the operatic achievements of our "serious" composers.

VIII

Third Style Period (American Folksong)
The Patriotic and Absolute Works
(1939-1955)

CHAPTER VIII is devoted to the second large classification of
Aaron Copland's American Folksong Period, the patriotic and
absolute works. Considerably fewer in number than the *Gebrauchsmusik* works, as noted in Chapters VI and VII, these
scores are remarkable for their seriousness of purpose and of
tone.

With the advent of World War II, Copland placed his gifts,
both personal and musical, at the service of the nation. Pursuing
a policy of unity and solidarity for the Western Hemisphere,
our State Department in 1941, and again in 1947, sent him as an
emissary of "good will" to our South American neighbors, of
both of which visits this chapter offers brief glimpses.

Enunciating democratic principles during those years of stress,
Copland's patriotic works include: *Lincoln Portrait; Fanfare for
the Common Man;* and *Preamble for a Solemn Occasion.* Except
for its lack of a serious tone, a fourth work, *Letter from Home,*
might conceivably have been placed among the patriotic works;
instead, as we have seen, its functional use places it in the category of "radio commissions."

The absolute works, numbering ten, include: *Piano Sonata;
Sonata for Violin and Piano; Jubilee Variation* (on a theme by
Eugene Goossens); *Third Symphony;* a large choral work en-
titled *In the Beginning;* a suite, *Four Piano Blues; Concerto for
Clarinet and String Orchestra; Old American Songs* (Sets I and
II), newly arranged for solo voice and piano; a song cycle en-
titled *Twelve Poems of Emily Dickinson;* and *Quartet for Piano
and Strings.*

The really close relationship existing between the patriotic and absolute works becomes apparent when it is realized that *Fanfare for the Common Man* is later used in the Finale of Copland's *Third Symphony*.

In spite of the marked success with which the American public greeted Copland's new aesthetic change of direction, i.e., writing simple music stemming from folk sources for a greatly expanded audience including schools, radio, the theater, and films, which brought him both fame and economic security, he was not artistically satisfied to remain simply a "peoples' composer."

Furthermore, his attitude regarding the reliance on "conscious Americanisms" (folksongs and folk rhythms) for music materials was undergoing a change, as his letter of June 2, 1941, to Oscar Thompson indicates. Observing that within the last ten years American composers had become more self-reliant, Copland continued: "I no longer feel the need of seeking out conscious Americanisms. Because we live here and work here, we can be certain that when our music is mature it will also be American in quality. American individuals will produce an American music, without any help from conscious Americanisms." [1]

Recognizing the wide gap existing between concert and popular audiences, two years later Copland remarked that the composers would have to find a musical style and language which would satisfy both the composers and the expanded audience, citing Shostakovitch as a contemporary composer whose most remarkable attribute was that he had made his music "come fully alive for a world audience." [2]

Virgil Thomson's theory of dividing musical composition into two categories apparently assisted in solving the composer's dilemma, for Copland was henceforth to write two main types of music: (1) more relaxed and easygoing compositions for popular consumption, including radio, ballet, film, and opera audiences (the music of Chapters VI and VII); (2) very intense and serious works, for concert hall audiences, that would satisfy the composer's own inner creative aesthetic (the music of Chapter VIII).

The Patriotic Works

Copland's patriotic works not only reflect that composer's reaction to a critical period in our nation's history (World War II) but also contain, in a measure, some aspects of his political thinking. Having forsaken his "ivory tower" and the abstract approach of the early thirties for a simpler language with which he might communicate with all mankind, Copland again gives evidence in these scores of outwardly reflecting the events of his time. Not to be finally placed among the composer's important works, these scores, nevertheless, represent a growing tendency on the part of our creative artists, writers, and composers to concern themselves with the political destiny of our country and to reaffirm in their works the democratic ideals which led to its founding and preservation.

Two of the patriotic works bear an outward resemblance to each other in that they employ highly divergent media, the spoken voice of the theater and the symphony orchestra of the concert hall. Thus both *Lincoln Portrait* and *Preamble for A Solemn Occasion* are scored for speaker and orchestra.

In January, 1942, André Kostelanetz commissioned Copland and several other composers to write musical portraits of great Americans. Giving up his first idea of writing a portrait of Walt Whitman, Copland discussed his second choice, Lincoln, with Virgil Thomson, who was to do a musical portrait of Fiorello H. La Guardia. Thomson wisely pointed out that no composer could hope to match the stature of Lincoln's greatness in musical terms. Believing that part of the problem could be solved by having Lincoln himself speak some of his great historical conceptions, Copland chose for a text excerpts from Lincoln's letters and speeches. Both the order and arrangement of the selections are the composer's own; yet, in expressing Lincoln's idea of democracy, Copland has chosen words that are as prophetic and applicable to our own critical times as they were in the Civil War years.

Begun in February, 1942, in New York, the preliminary sketch was finished on April 16 and the orchestration a few weeks later.

Combined with musical materials of his own, Copland has worked in two songs of the period: Stephen Foster's "Camptown Races" and a ballad published in 1840 under the title of "The Pesky Sarpent," but better known today as "Springfield Mountain." As in his use of cowboy songs in *Billy the Kid*, these tunes are presented freely and not literally to set the atmosphere of the *Portrait*.

Kostelanetz, to whom the work is dedicated, conducted the first performance of *Lincoln Portrait* on May 14, 1942, in Cincinnati, with the Cincinnati Symphony Orchestra and William Adams, speaker.

The work's first radio performance occurred on August 16, three months later, in New York, when Kostelanetz conducted it on his regular CBS Sunday afternoon broadcast. According to Robert Lawrence, Copland was present to speak a few introductory words regarding his tonal portrait, and Carl Sandburg read the text. Lawrence received the impression that the work would endure a long time, for Copland "has struck that common denominator of direct emotional appeal which unites the professional musician and the intuitive music-lover. Here, in its sinew and lack of rhetoric, is American music," he wrote; "and here, by virtue of its dramatic fire and avoidance of theory, is a work that maintains contact with an audience." [3]

Although *Lincoln Portrait* is the better of the two works untilizing a speaker and is serious and thoughtful in tone, as a work of art it is not entirely successful, for the composer was unable to completely reconcile its two opposing functional elements, the theater and the concert hall. On the other hand, *Lincoln Portrait* is a utilitarian and appealing work which fulfilled its purposes during the World War II years when certain fundamental American conceptions needed to be restated and emphasized in simple, direct terms. As an anniversary piece, the work is appropriate and entirely valid to the annual celebration of Lincoln's birthday.

Turning to the composer's second work of this type, *Preamble For A Solemn Occasion*, I believe from a study of the score and only one hearing of the work, a broadcast, that it is inferior to the *Portrait*. Commissioned by the National Broadcasting Company, and written between August 16 and September 5, 1949, at the composer's home in Sneden's Landing, New York, the work is cast in the composer's prophetic vein and enunciates heroic concepts. Maintaining a slow, stately tempo throughout the short one-movement work, the composer evidently conceived *Preamble* as a hymn, for the original manuscript bears that title crossed out. Instead of the warm, nostalgic folksongs developed as material for the *Portrait,* the composer's material for the *Preamble* consists of "pure" musical ideas derived from triads and descending scale passages subjected, at times, to a chromatic-harmony setting with a noticeably strong intertwining of contrapuntal textures. Offering less human appeal than the *Portrait* and couched in a more abstract language, *Preamble* relies for its dramatic effect on a short text, or creed, taken from the Preamble to the United Nations' Charter. The composer emphasizes their heroic content with an extended orchestral passage, *fortissimo,* and closes, as in the *Portrait,* with a rousing C major climax. The work's first performance was given by the Boston Symphony Orchestra, with Leonard Bernstein conducting, at Carnegie Hall, New York, December 10, 1949, with Sir Laurence Olivier as speaker.

Carrying out in America an experiment he had successfully essayed in London in 1921, Eugene Goossens, conductor of the Cincinnati Symphony Orchestra, commissioned ten American composers, including Aaron Copland, to write patriotic fanfares for performance during the 1942–1943 Cincinnati orchestral season. Aside from tributes to heroism, which had a high propaganda value during World War II, the fanfares also provide conductors with opportunities for virtuosic display of the brass sections of their orchestras.

Copland's contribution, *Fanfare for the Common Man,* scored for brass and percussion, forty-six bars in length, was composed in Oakland, New Jersey, during the fall of 1942. Its first performance took place in Cincinnati, March 14, 1943, with Goossens and the Cincinnati Symphony Orchestra.

In Copland's *Fanfare* two timpani tuned in fourths (F and B flat), reinforced by bass drum and tam-tam, establish a dramatic and ominous mood in the very deliberate rhythm ♩♪ ♫♪. Three trumpets, in unison, proclaim the fanfare theme, which contains two ideas, or germs, from which the short work is fashioned: a characteristic trumpet "flourish," and sustained tones which later form a choralelike theme. Both ideas are derived from the B flat and E flat major triads. Through simple but "absolute" musical means, Copland chose to do honor to the "common" man who performed no deeds of heroism on the battlefield but shared the labors, sorrows, and hopes of those who strove for victory. The *Fanfare* is later to become more significant and symbolic in the composer's *Third Symphony*, where it forms the introductory material for the great fourth movement.

The Absolute Works

The time span of the absolute works virtually coincides with the composer's connection with the Berkshire Music Center, for the summer of 1940 marked the beginning in America of a unique type of music school with which, from the start, Aaron Copland has been, and is, closely affiliated.

It had been Serge Koussevitzky's long-cherished dream to provide a school where musicians might add to their professional training and enlarge their artistic experiences under the guidance of eminent musicians. The gift, in 1936, of the 210-acre estate "Tanglewood" * to the Boston Symphony Orchestra, by the late Mrs. Andrew Hepburn and Miss Mary Aspinall Tappan, made possible the realization of that dream. Overlooking the majestic Stockbridge Bowl, the Berkshire Music Center was designed to provide an opportunity for music study in conjunction with the Berkshire Festival Concerts.

Supplementing a faculty chosen from the ranks of the Boston Symphony Orchestra with other distinguished musicians, Kous-

---

* Nathaniel Hawthorne lived at Tanglewood during the year 1850-1851, where he conceived his *Tanglewood Tales, The Wonder Book*, and wrote *The House of Seven Gables*. Tanglewood was also the meeting place of Emerson, Holmes, and Melville.

sevitzky invited Aaron Copland to join the school as head of its composition department. In June, 1940, the Berkshire Music Center first opened its doors.

At the close of Tanglewood's first season, Copland remained on at his summer headquarters in the vicinity of the school, where he composed the short organ "Episode," returning to New York in September, where he continued work on the *Piano Sonata,* begun in the summer of 1939. In the meantime he had started to put in book form certain articles, radio talks, and lectures presented about 1927, which pictured the high light of the "modern" movement as he saw it.

In April, 1941, Copland went to Key West, Florida, and from there to Havana, Cuba, where he completed his second book, *Our New Music,* published in the fall of that year.

On August 24, 1941, the New York *Times* carried the announcement that Aaron Copland had been selected as a representative American composer to be sent on a cultural mission to South America. Stating that he would visit Mexico and other Latin-American countries, the *Times* reported that Copland was being sent by the Committee for Inter-American Cultural Relations, an autonomous organization working through the office of Nelson A. Rockefeller, the President's Coordinator of Inter-American Affairs. During the four-month good-will tour, extending from August to December, Copland's duties would be to give lectures, arrange concerts, and possibly conduct some orchestras.

Traveling by plane, Copland took along a quantity of American scores to introduce to Latin-American audiences. His first stop was Mexico; then Colombia; September found him in Ecuador, Peru, and Chile. Arriving in Buenos Aires in late September, he was acclaimed as one of America's foremost contemporary symphonic composers.

According to the Buenos Aires *Herald,* the purpose of Copland's trip was twofold: he had come to South America to ascertain what was being written there, and to tell local musicians about serious symphonic and other musical advances in the United States. In addition to some chamber music concerts, two lectures by Copland were scheduled at the Teatro del Pueblo.

The *Herald* also informs us that on his way to Buenos Aires, down the West Coast, Copland met the American Ballet in Lima, where inhabitants of that city were privileged to hear him conduct a performance of *Billy the Kid*.

During the North American's stay in Buenos Aires a symphony orchestra under the direction of Juan José Castro at the Colón Opera House performed works by Mendelssohn, Ravel, and Copland, including the latter's *Outdoor Overture*.[4]

Arriving in Uruguay in October, Copland, according to the Montevideo *Sun* (undated) attended a reception and concert given by the United States Ambassador and Mrs. William Dawson at the Embassy in his honor. The program consisted of the following works: "Two Pieces for Organ" by Roger Sessions, played as a piano duet by Aaron Copland and Hugo Balzo; *Trio for Violin, Cello and Piano* by Roy Harris, performed by Juan Fabbri, Vincent Navatta, and Aaron Copland, respectively; the Second Movement of an unfinished *Piano Sonata* by Aaron Copland, played by the composer.

The *Sun* also noted that on the following day, under the auspices of the Good-will Broadcast, Copland would be heard in a local broadcast on the subject of "The Influence of Jazz on Modern Music," which would be illustrated by piano solos. Another Broadcast Talk with records of Copland's compositions would be heard at Amiges del Arte, 18:30 to 19:30, admission free. The following Sunday, the North American composer would be heard in a lecture on "Music in the Films" at Montevideo Radio City, at ten o'clock, to which the public was invited.

According to the New York *Herald Tribune* of October 12, 1941, Copland returned to Santiago de Chile for the week of October 18 to 25, to conduct the Orquesta Sinfónica de Chile in his *Outdoor Overture*, *Quiet City*, and *El Salón México*. In addition, the composer played his *Piano Concerto* there and gave lectures on American music. He spent the month of November in Brazil and, on his way home, stopped for several weeks during December in Havana, Cuba, continuing the same kind of musical activities in both countries.

In the wake of his survey of music in South America, the New York *Times,* with the news source given as Rio de Janeiro, published a report of an "Inter-American Plan." Finding the South Americans receptive to North American music whenever some representative visited their countries for a short time, lectured, or organized concerts, Copland stated that as soon as the visitor was out of sight, a pleasant memory was all that remained, with no permanent means to keep these countries in touch with North American products.

Citing the need of scores, orchestral parts, chamber music works, solo pieces, and pamphlets with explanatory notes about the composers and their work in the language of the respective countries, Copland believed that it would be a good plan to establish several music centers in South America which would be supplied with the principal published works of North American composers. The centers would stock enough copies of every work to make it available in various countries at the same time.

He further suggested that the principal South American radio stations be supplied with a collection of records so that more frequent broadcasts of North American music might be heard. If such a plan could be realized, according to the *Times,* Copland seemed sure that it would meet with success.[5]

Piano Sonata

Despite all the activity his semiofficial good-will tour entailed, Copland somehow managed to complete his *Piano Sonata* in South America. Played by the composer, the work received its first performance on October 21, 1941, in Buenos Aires, at an all-American concert sponsored by La Nueva Música. Composed over the two-year period 1939 to 1941, the *Sonata* is dedicated to Clifford Odets, who commissioned it.

Following in the more "serious" idiom of the *Piano Variations* and *Short Symphony,* the *Piano Sonata,* an "absolute" * work,

---

* John Rosenfield has defined "absolute" or "pure" music as "music that tells its own story and defies translation into pictures or words." Dallas *Morning News,* November 20, 1951.

and the first to follow after Virgil Thomson's second category
of musical compositions (i.e., "very intense and serious works
for concert hall audiences"), differs stylistically from the works
of the Abstract Period in that, although it relies on purely musically conceived materials, it has captured, in addition, the
warmth and humanness gained through the composer's contact,
during the interim, with folksongs. Containing themes that can
be hummed or whistled, with its over-all Slow-Fast-Slow design,
the *Sonata* calls to mind Beethoven's *Sonata*, Op. 111, Tschaikovsky's *Pathétique Symphony,* and Ives's *Concord Sonata,*
works all ending with slow movements.

Opening in the key of B flat minor, the first movement (*molto
moderato*) is in sonata-allegro form. Its first theme is based on
two familiar ideas: a polytonally harmonized, dramatic, descending B flat minor triad, recalling the B minor upward-curving
"motto" of the *First Symphony* (Example 1A), and the declamatory theme of the *Piano Variations* (Example 1B). The second

Ex. 1A

Ex. 1B

theme, in tender, flowing thirds (key of G minor), with a strong
modal flavor, is obviously a figuration of the first idea. The development section, free in character, reveals both themes in
varied lyric and dramatic guise. The recapitulation, in grandiose
vein, later presents the second theme as an accompaniment to
a theme derived from the first idea. The movement closes with
a brief recollection of the dramatic triad idea, expressing a mood
of utter finality.

The fast second movement, in scherzo vein, is delicate and
light with the character of a fleeting will o' the wisp. The composer's material is based on a melodic version of the harmonic
intervals of a major second, a perfect fourth, and a major sixth,
which he renders thus (Example 2). The moods are alternat-
ingly wistful and poetic, and, although the movement appears
to be derived from jazz sources, no actual jazz themes are found.
The trio, or contrasting section, is based on a theme harmonized
in intervals of sixths (Example 3).

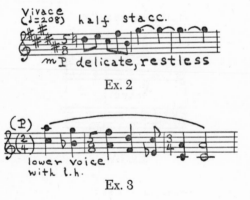

Ex. 2

Ex. 3

The third movement (*andante sostenuto*), free in form, opens
in prophetic vein with the sounding of three heavy chords, implying the tonality of G major. These chords are reiterated three
times and serve to introduce the melody from the contrasting
(trio) theme of the scherzo movement (Example 3), presented
here in the form of three short variations. Exhibiting the main
features of sonata-form, the third movement builds to a powerful

climax and then returns to the bell-like sonorities of the first movement's opening theme, thereby attaining a unification of the composer's musical and emotional thoughts through cyclic means. One of Copland's important works, the *Piano Sonata* marks the beginning of his mature expression.

John Kirkpatrick and his wife, Hope Kirkpatrick, soprano, had scheduled a New York Town Hall joint recital for January, 1943, on which occasion Kirkpatrick planned to introduce the new Copland *Piano Sonata*. He wrote the composer to invite him to the concert and to learn whether any other performances of the composition were likely to be forthcoming before January 9. Copland's postal-card reply, dated December 1, 1942, from Dellbrook Farm, Oakland, New Jersey, where he was at the time, reads:

Dear John:

Nice to hear you're planning a Town Hall shindig. No one to date has played the *Sonata* publicly in New York. There is no way of guaranteeing that no one will before Jan. 9, but it seems extremely unlikely.* I am playing it in Town Hall on Feb. 17 at an all-Copland Music Forum concert. I had thought that would be the *première* but am delighted at the prospect of your doing the "first time." Thanks for sending the programs. It will be good to hear about the real America from you.

Regards to Hope,

AARON

P.S. I'm living in the country and its lovely.

The New York *première* of the *Sonata* took place as planned, January 9, 1943, with the composer present. Noel Strauss acknowledged that Kirkpatrick, in whom our native composers had found one of their most ardent and accomplished champions, gave a reading of the Copland *Sonata* which could scarcely be improved upon, making it possible for the listener to follow easily all of the details of the work and its larger architectural aspects. Despite the pianist's zealous efforts to accord the *Sonata* an interpretation that would make friends for it, Strauss stated

* *The Piano Sonata* was published in the early part of 1942.

that the undue protractedness of each of the three movements did not permit the work to become communicative or to appear of genuine importance.[6]

Six years later, in 1949, in reviewing Leonard Bernstein's recording of the Copland *Piano Sonata*, Howard Taubman noted that on first hearing the work, some considered it "difficult in form and style and unyielding in content. But if you give yourself a fair chance to become well acquainted with it," he continued, "the sonata proves to be none of these things. On the contrary, it has simplicity, clarity and a great deal of touching, restrained feeling.[7]

In February, 1943, Copland left for an eight-month stay in Hollywood to complete his third studio assignment, the musical score for the film *North Star*. One of his most interesting Hollywood experiences during this time is indicated in a letter to Arthur Berger in which he recounted that Stravinsky invited him and George Antheil to dinner. Dated April 10, 1943, Copland's letter said that Stravinsky was extremely cordial to his guests and that after dinner "we played S.'s Symphony from off-the-air records. I don't think he's in a very good period," Copland wrote. "He copies himself unashamedly, and therefore one rarely comes upon a really fresh page—for him, I mean." [8] All of which is interesting, for it tells us what one celebrated composer thinks about the work of another.*

Following the completion of the serious *Piano Sonata* of 1939–1941, Copland produced six or seven works in a more or less easily understood "popular" style. During the year 1943, he completed another "serious" or absolute work, the *Sonata for Violin and Piano*. Lest confusion arise regarding the composer's artistic intentions in his lighter and more serious styles, it is well, at this point, to consider briefly some illuminating remarks that he made on the subject.

In a letter to Arthur Berger (dated April 10, 1943) relating to the latter's recent article on "Copland's Piano Sonata," † Cop-

---

* Mr. Copland recently said to the author that "in retrospect of twelve years, the above-expressed opinion does not reflect my current thought in the matter."

† Berger's article appeared in the *Partisan Review*, March-April, 1943. pp. 187-190.

land thought that Berger, in an effort to draw a sharp distinction between his (Copland's) "severe" and "simple" styles, rather overemphasized the line of demarcation between the two styles, leaving the inference that only the severe style was serious, which Copland did not think was true. Continuing, Copland wrote:

> What I was trying for in the simpler works was only partly a larger audience; they also gave me a chance to try for a home-spun musical idiom, similar to what I was trying for in a more hectic fashion in the earlier jazz works. In other words, it was not only musical functionalism that was in question, but also musical language. I like to think that in *Billy* and *Our Town,* and somewhat in *Lincoln,* I have touched off for myself and others a kind of musical naturalness that we have badly needed —along with "great" works.[9]

Sonata for Violin and Piano

Unlike the *Piano Sonata* which, as we have seen, had its inception in the principles of the Abstract Period of the composer's development and, as such, is an extension of that compositional aesthetic in terms of a new-found warmth and humanness gained from contact with North and South American folk music, the *Sonata for Violin and Piano* was conceived out of a pastoral, folksong aesthetic, although there are no literal quotations of folksongs. For materials Copland has used the residue, or distilled essence, of folksongs (including folk rhythms), and not the folksongs themselves. Both sonatas, nevertheless, represent different phases of the composer's most serious and developed methods. In comprehending the underlying aesthetic differences between these two works, we are provided with the key to their complete understanding and full enjoyment.

Perhaps, because he was composing the ballet *Appalachian Spring* (of folk origin and utilizing a Shaker hymn) virtually at the same time that he was writing the *Violin Sonata,* the character of the *Sonata,* in its opening introduction, projects two folklike ideas (a) a hymnlike, simple, devotional quality expressed by means of a gentle polyharmonic language;* (b) a fresh, sprightly, pastoral, springlike mood expressed by means of a buoyantly lyrical melodic phrase (Example 4). Bearing the general outline of sonata-allegro form, the real first theme soon enters, key of G, and reveals a close affinity to the b idea† and to the simple, homespun style and thematic material of *Our Town*. The second theme, in D major, is soon heard in the violin over a piano accompaniment of the first theme presented in canonic imitation with a derivative of the same theme (Exam-

Ex. 4

Ex. 5

* Note how the composer has simultaneously combined dominant harmonies with their tonic resolutions.

† Virgil Thomson ascribes to the French symphonists the tendency of modern composers to express "landscape and the picturesque" in terms of symphonic (sonata and otherwise) form. See *Music Right and Left* (New York: Henry Holt & Co., 1951), pp. 108-109.

ple 5). Both themes, as well as the introductory ideas, are developed. One derivative of the second theme, having the character of a *cantus firmus* in the Dorian mode (or of a primitive hymn), is considerably developed and later appears in an effective three-part canon at the unison.

The second movement (*lento*), strongly modal in sound, is in three-part song form with an A-B-A design. Opening with a short introduction on the piano, having the flavor of a Mexican folk tune in a retarded tempo, the A theme enters over a repetition of the Mexicanlike tune (Example 6). The B theme is made up of the descending form of the E minor and G major triads linked together by the tone C and is set with a polytonal harmonization that reiterates a familiar folk rhythm. Thus both themes of this movement reflect abstract materials expressed in terms of folk usage.

Ex. 6

Ex. 7

In the form of a scherzo and trio, without pause between, the third movement (*allegro giusto*) is in the tonality of G. Its first theme is a long, improvisatory, single-lined fugato-style theme

stressing the tone F natural, and stems from the following motive
(Example 7). The theme's fugato style is emphasized by the
entrance of the piano (at the twenty-sixth bar) in a development of the theme in canon, at a distance of four bars. A perfectly
beautiful derivative of this theme in a romantically classical
(Schubertian) setting follows, expanding freely until the second
theme, in D major, is reached, which is diatonic in outline.

The A theme of the trio, a derivative of the second theme of
the scherzo, in its rhythmic setting evokes memories of the cowboy rhythms in *Billy the Kid* (Example 8). (Compare Example
8 with Example 2, Chapter VII, and it will be seen that the
cowboy rhythmic derivative appearing in the *Violin Sonata* is
a distillation of the cowboy rhythm earlier used as a setting for
"Good-by, Old Paint.") The B section of the trio, a bell-like
theme, appears to be a derivative of the B theme of the second
movement and has a refrainlike folk implication.

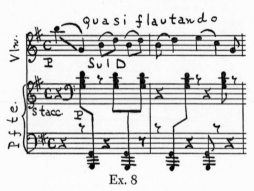

Ex. 8

A remarkable creation, the *Violin Sonata* presents easier audi-
tory and performance aspects than the *Piano Sonata*. With Ruth
Posselt, violinist, and Aaron Copland at the piano, the *Sonata
for Violin and Piano* received its first performance on January 17,
1944, in Times Hall, New York City.*

* On March 8, 1955, P. G-H wrote in the New York *Herald Tribune* of
Copland's appearance with Carroll Glenn, violinist, in a performance of the
Violin Sonata in Town Hall, New York: "Copland's Sonata is always good to
hear; it is one of his best works, and Miss Glenn's acute sense of style enabled
her to get right to the heart of this spare but moving work."

Over a period of years Copland had collected themes with the idea of someday writing another symphony. Upon receipt of a commission from the Koussevitzky Music Foundation,* in 1943, to write such a work, he began to actually plan the symphony. In July, 1944, he went to Tepoztlan, Mexico, for the express purpose of writing the new work. A remote village, where the population was largely Indian, Tepoztlan had the quiet atmosphere of Tlalpam, which Copland, on his first visit to Mexico, in 1932, had found so favorable for the completion of his *Short Symphony*.

As we have seen, the composer's previous essays in symphonic form had resulted in his *First (Organ) Symphony* (1924), stemming from a modern European aesthetic and a definitive expression of his French years of study; and the *Short Symphony* (1931-1933), combining an abstract aesthetic with jazz-derived materials and therein crystalizing the gains of the Jazz and Abstract Periods into the highest of all forms.

In the meantime the composer had passed through a *Gebrauchsmusik* phase, by means of which he had encompassed still a third period of development, the Folksong Style. But how was he to rationalize and consolidate the *Gebrauchsmusik* and folksong gains of the past decade into the symphonic form in such a way as to realize his own personal expression? It was true that the two *Sonatas* (for piano, and violin and piano) with their absolute content and adaptation of sonata form had crystallized the problem of style to some extent; but it still remained that, in order to achieve a complete synthesis of all style manifestations, the composer must come to grips with the problem of their amalgamation into symphonic form. This task was to confront him as the most artistically difficult of his entire career. Realizing the seriousness of his problem, Copland therefore sought seclusion in Tepoztlan, hiding himself like a recluse from the outside world for three months, so that only the symphony would engross his best thought. Here he also wrote the short *Letter from Home*, a commission from the American Broadcasting Company,

* Established in memory of the conductor's wife, Natalie Koussevitzky.

which received its first performance during the time the composer was still away.

After a stopover in Washington, D.C., to attend the world *première of Appalachian Spring,* Copland returned to New York City for a period of eight months.

During the first part of 1945 he wrote a brief *Variation* for the celebration of the Cincinnati Symphony's final Golden Jubilee concert in March, 1945, on a theme by Eugene Goossens, and also the musical score to the documentary film, *The Cummington Story.*

Meanwhile, he took up residence in Bernardsville, New Jersey, in order to get on with the composing of his symphony, remaining there from March through September; in April he completed the first movement. Finishing the symphony's second movement in August, Copland returned to New York for the months of October and November, 1945. Finding that other musical activities were interfering with the symphony's progress, Copland secluded himself in Ridgefield, Connecticut, where he remained from December to May, completing the third movement in January, 1946, and beginning work on the Finale. In May he returned to New York for a month, and in June he went again to the MacDowell Colony, which he had not visited since 1938, to continue work on the symphony.

With the Allied victories over both Germany and Japan realized, the country began to pursue its normal peacetime activities. Closed during the war years (1943–1945), the Tanglewood School reopened for its fourth season in July, 1946, at which time Copland was appointed to the post of assistant director. During the school's session he resided at nearby Stockbridge.

Jacob Avshalamoff has given us a glimpse of Copland's activities during the summer of 1946. "Some new music had more intimate hearings at the weekly composers' gatherings under Copland's direction," he wrote. "Those studying at Tanglewood, as well as visitors, met each Sunday evening for informal programs of works recently written." According to Avshalamoff, the final Sunday evening was devoted to a program of music by several of the many South American composers in attendance at the school's summer session.[10]

During August and September Copland worked feverishly on the symphony in Richmond, Massachusetts, where, on September 29, he completed the finale, barely in time for the necessary copying of parts for the first performances with Koussevitzky and the Boston Symphony, which took place in Boston, October 18 and 19, 1946.

Third Symphony

I. The First Movement (*molto moderato*), bearing no relation to the sonata allegro with which most symphonies begin, is broad and expressive in character and begins and closes in the key of E major. There are three themes: the first, immediately stated in the strings (without introduction) establishes the work's pastoral mood in which the second phrase, of nine tones (Example 9), bears a striking resemblance to the opening hymn-like theme (of eleven tones) in *Appalachian Spring* and to the sustained tones of the theme from *Fanfare for the Common Man;* the second, in similar mood, is heard soon after in the violas and oboes; the third, of a more vigorous nature, is announced by trombones and horns (Example 10). Both the first and third themes appear in later movements of the *Symphony.* The overall mood of the first movement appears pastoral, expressing simple religious piety combined with a sense of strength, well-being and quiet contentment.

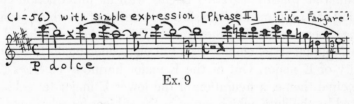

Ex. 9

Ex. 10

II. A scherzo (*allegro molto*), with first part, trio, and repetition, forms the Second Movement of the *Symphony*. A brass introduction, evocative of hunting calls rather than of the military, apparently derived from the trombone theme of the first movement and here presented in diminution, leads to the main theme, brisk and marchlike, which is first heard in the horns and violas and later, clarinets (Example 11). After reaching a climax, the trio follows without pause, introducing a quiet melody first sung by the oboe and developed by other wood winds in canonical style. The mood of the trio is pastoral and quietly devotional, providing admirable contrast to the brisk scherzo theme.

Ex. 11

Ex. 12

III. Freest of all in formal structure, the Third Movement (*andantino quasi allegretto*) begins with an introduction consisting of a rhythmically transformed version of the third (trombone) theme of the first movement. This is briefly developed in contrapuntal style, coming to a full close once again in the tonality of E major. Out of the E major harmony emerges the principal theme, a figuration of the lower E major tetrachord, stated by the flute, which serves as the subject for what may be termed three continuous variations (Example 12).

At first this theme, set for wood winds and strings, contrapuntally weaves a mood of quiet nostalgia; the second version, with the strings marked *ritmico*, presents dancelike aspects of the

theme exposed to a rhythmic development, with the addition of
a trumpet and horn to the instrumentation; a third version,
quieter and simpler, adds harp and celesta to wood winds and
strings; the final version, vigorous and direct, and emphasizing
the device of imitation, gradually floats back to the introductory
theme. With the exception of a single horn and trumpet, the
third movement omits the brass section.

IV. Following without pause, the Finale *(molto deliberato)*
is the longest movement of the symphony and closest in structure to the sonata-allegro form. The opening fanfare, which
serves as an introduction to the movement, is based on the composer's *Fanfare for the Common Man*, composed in 1942 (Example 13). Following this military introduction, the usual two

Ex. 13

themes are presented: the first, in a fast sixteenth-note rhythm
introduced by the oboe; the second, broader and more songlike.
A full development ensues, followed by a unique return to the
earlier material of the movement which leads to a peroration.
An unusual feature of the second theme, which exudes a Mexican or Latin-American folklike flavor in jazz rhythm, finds it not
in its usual place, following the first, but, instead, tucked away
in the development section (Example 14). Instead of a recap-

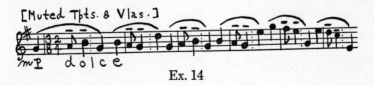

Ex. 14

itulation in the usual way, the composer has intertwined the various themes of the symphony, thus emphasizing its cyclic structure, and concluding with a massive restatement of the opening phrase with which the entire work began, closes with a triumphant full D major final cadence.

The note of an American baroque, first sounded in the variations on the Shaker hymn "Simple Gifts" in *Appalachian Spring,* is strongly sensed throughout the *Third Symphony.* Evolved out of a folk source in the ballet, the baroque character is more forcefully established in the symphony for the reason that the work presents pure or absolute music materials tinged, however, with jazz and folk (including hymn) distillations, which are worked out in terms of baroque contrapuntal techniques, resulting in a higher, more personal expression of the composer's thought. To the national style fund of Americanisms, already present in Copland's music was now added American hymnody which, in the *Third Symphony,* fuses with the declamatory style present in his work since the early twenties.

Following the Boston Symphony's first New York performance of Copland's *Third Symphony* on November 16, 1945, Virgil Thomson wrote at length on the new work. Stating that the symphony's expressivity is pastoral and military, Thomson averred that these two subjects are contrasted through three movements which do not differ greatly, either thematically or emotionally, from one another. "They are resolved in the fourth," he continued, "by a transformation of the chief military material into a hymn and of the first theme, hitherto pastoral and meditative, into a sort of triumphal affirmation of faith in the pastoral virtues."

Acknowledging that there was nothing to question about such a program, or the composer's choice and handling of musical materials, Thomson was of the opinion that the mature Copland had said what he meant to say with emotional sincerity which, if true, stamped him a "great man" and the work, regardless of whether it ever became popular, "great music."[11]

Returning to New York in October, 1946, Copland took a stu-

dio at 3 Riverview Terrace. Receiving a commission for a large
choral work from the committee in charge of the impending
Harvard Symposium of Music and Criticism, the composer went
to Boston in February, 1947, where, during the next three
months, he wrote the *a cappella* score *In the Beginning*.

In the Beginning

In one extended movement, with the mezzo-soprano as leader,
singing in recitative style and announcing the creation of heaven
and earth (in a gentle, narrative manner, like reading a familiar
and oft-told story), followed by the mixed *a cappella* chorus
which is first heard in two parts, *In the Beginning* at once invokes
the spirit of God moving upon the face of the waters. Chroni-
cling the division of the firmament into day and night, the chorus expands to three parts, completing the introductory section.

Utilizing the device of choral chant to establish the creation
of the evening and the morning of the first day, key of C flat major, sustaining the final chord over six bars, the solo voice enters
with the polytonal harmony of A flat major, sounding C natural
against C flat, giving a characteristic "blues" polyharmonic connotation (Example 15).

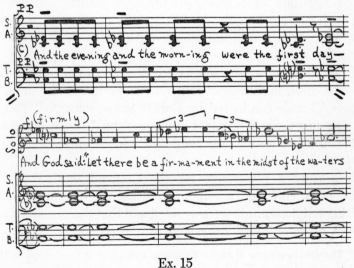

Ex. 15

This material serves as a link or refrain to establish the religious atmosphere for each of the six days' creation, progressing upwards, diatonically, throughout the work, from C♭ to D♭, E♭, F♯, and G to vary the principal tonal centers. The events in the creation of each separate day are unfolded according to the composer's inner conception of the Biblical text, portrayed in these varied moods: antiphonal and jubilant; modally ecclesiastical; archaically pastoral; rhythmically ecstatic, fervent (implying a Negro spiritual connotation); flowing and lyrical, notably the lovely E flat 6/4 section, which is the musical epitome of the text, "Let the waters bring forth abundantly"; the dramatic creation of man, contrapuntally developed. Throughout, the solo voice appears as narrator, setting the scene, as it were, and creating the mood and atmosphere for the subsequent unfolding of the events of each day.

A further expression of the American baroque spirit, the American national imprint is sensed in three ways: by the composer's adaptation to his own needs of American traditional hymnody and religious music sources, without, however, actually using such material literally, which here again has been fused with his declamatory style; in the aura of "blues" and Negro spirituals which permeate the work without actually using such sources literally, blending these distillations with his prophetic style; and in the definitive American rhythms sensed in the fast sections.

In the Beginning received its first New York performance on May 19, 1947, in Carnegie Hall and was performed by the Collegiate Chorale conducted by Robert Shaw, with Nell Tangeman singing the solo passages of the narrator.* It was presented between Hindemith's *Last Judgment* and Mozart's *Mass in C Major.*

Indicating a preference for the Copland work over the Hindemith, Howard Taubman noted that the obvious tricks of writing religious music were avoided and that the sweetness and power of the Biblical story were conveyed. "[The composer]

---

* The world premiere of *In the Beginning* took place at Cambridge, in Harvard Memorial Church, May 2, 1947, by the above mentioned group.

does not hesitate to use a jazz idiom at certain moments in the text, [i.e.,] 'And let there be light in the firmament of the heavens to give light upon the earth.' And oddly enough," commented Taubman, "this device has the affecting quality of some of Marc Connelly's 'Green Pastures.' " [12]

Soon after the Boston and New York performances of *In the Beginning,* Copland was invited by Carlos Chávez to conduct the Mexican *première* of his *Third Symphony,* which took place in June, 1947, performed by the Orquesta Sinfónica.

Regarding Copland's second and third efforts in the symphonic form, Rodolfo Halffter, critic for *El Universal Grafico,* commented that between the "audacious" *Short Symphony* and the *Third* there is a deep abyss. He pointed out that the two works are separated not only by the passing of fifteen years (very important in the life of a genuine artist), but also by the evolution which the composer had undergone. "The aggressive Copland, the 'enfant terrible' of the early 1930's," Halffter continued, "has become the lovable and grave. The 'tight-mouthed' Copland of those years is now a being approachable and talkative, tender and sentimental. . . . in the 'Third Symphony' Copland speaks to the audience with his heart in his hand." [12] Halffter described the composer-conductor as an "exacting director."

Following the Mexican performance of his *Third Symphony,* Copland returned to Tanglewood for his fifth summer, residing in the nearby village of Richmond, Massachusetts.

In the latter part of August he left for a four-month sojourn in South America, his second tour for the United States Department of State, made under its program of exchanging professors in various fields with Latin-American countries.

In addition to visiting the north coastal towns of Brazil, including Recife (the capital city of Pernambuco), Bahia (Salvador), and Fortaleza (in the state of Ceará), where, to his knowledge no one had ever before seen a North American composer, Copland's itinerary also included the larger cities such as Montevideo, Buenos Aires, Rio de Janeiro, São Paulo, and Pôrto Alegre.

In all of these places our national government was cooperating with local persons to maintain cultural centers for the teaching of English and the spreading of ideas about our civilization. In an effort to give the local citizens a truer picture of the United States than is conveyed by a typical Hollywood movie, the cultural centers, putting into practice Copland's "Inter-American Plan" (devised after his 1941 South American tour), loaned books, phonograph recordings, and printed music, and organized lectures and concerts relating to our culture.

In Recife, the inhabitants honored Copland by devoting an entire evening to a demonstration of their popular arts. Most interesting was the "frevo," a solo dance, whose accompanying music is derived from street marches (like New Orleans jazz) and has, according to Copland, a "terrific bounce." For the North American's benefit an army band of twenty-eight men was collected and performed "frevos" in a characteristic way. In Bahia Copland also heard for the first time a new instrument called the *berimbau*, which is believed to be of Moorish origin.

Although these side tours into Brazilian popular music were highly diverting, Copland's main concern was with the concert life in Rio, São Paulo, Montevideo, and Buenos Aires. In its relation to North American music the situation, in general, appeared better than on the occasion of Copland's first Latin-American tour, six years earlier. At least people were familiar with the names of our composers if not with their music.

Since most of the "live" performances of North American music, including chamber music, piano pieces, and songs, occur occasionally at the Argentine League of Composers or the Brazilian Chamber Music Society, both avant-garde groups, the "big" public gets its contact with our music solely through recordings. In addition to Gershwin, whose music is universally known and liked, the names of Samuel Barber, Roy Harris, Walter Piston, and William Schuman are most familiar.

In each city Copland made inquiries about the younger composers and found that Buenos Aires, thanks to an active concert life and several competent teachers, has produced an impressive group of younger men. While Brazil has many excellent

composers, it had but few good teachers. Noting that the French
school no longer exerted so general an influence on the younger
generation as was true of their elders, Copland thought this was
a step in advance. He named Camargo Guarnieri, Luis Gianneo,
José Maria Castro, and Alberto Ginastera as leading South
American composers.[14]

With a dateline of Buenos Aires, November 16, 1947, the New
York *Times* reported that on the previous night the Colón Opera
House was packed for a symphonic concert at which the American composer, Aaron Copland, conducted the entire program,
made up of his own works. Sponsored by the United States Embassy, the event was attended by the Ambassador and Mrs.
James Bruce and many other members of the American colony.
It was noted that a large number of Buenos Aires students were
also in the audience.

"Argentines, with their love of the modern," continued the
Times dispatch, "have always regarded Copland highly, and
last night he received a tremendous ovation at the conclusion
of his *Third Symphony*. It was heard for the first time here, on
this occasion, as was the ballet suite *Appalachian Spring*."[15] The
concert also included *An Outdoor Overture* and *Lincoln Portrait*, in the latter of which Jorge Danton, as narrator, spoke the
words of Lincoln in a Spanish translation.

As was his custom, Copland, between his official musical duties
connected with the tour, was composing. His principal effort during this time was a clarinet concerto, commissioned by Benny
Goodman, in which he incorporated Latin-American themes
and rhythms.

Returning to New York, to his home at Sneden's Landing,
Palisades, New York, Copland spent only the month of January
there. In February he was off again to Hollywood, to complete
his fourth film assignment, the musical score for *The Red Pony*.

Returning to New York in April, 1948, Copland wrote a fourth
"Blues" for piano, which with three others written in 1947, 1934,
and 1926, form an engaging piano suite, *Four Piano Blues*. Not
to be counted among the composer's important works, these
short (and not difficult) piano pieces nevertheless offer aspects

of the composer's style development as applied to the slow, nostalgic, blues element of jazz.

The first (of the published volume), composed in 1947, presents a buoyant, songlike conception of the blues, reflecting the composer's Folksong Period, featuring the diatonic ascension of the harmonic intervals of major seconds and a dominant-seventh cadence. Although written in 1934, "Blues No. 2" does not present any aspects of the composer's Abstract Period; on the contrary, it harkens back to his first usage of literal jazz materials, stressing ornamental grace notes and reiterated-tone syncopations. Curiously, "Blues No. 3," composed in 1948, reflects the composer's second or Abstract Period with its vague, indistinct melodic outlines and more stringent harmonies; it is more nearly a manifestation of the composer's serious or absolute style in terms of blues material. "Blues No. 4," composed in 1926, already discussed in Chapter IV, represents the composer's first exuberant, lusty use of literal jazz materials and stands up well beside the other three. Its fast tempo provides the contrast lacking in the first three "Blues" and brings the suite to a satisfactory close.

Concerto for Clarinet and String Orchestra

Returning to Tanglewood for the sixth summer during July and August, and again residing in Richmond, Copland continued work on the *Clarinet Concerto*, which he completed in October, 1948, at Sneden's Landing. Dedicated to Benny Goodman, the *Concerto* is scored for solo clarinet and string orchestra with harp and piano. Its first performance took place on November 6, 1950, when Benny Goodman broadcast the work with the NBC Symphony Orchestra.

Like the *Piano Concerto* of 1926, the *Concerto for Clarinet and String Orchestra* is cast in two-movement form, Slow-Fast, played without pause, the two movements of which, unlike the *Piano Concerto*, are connected by a cadenza for the solo instrument. Conceived in an A-B-A song form, the first movement (slowly and expressively) is in a dreamy 3/4 meter, recalling the vein of the waltz movement from the composer's earlier *Dance Symphony*. (It is worth recalling here that Copland is not much given to using 3/4 meter, preferring, instead, 2/4 and 4/4.) One of Copland's intense, songful utterances in an almost romantically lyrical vein, this work, in the opinion of the author, loses much of its inherent effect by the arbitrary slow, weighty tempo established by the composer, who recently conducted a recording of the work with Benny Goodman. The B section of the movement, hymnlike in mood, recalls the religious calm of *Our Town, Appalachian Spring*, and the *Violin Sonata*. Thus the two dominant moods of the first movement of the *Clarinet Concerto* appear to be worldly and religious, and have their counterpart in French music in Debussy's two *Dances* ("profane" and "sacred") for harp and string orchestra. The principal tonal centers involve C major, G minor, and C major relationships.

A connecting cadenza, the material of which consists of broken chords and scales, leads into the second movement, which has the atmosphere of one of the composer's characteristic jazzy scherzos.

Having completed the first movement of the *Concerto* in Rio, during his 1947 South American tour, it is not surprising to find a Brazilian popular theme present in the rather free rondo. Following a pianissimo, somewhat brittle, and wraithlike introduction, the A theme is introduced in the orchestra and then taken up by the clarinet, developed in the composer's familiar cumulative style. Both its melodic and harmonic contours indicate that this theme has an affinity with the second jazzy, ragtime theme of the second movement of Copland's earlier *Piano Concerto*. In fact, this movement is chuck-full of the same kind of jazz materials, now ultra-refined, that proved of such potent value to the *Piano Concerto*.

In addition to the jazzy A section, the rondo features a B section which recalls an episode from the first movement; a C section derived from the cadenza; an A-A-C-D rhythmic section featuring the Charleston rhythm used as an ostinato; an E section made up of a Brazilian popular tune which later has rhumba implications (Example 16). Other American dance rhythms present in

Ex. 16

this movement include syncopations, tone clusters, another ostinato based on the Charleston, followed by a "boogie-woogie" ostinato. Over this the composer has worked a peroration of themes which leads to an effective brief stretto and following seven repetitions of a highly dissonant C major chord, closes with a typical clarinet scale and glissando (smear) in "pure" C major.

As to whether the *Clarinet Concerto* is to be classed among the composer's great works, we are much too close in time to judge. However, in formulating even a temporary judgment of the work, we must again reflect on the composer's intentions. A commission for Benny Goodman (to perform himself), who is generally regarded as our most outstanding "popular" clarinetist and one of our significant swing-band leaders whose strongest appeal is to the youth and lay audiences of the country, would scarcely be expected to pose the same aesthetic problems (or situation) to the composer writing a work for the first clarinetist of one of our major symphony orchestras. In view of the fact that Mr. Goodman performs both popular and serious music, the latter when he can, and for less critical audiences than those, for example, in the concert halls of New York, we must regard this work as *Gebrauchsmusik*, absolute in form, and relying, for its materials, on jazz, "Exotic Travel Souvenirs" (both French and Brazilian), and North and South American folk derivatives. On the basis of the composer's having accomplished what he set out to do, the *Clarinet Concerto* is a completely successful work.

In March, 1949, Copland began work on a song cycle subsequently to be called *Twelve Poems of Emily Dickinson*, his first work for solo voice and piano since the "Vocalise" of 1928.

In May, 1949, he made a two-month visit to Europe, his first since 1938, among other activities performing his *Piano Variations* in a concert at the American Embassy in Paris. During the wartime and recovery interval of eleven years when he did not visit Europe, Copland had, through his almost exclusive contact with North and South American cultures, become thoroughly American in his musical outlook, having shaken off the last vestiges of a European influence on his musical style .

Arriving in Tanglewood, in July, for his seventh summer, at the close of the school session, Copland returned to his home at Sneden's Landing where, between August 16 and September 5, 1949, he wrote the *Preamble For A Solemn Occasion*. Shortly afterwards, upon receipt of a commission from the Elizabeth Sprague Coolidge Foundation for a chamber work in celebration of the Foundation's twenty-fifth anniversary, Copland began work on his *Piano Quartet*.

Twelve Poems of Emily Dickinson

Composed during the twelve-month interval between March, 1949, and March, 1950, the *Twelve Poems of Emily Dickinson* are a major achievement not only in the career of Aaron Copland but to contemporary literature. Established as a classic-romantic form through the contributions of Beethoven, Schubert, Schumann, and Brahms, the literature of the song cycle has been steadily increased during contemporary times with such notable works as Mahler's four cycles, including *Lieder eines Fahrenden Gesellen*, Fauré's *La Bonne Chanson*, Schoenberg's *Hängenden Gärten*, Ravel's *Shêhêrezade* and *l'Histoires naturelles*, Milhaud's *Catalogue des Fleurs*, and Hindemith's *Marienleben*. Copland's *Twelve Poems of Emily Dickinson*, by virtue of their serious tone and perfect musicianship, give America an excellent representation in the above-mentioned imposing contemporary list.

Of approximately twenty seven and a half minutes' duration,

the *Twelve Poems of Emily Dickinson* must be placed among Aaron Copland's large and important works. Almost completely homophonic in texture (voice with piano accompaniment), the piano accompaniments are exceedingly expressive, having captured the mood and introspective quality of the poems.

The difficulty in the understanding of these songs on the part of both critics and public may be attributed to their newness (they are scarcely five years old), and to the fact that a melodic line to the composer often means diatonic steps and wide angular skips regardless of whether intended for solo voice or instruments, the range proving the one limiting factor. (This statement may be verified by a glance at Copland's three earlier songs for solo voice). Naturally, this standard of writing demands first-rate singers, with good voices, musicianship, intelligence, and the ability to communicate sincere emotions. It must also be kept in mind that although the poems themselves make certain programatic allusions, basically they treat of more abstruse matters—philosophical thoughts about Nature, Death, Life, and Eternity. For their musical counterpart the composer has, as in all of his absolute works composed since 1940, appropriately turned back to the abstract techniques of his second style period, which fact provides the key to the complete understanding of the Dickinson songs.

We note that four of the *Twelve Poems*, Nos. 1, 2, 6, and 8 belong to the classification Poems about Nature; these are "Nature, the gentlest mother" (4/4, quite slow), with its nine-bar introduction containing florid thirty-second-note flutterings and repeated grace notes, suggestive of woodland stirrings and bird warblings, which admirably set the pastoral mood of the song; "There came a wind like a bugle" (2/4, quite fast) with its rushing, ascending A major scale in parallel ninths and the voice enunciating a buglelike melody (Example 17); "Dear March, come in!" (6/8, with exuberance) with its undulating ostinato of broken ninth and tenth intervals in the piano accompaniment, breathing the excitement of spring's return, over which the voice, dipping joyously over frequent large skips, ecstatically welcomes the coming of March; "When they come back" (2/4,

Ex. 17

moderately, beginning slowly), one of the simplest and most
nostalgic of the poems, based on triads for its musical expression,
tender and contemplative of the return of blossoms, robins, and
the pangs of a beautiful May, on which "we might not look
again."

Under the classification of Poems about Death there are two
(Nos. 4 and 9): "The world feels dusty" (3/4, very slowly)
with its gentle swaying, almost berceuselike motion in the piano
accompaniment, over which the voice, in the first phrase, gradually spans the octave D after rising from the tonic, to the fifth,
to the seventh, pushing upward to high D, presenting the aspects
of a typically Copland melodic line; "I felt a funeral in my brain"
(2/4, rather fast), undoubtedly the most dramatic of all the
songs, opening with a macabre ostinato in the piano accompaniment in the bass, and heavy, foreboding triads in the right hand,
over which the voice thunderingly proclaims its gloomy song
(Example 18). Two features of the piano accompaniment are
the thud of drum beats which serve as an ominous ostinato to
the frenzied cries of the text, and the toll of the bells which mark
the reality of solitary silence. Two other songs (Nos. 5 and 12)
appear to overlap the classification of both Death and Life:
"Heart, we will forget him," with No. 12, "The Chariot," also
overlapping Eternity.

Ex. 18

Appearing under the classification Poems about Life is the most romantic of the songs, "Heart, we will forget him," which bears the imprint of Mahler and other late nineteenth century German romanticists. In order to capture the romantic intensity and deep yearning expressed in the poem, Copland adapted the *essence* of that chromatic reservoir to his own needs just as he had delved into other sources, i.e., folk or even twelve-tone materials, for the purpose at hand. One of the memorable songs of the cycle, its contrapuntal texture is to lead on directly to the "tone row" which is to provide the basis for the composer's notable *Piano Quartet*. In addition to this song are No. 7, "Sleep is supposed to be" (C, moderately slow), which marks the end of the approximately first half of the cycle, and No. 10, "I've heard an organ talk sometimes," which recalls the gentle hymnlike mood so characteristic of the composer's mature thought.

The first of the two songs about Eternity, No. 3, "Why do they shut me out of Heaven?" (moderately) is naive and childlike in the Dorian simplicity of its opening phrase, while the

second, No. 11, "Going to Heaven" (fast) has the quality of a
joyous, fervent Negro spiritual.

The twelfth song, "The Chariot," is one of the most abstract
songs in content. However, the composer has assisted the less
acute ear of the audience to a greater comprehension of the
song's meaning by recalling the opening material of No. 7, which
is about sleep, a quality of Life. Lending a cyclic summarization
to the form, the composer eloquently closes his song cycle, combining thoughts of Life, Death, and Eternity.

As was his custom (and as we have heretofore seen), Copland
relaxed between composing the "serious" song cycle and *Piano
Quartet* by arranging, in 1950, a first set of five *Old American
Songs*,* thereby presenting new settings of early Americana.
Scored for solo voice and piano and forming a kind of vocal suite,
the accompaniments, practical but exceedingly attractive, offer
moods by turns nostalgic, energetic, sentimental, devotional,
and humorous. Presenting characteristic facets of our early native song improvisations, the five songs comprise the following:
"The Boatmen's Dance" (Minstrel Song of 1843); "The Dodger,"
a campaign song of the fast "patter" type, featuring a banjo-
style accompaniment; "Long Time Ago," a sentimental English
(or Irish) type of ballad; "Simple Gifts," an effective harmonization of the Shaker hymn used as the subject for the variations in
Appalachian Spring; and "I Bought Me a Cat," a children's or
American "nonsense" song. The set was first performed by Peter
Pears and Benjamin Britten, June 17, 1950, at the Aldeburgh
Festival, Suffolk, England. In America, these songs have been
performed with much success by William Warfield. In affirmation of their *Gebrauchsmusik* content, Irving Fine has made
choral arrangements of these *Old American Songs* which are
suitable for performance by college or university choral groups.

---

* The Second Set, published in 1954, includes the following: 1. The Little
Horses (Lullaby); 2. Zion's Walls (Revivalist Song); 3. The Golden Willow
Tree (Anglo-American ballad); 4. At the River (hymn tune); 5. Ching-a-ring
Chaw (minstrel song).

Quartet for Piano and Strings

As we have seen, the absolute works composed after 1940 have gradually shifted back toward the second or abstract style, to which the folksong gains lent warmth and humanness. That the composer feels he has achieved his most individual expression through the more abstract approach and believes that the absolute works are more truly representative of his best creative thought must, therefore, be acknowledged. In Copland's final large work to be considered in this study, the *Piano Quartet* (1950), he reverts to his first method of approach, to the twelve-tone or "serial" technique, exemplified by the experimental "Song" written twenty-three years earlier, using an eleven-note "tone row" as a subject for the *Quartet*. Copland's return to this twentieth century compositional development during his mature years may be attributed to two factors: Arnold Schoenberg's presence and teaching in America from 1933 until his death in 1951, during which time he developed a vigorous school of Twelve-tone Composers; the fact that the twelve-tone technique was the only one of the twentieth century advances with which he had not come to final grips.

Approximately of twenty minutes' duration, the *Piano Quartet* is more nearly related to the *Piano Variations* (1930), with its four-note tone row, than to any other of the composer's work. Not at all related in form, the relationship between these two highly divergent works lies in a similar harmonic conception of twelve-tone principles without totally relinquishing either tonal or polytonal centers. A growth in contrapuntal textures is noted in the *Quartet* as opposed to the homophonic texture of the *Variations*.

I. The first movement (*adagio serio*), developed in fugal style, is based on an eleven-note tone row (*cantus firmus* like subject) having both whole-tone and diatonic implications in its melodic contour (Example 19). Mainly atonal in harmonic outline, in the progress of the movement's contrapuntal lines, to relieve the amount of dissonance, the composer has adroitly set up frequent tonal centers at the point where the "subject" ends and the "answer" begins. Unlike purely tonal fugal movements, the expositions of which are based on tonic and dominant

Ex. 19

Ex. 20

relationships, Copland has, instead, established interval relationships of major and minor thirds. Thus in the exposition section of the first movement, the ears glides over such tonalities (approximately at every five bars) as B flat, G flat major, E flat minor, C minor, C major, and, after a longer interval of twelve bars, F major. Here enters the second subject, a retrograde form of the original tone row, announced by the cello and immediately imitated in the piano. The material of the entire movement is derived and developed contrapuntally from the tone row and ends with an atonal harmonic impression.

II. The second movement (*allegro giusto*) is in the form of a scherzo having sonata-form implications, with the principal material developed from a two-measure jazz-derived motive, sounded in octaves in the violin and cello and emphasizing the tonality of B flat (Example 20). More full-bodied (contrapuntal) than either the scherzi to the *Piano Sonata,* or the *Short Symphony* (*Sextet*), this scherzo appears almost Hindemithian in its angular, busy, dissonant counterpoint. It features a second theme presented in fugato style and a closing theme of clangorous, widely spaced, syncopated chords in open fifths. An extended section devoted to South American polyrhythms (including the *frevo*) occurs in the development section, over which the first four notes of the tone row (from the first movement) appear in a syncopated refrain.

III. The third movement (*non troppo lento*) presents an A-B-C-A-B song-form design, contemplative in mood, with section A featuring the strings (without piano) in a harmonization including secondary ninth and eleventh chords. Soon is heard a bell or chime sound, easily recognized as the first three tones of the tone row,* harmonized in thirds, which forms an ostinato accompaniment to the B section, a melody characterized by wide skips and diatonic movement with deep curves, abstract in conception (Example 21). This leads into C, a hymnlike melody for the strings (*con energia, forte*), underneath which the piano plays a counterpoint of bell-like, pedestrian, quarter-note values. This section builds to a climax and then subsides. Both A and B sections return and the *Piano Quartet* ends with a last reminder of the chimelike motive from the tone row, quietly devotional and peaceful in spirit. Thus the tone row fulfills its purpose as the unifying element of the three movements, strengthening the work's cyclic form. To the composer's fund of materials that already contained the residue of jazz, abstract, folk, hymnody, and exotic materials, the *Piano Quartet* adds the twelve-tone technique, into which larger reservoir he may continue to reach, at will, for the musical function at hand.

* This material recalls the same motive, identified in *Music for the Theatre* as "Three Blind Mice," one of Copland's favorite melodic figures.

Ex. 21

Completed on October 20, 1950, at Sneden's Landing, New York, the *Quartet for Piano and Strings* received its first performance on October 29, 1950, in the Coolidge Auditorium, the Library of Congress, Washington, D.C. It was heard in the fourth program of the Eleventh Festival of Chamber Music, celebrating the Twenty-fifth Anniversary of the Elizabeth Sprague Coolidge Foundation, and was performed by the New York Quartet comprising Alexander Schneider, violin, Hermann Busch, violincello (substituting for Frank Miller), Milton Katims, viola, and Mieczyslaw Horszowski, piano. Those of us who were fortunate to be present at the *première* performance of this majestic work received a great and moving aesthetic experience that was even intensified in the second performance, which took place a week later, on November 5, at the Museum of Modern Art, New York City

Although the austere mood of the Quartet causes it to proceed slowly in winning the acclaim of the general public, still the following reviews indicate that the work is gradually attaining its rightful place in the contemporary chamber music repertory. Performed in Italy on the April 12, 1954 concert of the Rome Conference on Twentieth Century Music, Copland's Piano Quartet, observed Michael Steinberg, ". . . already has made its mark as one of the composer's finest works, although the scherzo is not as fetching as the two serene slow movements framing it." [16] On February 26, 1955 the New York *Herald Tribune* noted that on the previous night Copland's "austere" Quartet was given a "dynamic performance with the composer himself at the piano; it is a highly dissonant work, full of tensions that craggily build and subside. The ending Lento section has a deep mood, and with it comes the conviction that Copland ever evokes in this, his most introspective and personal vein." [17]

That Copland is steadily producing new vocal repertory works is evidenced by his latest song, "Dirge in Woods" (text by George Meredith), composed last year to honor Nadia Boulanger on the fiftieth anniversary of her teaching career. First performed at the Fontainebleau School of Music summer 1954, the first New York hearing of this three-and-a-half-minute work was given by Adele Addison, soprano, in Carnegie Recital Hall, March 28, 1955, as one of a group of American songs in the second concert presented by the newly merged League of Composers and United States Section of the International Society for Contemporary Music.* Despite the word "dirge" in the title, Ross Parmenter stated that the song's mood is hardly sad. "Rather," he continued, "the feeling is one of serene acceptance that all living things must drop and die, like the needles and cones from the pines in the forests." Terming the work a "beautiful new song," Parmenter noted that "the vocal line is long and floating and the piano accompaniment ripples gently under it." [18]

Copland's newest work, *Canticle of Freedom*— commissioned by the Massachusetts Institute of Technology—was first performed in Cambridge, Massachusetts May 8, 1955.

* Songs by Roger Sessions and Charles Ives completed the song group.

IX

Critical Works and Influence
(1924-1955)

No STUDY of the life and work of Aaron Copland can be complete without a glance at his critical works, for his three published books and approximately sixty-five periodical and newspaper articles, devoted almost exclusively to different phases of contemporary music, denote the composer's fully rounded artistic life and suggest (without defining the limits) the scope of his influence in the world today. This chapter undertakes, therefore, to show the really close relationship existing between the composer's tangible critical works and the probable scope of his influence, the latter which, though obviously immeasurable, is clearly indicated in Aaron Copland's musical and critical works, his teaching, and his travels.

Finally, on the basis of his entire musical and critical production, his organizational activities of contemporary American music, some aspects of his influence on the younger composers through his music, travels and teaching, and professional critical opinions of his works between 1919 and 1955, Aaron Copland's position in and contribution to contemporary American music is more nearly determined.

Critical Works

It will be recalled that the early chapters of this study brought out the fact that young Copland, in order to supplement his earnings as a composer, preferred to lecture and to write musical criticism rather than to support himself by teaching. Thus his critical writing had both a functional and artistic purpose.

It is significant that his first critique, written as a young student in Paris, in 1924, was concerned with the subject of a contemporary composer of that day, "Gabriel Fauré: A Neglected Master" (undoubtedly inspired by Mlle Boulanger); while his latest, written thirty-one years later, from the vantage point of a leader of contemporary music in America, is appropriately titled, "Modern Music: 'Fresh and Different' " * During this approximately one-third century, both contemporary music and Aaron Copland have carved out secure niches in posterity for themselves, while his critiques, depicting various aspects of contemporary music's growth, point like signposts along the rugged path each has trod.

Turning to Copland's three books, *What to Listen for in Music* (1939), *Our New Music* (1941), and *Music and Imagination* (1952), we note in passing that the first of these is the published version of fifteen lectures given under the same title at the New School for Social Research in New York City during the winters of 1936 and 1937; and that the second, *Our New Music,* traces the growth of contemporary music in America and contains excerpts from some of the composer's critiques published earlier in *Modern Music, The New Republic,* and the *American Mercury.* The third book, *Music and Imagination,* comprises six lectures presented by the composer as occupant of the Charles Eliot Norton Poetry Chair at Harvard University during the 1951–1952 academic year. This book follows those of two earlier composer occupants of the Poetry Chair, Stravinsky and his *Poetics of Music* (1947) and Hindemith with his *The Composers World* (1950). It is of the utmost significance to American music that Aaron Copland was chosen as the first native composer to fill this place of honor.

In compiling a list of Aaron Copland's critiques, I note that more than half of the periodical and newspaper articles treat various aspects of contemporary music in America; twelve are devoted to the contemporary music (and composers) of Europe; four relate to festivals of music, three of which are reviews of

---

* A chronological listing of Aaron Copland's critical works, extending from 1924 to 1955, has been placed in Appendix III.

European festivals; nine are reviews of new books about music; and three are reviews of musical recordings. Two final ones are devoted to personalities that were important forces in the advance of contemporary music, Nadia Boulanger and the late American critic, Paul Rosenfeld, and are cited among those concerned with American music.

In view of the fact that an entire study might easily be developed around Aaron Copland's critical writings and influence, this final chapter must, of necessity, limit the discussion of these critiques to those that reflect the American scene, inclusive of both North and South America.

Copland's first critique about an American composer, "George Antheil," was written in Paris, in 1924, at the time that young man was the leading American *enfant terrible* in Paris music circles. Believing that Antheil, a young man of his own age (twenty-three), was essentially a very sincere musician, completely absorbed in his work and oblivious to the opinions of everyone, Copland praised him for his "perfect musicianship" and censured him for his structural weaknesses in form and for his "unconscious plagarisms" from other composers. According to Copland, Antheil had not, at that time, found his personal idiom.[1]

"America's Young Men of Promise," Copland's fourth critique in chronological order, begins by stating that it has always proved a fascinating diversion to discover the important composers of tomorrow from among the young men of today. In addition to Franz Liszt, who concerned himself with the rising young European talent of his day, Copland recalled that Erik Satie, Busoni, Schoenberg, and Casella, more recently, had gathered about themselves the significant young men of their immediate spheres of activity.

In America, Copland observed, there had been no "godfather" to nurture our young composers. They had been left to shift for themselves. Furthermore, he charged that in America "when, as occasionally happens, a young talent does emerge from obscurity, this can almost always be attributed to the sensational element in his work, never to its purely musical merits."[2] But, of the many other composers who continued to write with little or no hope of having their works performed, if they could not be heard, they could at least be heard about (through the good offices of Mr. Copland and *Modern Music*). Perhaps, on hearing about them, some one might be induced to let the American public hear their music.

Copland then offered a list of seventeen names of composers, born here, whose ages lay between twenty-three and thirty-three, and whose music he believed was worthy of special note. He divided this list of composers into the following categories: (a) four Prix de Rome men: Leo Sowerby, Howard Hanson, Randall Thompson, Herbert Elwell; (b) three revolutionaries: George Antheil, Henry Cowell, Roger Sessions [Copland's own name would fit into this category]; (c) five free lancers: Roy Harris, Avery Claflin, Edmund Pendleton, Richard Hammond, Alexander Steinert; (d) three pupils of Ernest Bloch: Bernard Rogers, Quincy Porter, Douglas Moore; (e) two pupils of Nadia Boulanger: Virgil Thomson, Quinto Maganini. In this critique, written about his contemporaries, we have one of the first evidences of Copland's assumption of the role of "godfather" to American music, one that he has so distinguishedly filled for more than a quarter century.

Regarding Emerson Whithorne's query, "Where Do We Go from Here?" [3] which problem seemed to be disturbing to a number of our young composers in 1926, Copland replied in his ninth critique, "Music Since 1920," with the following answers. Stating that the innovations of Strauss and Debussy actually did not extend beyond the decade 1900 to 1910, and that the radical experiments of Schoenberg and Stravinsky belong to the decade from approximately 1910 to 1920, Copland reasoned that only the products of the years 1920 to 1928 could truly be termed "modern music"; for him the modern composers of these latter years were Hindemith, Milhaud, Prokofieff, and Křenek. For the present, he concluded, the answer to "Where do we go from here?" was: "Nowhere. Let us be content to rest awhile, to till the ground others have cleared." [4] And for now (1928), he counseled, the young composers' faith in the music of the present must rest with men like Hindemith, Milhaud, Honegger, and Prokofieff.

Just as Copland had made propaganda for Fauré, Antheil, Mahler, Stravinsky, and other composers in critiques relating to their works, so he did the same for Chávez,* in a critique entitled "Carlos Chávez—Mexican Composer." Copland had timed his propaganda well, immediately after a performance of the young Mexican's works at the first Copland-Sessions concert, April 22, 1928.

Noting that Chávez is a native of a country virtually without composers, without organized orchestras, or even an art-music tradition, Copland asserted that his friend had been able, nevertheless, to create not only a markedly individual style but one that is recognizably Mexican. Virtually self-taught in harmony and theory, although he had studied piano with his sister in Mexico City, it was not until he was twenty-one that Chávez composed his first ballet, *The New Fire*, in which he employed the ritualistic music of the Mexican Indian as themes. In addition to a second ballet, *The Four Suns* (based on an Aztec legend), his most mature work written to that date was his recently completed *Piano Sonata*. Discerning two limitations in Chávez's music, scope, and possibly form and melody, Copland insisted, nevertheless, that Chávez was one of the few Americans who was more than simply a reflection of Europe. Though he was still at the beginning of his career in 1928, Copland believed it was not too soon to say that Chávez's work presented one of the first authentic signs of a New World with its own music.[5]

Both Chávez and the Mexican folksong were to prove important influences upon young Copland, of which this critique suggests an inkling, for it was a Mexican folksong that became the springboard to his third style development, that of the American folksong.

Finding that he could not attend the official celebration of the Fontainebleau School of Music's Tenth Anniversary, Cop-

---

* According to Copland, the young American composers living in and around New York at that time regarded Chávez as "one of us," i.e., an American composer.

land contributed a critique to the *Fontainebleau Alumni Bulletin* entitled "A Note on Nadia Boulanger". Stating that he had long wanted to write down his impressions of his former teacher while they were still fresh in his memory (which opportunity the *Bulletin* so admirably provided), Copland asserted that it was Boulanger's "miraculous" love of music which had created within her a burning desire to know everything about music, whether old or new. What distinguished her from the routine professional musician was her enthusiasm and interest in contemporary music.

Copland averred that it was Boulanger's practice never to single out an American composer as different from a French or a Spanish composer. Instead, she searched for the profound personality that could create great music, considering such a personality as beyond the limits of territorial boundaries. With this attitude she caused each pupil to rely on the strength or weakness of his own individuality, and in so doing she made him stronger. Her faith in the future of American music was great, according to Copland, for it rested on the testimony of works she already knew. A partial list of her American pupils included: William Ames, Marc Blitzstein, Robert Russell Bennett, Theodore Chanler, Israel Citkowitz, David Dushkin, Robert Delaney, Herbert Elwell, Roy Harris, Quinto Maganini, Douglas Moore, Walter Piston, Quincy Porter, Melville Smith, and Virgil Thomson. Others who had benefitted by her criticism were named by Copland as: Bernard Rogers, Richard Hammond, and Roger Sessions.[6]

As a final rebuttal to the 1931 Yaddo critical controversy, Copland wrote his seventeenth critique, "The Composer and His Critic," in which he clearly outlined the responsibilities of the daily music critic toward the development of American music. Here we view an angry, militant, dynamic Copland, demanding that the composer be granted his rightful place in the scheme of things.

Acknowledging that the writer on music in our daily press influenced the opinions of his readers to an extent unknown in European countries (not because our music critics were more

oss, Paul Bowles, Hunter Johnson, and Samuel Barber. Those who were somewhat older and of more mature talents were Marc Blitzstein, Israel Citkowitz, Gerald Strang, Ross Lee Finney, Elie Siegmeister, Irwin Heilner, Lehman Engel, Paul Creston, and Edwin Gershefski. Those not yet twenty-five were Henry Brant, David Diamond, and Norman Cazden.[12]

Introducing Silvestre Revueltas, whose Mexican film *Redes* was being exhibited at that time (1937) in New York, Copland wrote a critique entitled "Mexican Composer—Silvestre Revueltas."[13] Stating that the need for musical accompaniments to films by serious composers was gradually becoming evident even to Hollywood, Copland affirmed that, in choosing Revueltas to compose the music for *The Wave,* it was very much like the U.S.S.R. asking Shostakovitch to write the musical scores for its best films. Anyone who was interested in the development of music in the Western Hemisphere, concluded Copland, could now hear the music Revueltas wrote for Paul Strand's "memorable" film of Mexico.

"The Composers Get Wise" is concerned with the economic plight of the professional composer. Copland cited three main sources of income for "practicing" composers as follows: (1) commissions to write a specific work, such as the incidental music for a stage play, a symphony, a ballet, a film score; (2) royalty payments derived from the retail sale of published music; (3) fees collectible on the performance rights of a composition protected under the copyright law. It is with the latter category, the newest source of income for composers, that the critique is chiefly concerned. Authoritatively written, for it was one of the serious problems that confronted Copland as President of the American Composers' Alliance, the critique reveals that when the occasion demanded the imaginative composer was also a realistic and practical man of business.[14]

Two critiques published in 1942 were the result of Copland's first South American tour, in 1941, undertaken at the behest of the State Department. These were "The Composers of South America" and "Latin-Americans in Music." Taking up the first one, Copland informs us that during his four-month sojourn he had examined the works of sixty-five composers in seven countries and had found no Bach or Beethoven among them. He noted that the Argentine composers were more cultivated and better professionally prepared than any other group in Latin-America, designating José Maria Castro, Juan Carlos Paz, and Alberto Ginastera as the outstanding composers of Buenos Aires.

Acknowledging that Heitor Villa-Lobos was the dominant musical figure not only in Brazil but in all South America, other important Brazilian composers named by Copland were Francisco Mignone, Lorenzo Fernandez, and Camargo Guarnieri, calling the latter the "most exciting 'unknown' talent in South America."*

According to Copland, the outstanding composer of Chile was Domingo Santa Cruz, Dean of the Fine Arts Department of the University. Other mature Chilean composers were Humberto Allende and Carlos Isamitt. Two "promising" composers, in their early thirties, were René Amengual and Alfonso Letelier.

Noting that the musical life of Uruguay was confined almost entirely to the capital, Montevideo, one of its most impressive talents was a youth of eighteen, Hector Tosar, whose vivid imagination, dash, and *élan* reminded Copland of Shostakovitch.

Finding that musical composition in Colombia, Peru, and Ecuador was still in its infancy, Copland stated that the European-trained Guillermo Uribe Holguin, of Colombia, and André Sas, of Peru, were the only composers whose works deserve serious consideration.[15]

In "Latin-Americans in Music," Copland revealed that his first contact with South American music occurred one afternoon in 1923, when he was introduced to Heitor Villa-Lobos, at the Paris apartment of Nadia Boulanger. His second was in New York's Greenwich Village around 1927, when Carlos Chávez, in a tiny one-room apartment where he then lived, played his Mexican ballet, *The Four Suns*, for him.

Observing that world conditions (and political expediency) had provided an unexpected impetus to our musical relations

---

* Guarnieri has since become well known in New York.

with neighboring American countries, Copland was of the opinion that much good might come from an interchange of musical experiences of every kind. Recalling that Chabrier, Debussy, and Ravel enriched their musical palettes by borrowing from typical Spanish sources, Copland saw no reason why we should not hope for similar inspiration from Ibero-American sources.

Acknowledging that up to now both North and South America had faced in the direction of Europe for musical sustenance, Copland asserted that it was now time to turn about and face each other. "If the nineteenth century was able, in a remarkably short period, to add Russia as a revivifying element to the musical scene," he hopefully concluded, "there is every reason to expect that the twentieth century will mark the entrance of the countries of the Western Hemisphere into the concert of musical nations."[16]

In the thirty-fifth critique, "From the '20's to the '40's and Beyond," Copland observed that although things "were beginning to happen" at the turn of the century, American music had come a particularly long way in the last two decades, listing the following advances: (1) "composer economics" was arrived at during the thirties, when the idea gradually took hold that a composer ought to receive his major income from the performance rights in his compositions; (2) the idea of "government in music," the sponsorship of a music program in the Works Progress Administration (Copland explained that governments need composers on the home front to stimulate and inspire love of country, and that composers have contributed to the betterment of Latin-American relations); (3) the number and quality of our younger composers,* who rival the technical dexterity of their elders and who look to them, instead of toward Europe, for their influences. Differing from the older generation in that they are satisfied to wait around until their elders see that their works are performed, the younger members, said Copland, nevertheless see clearly the new functional use of their

---

* Copland cited the younger composers as follows: Samuel Barber, William Schuman, Robert Palmer, Paul Bowles, John Cage, David Diamond, Robert McBride, John Lessard, Norman Dello-Joio, Edward Cone, Jerome Moross, Earl Robinson, Alexi Haieff, David Van Vactor, and Harold Shapero.

music in radio, films, high school, and the Broadway show.

Among the failures of the two past decades, Copland listed these: (1) no one had found out how to exploit many excellent works composed during that period by Stravinsky, Schoenberg, Bartók, Milhaud, Berg, Hindemith, Křenek, Martinu, Walton, and the Americans, Chávez, Harris, Piston, Cowell, and Ruggles; (2) there had been a lack of serious, critical, full-length studies of the works of American composers. Citing Paul Rosenfeld's *One Hour With American Music* (1929) as an isolated example of a first-hand survey of the field, Copland averred that we badly needed a critical survey of the last twenty years of musical development in America to know what we had accomplished.

Although nobody wants to write "modern music" anymore, he acknowledged, the modern movement had been "historically sound and musically fruitful." We should be lucky, he concluded, if the music of the next twenty years could be regarded as vital.[17]

In recognition of Koussevitzky's twenty-year leadership of the Boston Symphony Orchestra, Copland summarized the conductor's efforts in behalf of American music in a critique entitled "Serge Koussevitzky and the American Composer," which appeared in the spring of 1944. One of the composer's most intimate revelations of a long association and friendship with one of the leading artistic figures of contemporary times, it must suffice here to mention that between 1924 and 1944 Koussevitzky gave "first performances" to sixty-six American composers and performed a total of 163 American works. Nine of these were works by Copland, four of which were first performances.[18]

Copland's thirty-eighth critique, "The American Composer Today," appeared in 1945, in a U.S. Government publication designed for circulation in foreign countries. Presenting a brief historical account of the development of American music from the time of Dvořák's New York sojourn to 1945, the critique included a listing of our composers' major achievements in respect to orchestral music, opera, chamber music, and ballet. Noting the presence of Europe's leading contemporary composers in the United States during the period 1930 to 1941, it would seem self-evident, said Copland, that the future of European music would be closely allied with the course which music took in the Americas.[19]

The forty-first critique, "Memorial to Paul Rosenfeld," was first given in the form of a reading by Copland on October 29, 1946, over Radio Station WQXR, as a part of a tribute paid the late critic.[20] Contemporary American Music therefore sustained two severe blows during 1946, the loss of its most loyal and understanding critic, and the suspension from publication of the forward-looking *Modern Music*.

In "The New 'School' of American Composers," Copland recalled that in his twenties he had had a "consuming" interest in the work other American composers of his generation were producing and that he had instinctively thought of himself as belonging to a "school" of American composers. Now, toward the end of the forties, he and his contemporaries, of necessity, counted themselves among the "spiritual papas" of a new generation of composers, toward whose work Copland signified his interest was just as acute as it ever was. "For it is obvious," he wrote, "that you cannot set up a continuing tradition of creative music in any country without a constant freshening of source material as each decade brings forth a new batch of composers."[21]

To those who considered themselves the "guardians" of musical tradition in the Western Hemisphere (where the creative musical movement is still relatively new), Copland stated that it was an important function of his generation to nurture well the younger composers' "delicate roots," to see that they received a sound musical training, to aid their first successful efforts to be heard, and to see that they felt themselves a part of the musical movement in their country.

Unlike the composers of Copland's generation, most of the young composers, who sprang up in the forties, had not studied in Europe for the reason that Europe, instead, came to them. Thus, most of the younger men had had contact with Stravinsky, Hindemith, Schoenberg, Milhaud, and Martinu, all of whom, in 1948, were living and composing in the United States.

Added to the European influences (acquired in America) upon the younger men was that of the influence of their older American colleagues, which struck a new note in American music. It was significant, he thought, that nowadays the young American composers were just as likely to be influenced by Harris, Schuman, or Copland as they were by Stravinsky, Hindemith, or Schoenberg.

Rather than any one unified tendency, the works of the youngest generation, in general, reflected a wide variety of compositional interests, a condition Copland found healthy and natural. Copland cited as some of the "best" among the new generation the following composers, who ranged in age from twenty-four to thirty: Robert Palmer, Alexei Haieff, Harold Shapero, Lukas Foss, Leonard Bernstein, William Bergsma, and John Cage. Offering a short biographical sketch of each, Copland discussed briefly the compositional tendencies found in these composers' work.

In addition to the two critiques about film music discussed in Chapter VII, Copland wrote a third, "Tip to Moviegoers: Take Off Those Ear-Muffs," in which he expressed dismay at the general movie public's apathetic indifference to his own and other serious composers' wholehearted efforts to write first-rate, expressive music for films. "One's appreciation of a work of art," he stated, "is partly determined by the amount of preparation one brings to it."[22] Since the great majority of movie patrons were musical to some degree, Copland believed that by "taking in," through careful listening, the musical background of a picture, the moviegoers would enrich both their musical and cinema experiences. He defined film music as a form of dramatic music, related to opera, ballet, and incidental theater music.

Taking issue with the current tendency to condemn concert suites that had been extracted from film scores, Copland argued that if Grieg's *Peer Gynt* could be made from nineteenth century incidental stage music, there was no reason why a twentieth century composer cannot do the same with a film score. And as for the picture score, the composer really wanted to know how many of the millions in the theater were actually listening to the musical background. Urging the general public to "be on the composer's side," Copland facetiously counseled: "Remove those ear-muffs."

Copland's fiftieth critique is aptly titled, "A Modernist Defends Modern Music." Noting that after about fifty years of "modern music" there were still thousands of music-lovers who thought it sounded "peculiar," Copland said that it had occurred to him to wonder whether it wasn't possible to help the "listener of good-will" hear it his (Copland's) way. To bring some order into the apparent chaos of contemporary composition, Copland had divided its leading exponents into categories of relative degrees of difficulty that the understanding of their respective idioms presented.

The music of the composers Shostakovitch, Khatchaturian, Poulenc, Satie, early Schoenberg and Stravinsky, Vaughan Williams, and Virgil Thomson fell into the category of "very easy." The music of Prokofieff, Harris, Villa-Lobos, Bloch, and Walton was termed "quite approachable." Late Stravinsky, Bartók, Chávez, Milhaud, Schuman, Honegger, Britten, Hindemith, and Piston were composers whose works were "fairly difficult." Middle and late Schoenberg and the works of Alban Berg, Anton Webern, Varèse, Křenek, Charles Ives, and Roger Sessions were designated "very tough."

In approaching a "new" musical work of serious pretensions, the listener must first acquaint himself with the composer's objective* and then expect to hear a different treatment of harmony, melody, timbre, texture, for these elements, like the world itself, have undergone constant change.

Copland developed the critique with a brief discussion of the contemporary problems of the lay listener which were based on the following questions: "Why must new music be so dissonant?"

---

* Copland defines the composer's aesthetic as the following: "A composer writes music to express and communicate and put down in permanent form certain thoughts, emotions and states of being." Formed by the contact of his personality with the world in which he lives, the composer expresses these musical thoughts (which are not to be confused with literary ones) in the musical language of his own time.

"Is it true that the new composers care little about melody?" "Is contemporary music supposed to be without sentiment or feeling?"

Before concluding, Copland asked a pertinent question of his own of the lay listener: "Why is it that the musical public is seemingly so reluctant to consider a musical composition as, possibly, a challenging experience?" As for himself, when he heard a new piece of music he did not readily understand, he stated that he was "intrigued" and wanted to hear it again at the first opportunity.

New music still sounded "peculiar," Copland believed, because of the fact that most of the music heard on radio and concert programs, on records, and in our school curricula was devoted principally to the music of the past. Unless audiences demanded that music producers let them hear more of contemporary music, it was likely to remain "peculiar," he concluded.[23]

"Creativity in America" was presented by Mr. Copland on May 25, 1952, in the form of the Blashfield Address for the Joint Ceremonial of the American Academy of Arts and Letters and the National Institute of Arts and Letters. This critique is remarkable for its definitiveness of the creative personality in relation to the community and points toward the day when respect for our native creative artists will stamp America as a truly civilized nation.

Observing that a civilization that produced no creative artists was either provincial or dead, Copland stated that a mature people recognize the need to leave evidence of its essential character in art works, thereby contributing an incentive toward the will to live.

Posing the question: "What . . . does creativity mean in the life of a man and of a nation?" Copland averred that "the creative act affirms the individual and gives value to the individual, and through him to the nation of which he is a part.[24]

Then he asked, "Does the average American really grasp the concept included in the word: creativity? Have the artists of America succeeded in impressing themselves . . . in the deepest sense—on the mind of Americans?" Answering these questions in terms of his own observation and experience, Copland was of the opinion that the creative artist played a less important role here than in other countries; and that our native artists must make clear to all Americans the intrinsic value attached to the idea of the creative personality.

Stressing the fact that all of our citizens must become fully aware of the civilizing force that works of art represent, Copland expressed the fear that unless this was achieved, art, although it would not be "crushed" in the United States, would not be "noticed sufficiently to matter."

Copland believed that, as soon as the government showed more concern for the welfare of art in America, then our people would show more concern for their artists. As a result of government interest in education he noted that music in the schools had developed in an astonishing way, manifested by symphony orchestras and choral ensembles composed of almost unlimited numbers of young people. However, he did not think that these young people took any but the most conventional attitude to the composers whose works they performed. Creativity in our country depends largely on the fostering and understanding of the role of the creative artist; he and his work must be made meaningful to each community. "When [creativity] is understood as the activity of free and independent men, intent upon the reflection and summation of our own time in beautiful works," he concluded, "art, in America will have entered on its most important phase."

A single quotation from the address given by Copland on the theme "Music: As an Aspect of the Human Spirit," in December, 1954, over the Columbia Broadcasting System, as part of Columbia University's Bi-centennial celebration, must suffice here. Taking note of the development of musical instruments of the future which doubtless will include the invention of an electronic master instrument with unheard-of microtonic divisions of a scale, thereby producing totally new sound possibilities, Copland, nevertheless, is certain that "however arrived at, the process of music and the process of life will always be closely conjoined. So long as the human spirit thrives on this planet," he hopefully concluded, "music in some living form will accompany and sustain it and give it expressive meaning." [25]

Copland's final published critique to date entitled "Modern Music: 'Fresh and Different'," is the composer's positive answer to Henry Pleasants' negative article "Modern Music: A Dead Art," both of which appeared simultaneously in the New York *Times* recently. The oldsters, or conservatives Pleasants might have attracted, on the one hand, to his banner of wholesale condemnation of the Modern Movement must find it difficult, on the other hand, to swallow his untenable argument that of all the Twentieth Century musical developments only jazz remains vital and creative.

Like the alert fire horse impatiently champing at his bit at the sound of the alarm bell, Copland, Defender of the Modern Music Faith, rises to the fray only to find that "according to his own analysis, Henry Pleasants is pummeling nothing but a carcass." Because of the composer in our century music now behaves differently, in respect to textures, to melody, to suddenly attained heights, to precipitous descents and even in respect to its stops. "But," Copland continued, "[our modern music] shares with older music the expression of basic human emotions, even though at times it may seem more painful, more nostalgic, more obscure, more hectic, more sarcastic. Whatever else it may be, it is the voice of our own age and in that sense it needs no apology."

Noting that, in general, Americans take pride in the accomplishments of our popular composers, Copland finds the notion that anyone could imagine that "serious music is endangered by the wide acceptance of our popular music [both at home and abroad], or that one may be substituted for the other, is to be utterly naïve as to comparative musical values." [26]

Influence

Turning to the immeasurable quality of influence, we have, nevertheless, certain specific evidences that Aaron Copland's influence on the music of his time is wide in scope and direction, being of several kinds. His assumption of the role of leader of the "modern movement" in America, in 1924, upon his return from several years of European study and travel, was both natural and historically essential to our musical development; for our younger composers, who had up to that time struggled singly and to some extent without a clear direction for recognition of an American art music, under Copland's leadership were organized into a forceful group, united in aims and purposes and equipped with a similar compositional aesthetic. Proof that this development in America, stemming from Copland, was underway has been offered in the performances of his music by our leading orchestras, related in Chapter IV of this study, and in his first critiques devoted to American music, which are an integral part of this chapter. Proof that Copland wielded a strong influence on his American contemporaries in that he was the American source of the most dominant influence in our music during the twenties and early thirties, that of the modern French school, is to be found in the fact that eighteen American composers up to 1930, following his example, had studied with, or benefited from criticism of, Nadia Boulanger.* As Copland himself grew as an artist and man, his influence gradually extended to each successive new generation of younger composers, throughout the twenties, thirties, and forties, becoming a dominant influence in the fifties.

Upholding a high moral and artistic tone in his music and critiques, this influence was further projected through the composer's lectures at the New School for Social Research (for approximately ten years) and elsewhere professionally; through the Copland-Sessions Concerts (1928–1931) which featured the works of the younger men, and the Yaddo Festivals of American Music, 1931 and 1932; his attempts to give the composers of his time financial security through the American Composers' Alliance, of which he was president from 1937 to 1944; through his teaching, at Henry Street Music School, at Harvard University, and at Tanglewood. But most of all, Copland has influenced the younger composers through his music. By his conscious

* *cf.* p. 268 of this study.

efforts to seek out an American idiom, then unconsciously stumbling upon it, his folksong aesthetic has influenced almost all the younger American composers of his time.

Copland has exerted a strong influence in Mexico and South America by his presence there, intermittently from 1932 through 1954, notably during his two "good-will tours" for the State Department in 1941 and 1947 when he examined the works of most of the younger composers; through many performances of his works, which took place as early as 1929, in Mexico; and by his presence in Caracus, Venezuela, in December 1954, where he attended a First Festival of Orchestral Works by Contemporary Latin-American Composers. That the composer, in turn, was influenced by the rhythm and folk music of the Latin-American countries has been indicated in the musical analyses of his works. Nevertheless, he influenced Juan O. Salas and Alberto Ginastera away from the French aesthetic to that of folksong.

In Europe, which proved a dominant influence on Copland up to 1925, his influence has grown steadily since 1926, when Koussevitzky first performed his "jazz-inspired" *Music for the Theatre* at the Paris Opera House. Followed by performances of other works, at intervals, this influence appeared to make a big up-swing in June, 1938, when his *El Salón México* was performed at the Sixteenth Festival of the I.S.C.M. at London and, in the following year, at Paris. It is very probable that Copland's influence on the young Englishman, Benjamin Britten, stems from this time.

That his influence has been felt in the newly created state of Israel is indicated in a brief visit he made there in 1951, flying over from Rome where, at the time, he was in residence at the American Academy, the recipient of a Fulbright Award.

Since Copland's influence on the younger composers undoubtedly will be significant to the future development of American music, let us examine specific facets of that influence as it exists today, going to the composer himself and three of the outstanding Tanglewood group of young composers as our primary sources of information.

Acknowledging that he has had considerable influence on the

younger generation of composers, Copland believes that it has not been brought about through his teaching of them. Preferring to lecture, rather than to teach, his really first teaching in a school, as previously mentioned, was during the winters of 1936 and 1937, at the Henry Street Music School in New York City. Even in this instance he arranged for the pupils to come to his studio instead of going to the school.

In 1935 and again in 1944, Copland substituted for Walter Piston at Harvard University, conducting classes in composition and giving lectures during two spring semesters. Other than that, he taught only two of the younger composers, Paul Bowles and Israel Citkowitz, stating that he accepted these young men as pupils because at the time they had no money to pay any teacher and asked for his help.

Obviously the Berkshire Music Center (Tanglewood), with which he has been associated since its founding in 1940, has provided Copland with his most significant school contact with the younger composers, for it attracts students from all over the country. It gives him a chance for contact with what is being done by an even younger generation than those now composing. Each year, according to Copland, Tanglewood receives approximately fifty applications for composition study, from which are selected about sixteen students on the basis of compositions they have submitted earlier. The average age of students ranges from twenty-one to twenty-five, although an exceptional boy of sixteen was admitted during the 1949 session.

Since Tanglewood maintains only a six-week session there is not much time for writing at the school. In general, Copland seeks to give a general diagnosis of the big scores the students have already written and to state clearly what these scores lack. Occasionally an orchestral work by one of the composition students is selected for performance by one of the several orchestras in residence at Tanglewood. Copland's Tanglewood classes have not only attracted students from all sections of North America, but have also included students from Latin-America, Czechoslovakia, Sweden, and Israel.

A friendship with Koussevitzky, dating from 1924 in Paris, had kept Copland familiar with Koussevitzky's dreams and aspirations regarding a school in America. It was Koussevitzky's idea to appoint Copland as a more or less "permanent fixture" of the composition department and to supplement his work with that of a European composer of note, invited as a guest teacher each summer. Among the European composers who have taught at Tanglewood are Hindemith, Martinu, Honegger, Milhaud, Messiaen, and Dallapiccola. Carlos Chávez was guest teacher in the summer of 1953.

In addition to his teaching, Copland is active in the Tanglewood Forum which, as moderator, he conducts much in the manner of a Town Hall Forum. The procedure is to choose a number of subjects which have a musical interest and to invite a panel of speakers, each of whom is allotted ten minutes. Some of the discussions during the summer of 1949 were developed around these topics: "Nationalism in American Music," "The Future of Opera in America," "Should the Government Help the Arts?" and the entrancing but illusive subject of "Inspiration."

During the summer of 1951, I attended an opera forum in the Lenox Library, at which time the speakers' panel included Luigi Dallapiccola,* Italian guest teacher of composition, Boris Goldovsky, Leonard Bernstein, and others. In addition to his duties as moderator, Copland performed a brilliant "on the spot" translation of Dallapiccola's remarks which, due to that composer's unfamiliarity with English, were delivered in French.

On a visit to Tanglewood in 1949, I visited one of Copland's lecture classes, devoted on that occasion to the music of Anton Webern, exponent of the twelve-tone style. Presented in an atmosphere of easy but serious informality, the lecture began with a brief discussion of Webern's background, outlined by Copland, followed by a performance of Webern's short wood-wind *Quintet*, which was repeated. Having prearranged that Bernstein and Foss would take opposing viewpoints regarding the value of this work, Copland soon had the entire group of students in an enthusiastic discussion of music it had never before experienced.

---

* Dallapiccola's opera, *The Prisoner*, in twelve-tone style, received its American *premiere* during the 1950-1951 season at the Juilliard School.

I left the lecture that afternoon convinced that whether these young people ever became Webern "fans" or not, they had had the great experience of being guided in how to listen to and appraise the artistic qualities of an unfamiliar "modern" work. In 1947, with the help of Leonard Bernstein and Irving Fine, Copland presented a course of lectures on "American Music"; in 1949, he lectured on "Music of the Twenties," covering American and European music of those years.

At Tanglewood it is also Copland's province* to arrange concerts on Sunday nights of works composed by the students themselves, which are performed by students drawn from both the composition and instrumental departments.

During the 1949 visit to Tanglewood, at my request interviews were arranged with several composers who have been associated with Copland for some years and whose works, according to professional newspaper criticism, have shown a Copland influence. It was my purpose in these interviews to receive an expression of opinion from these young men as to the probable scope of Copland's influence on American music as a whole, and to inquire to what extent they believed their works have been influenced by their older colleague. These young composer's were Lukas Foss, Leonard Bernstein, and Irving Fine.

Lukas Foss, born in Berlin, regarded as a *Wunderkind,* came to New York with his parents at the age of fifteen, and was for several years the official pianist of the Boston Symphony Orchestra. In regard to Copland's influence on the younger composers, Foss believes that David Diamond has been most influenced by his older colleague, in almost every work, particularly in his quality of style. Crediting Chávez and Stravinsky with having had rhythmic influences on Copland, Foss believes that the Copland "flavor" was influenced by Milhaud, in France. All of these influences which have made the Copland style are, in turn, expressed in the Diamond style. In the earlier works of Harold Shapero, particularly his four-hand *Sonata,* the slow movement, Foss notes a Copland influence in the general mood and in the

* Koussevitzky appointed Copland Assistant-Director of Tanglewood in 1946, a position he continues to hold under Koussevitzky's successor, Charles Munch.

melodic inflection. He also named Elie Siegmeister's *Ozark Set*, Louise Talma's *Piano Sonata*, and Samuel Barber's song for soprano voice and orchestra, "Nocturne," as works that reveal Copland's influence. According to Foss, Menotti, in his opera scores, has revealed a knowledge of Copland's music.

Of Copland's scores, Foss stated that he had been most impressed with *The Second Hurricane* and *Billy the Kid*. In America, Foss thinks that Stravinsky, Hindemith, Schoenberg, Bartók, and Copland have had the most influence on the younger composers and that Copland's influence is equal to both that of Stravinsky and Bartók.

Turning to his own works, Foss believes that his choral work *The Prairie* (text by Sandburg) was very much influenced by Copland, and that it would be almost unnatural to avoid the whole Copland "atmosphere of Americana." It is Copland's "open-air quality," not really his own but a reflection of folklore, according to Foss, that is present in the younger composers' work. Although he has had no formal study with Copland (his teachers were Stravinsky and Hindemith), Foss has shown Copland his music and discussed his scores with him on numerous occasions. According to the younger man, the relationship between them has been one of a professional exchange of ideas. In examining a musical score for the first time, Foss said that he and Copland look for different things: "Copland looks for originality in a score and is disappointed when he finds it eclectic; I look for evidences of musicality rather than originality." Believing that composers often cannot recognize another composer's influence in their work, Foss further explained: "Sometimes in my music I point out a particular passage to Aaron which I think sounds like his music and ask, 'Isn't this like you?' 'No, it's you,' he replies. So a composer is not always aware when he has made something of someone else's his own, which is the way all composers have generally worked. Schubert set out to write in the Beethoven style and ended up by writing himself." *

Leonard Bernstein, born in Lawrence, Massachusetts, was

---

* The interviews with Foss, Bernstein, and Fine took place on July 13, 1949.

educated at Harvard University, where he studied composition with Walter Piston and Edward Burlingame Hill. At the Curtis Institute he studied orchestration with Randall Thompson. Bernstein was of the opinion that the most important general contribution Copland has made to American music is that he was made the agent for simplifying music, which tendency occurred in the thirties. Acknowledging that Copland was influenced by the Paris movement, the "antiserious" expression of *Les Six*, Bernstein remarked that the twenties were notable for their "acrid" emphasis on originality. Although he does not believe that Virgil Thomson has written great music, Bernstein thinks that his music has exerted an influence on Copland, in its expression of a primitive kind of simplicity, particularly his use of Baptist hymns. All of this affected Copland and in *The Second Hurricane* he discovered he too could write simple music which had originality. Every work since then, according to Bernstein, has capitalized on this discovery, which runs through all the ballets, simplicity with originality, and in these works Copland rediscovered the triad via Thomson and the Paris group. Stating that Copland has influenced all the younger American composers by this aesthetic, simplicity with originality, Bernstein cited William Schuman as one who has been most strongly influenced. Recalling that at first Schuman (who is not noted for his originality) wrote difficult, stony music, Bernstein said that all of a sudden he began to write simple themes with a strong lyrical feeling.

Bernstein thinks that his own *Jeremiah Symphony* is his most Copland-influenced work, particularly the rhythmic quality of the scherzo, which he believes was influenced by *El Salón México*. He named Copland's *Piano Sonata* as one of his "favorite pieces in the world," finding it a synthesis of the composer's complicated and simple styles. He defined Copland's American style as consisting of his own particular rhythmic way combined with a harmonization which expresses plain sentimentality.

Irving Fine, also a Harvard graduate, is at present an assistant professor at Brandeis University. Fine first began to know Copland when the latter came to Harvard as Horatio Lamb Lecturer during the 1944 spring semester. Emphasizing that Copland's music is a reflection of his own taste, Fine stated that his experience has been that Copland seems to "needle" the young composers to assert their independence. He constantly urges them to find their true personalities. One of Copland's larger aspects, according to Fine, is that of his contemporaneity; he is a composer of today, not hampered by tradition, not slavish to rules, and he is not a composer living in a dream world to write the music of the future. Fine believes that Copland's influence lies in the music he has written and described how this influence finds its way into other composers' work: "You admire his music, it appeals to you. He has certain general qualities that you wish to acquire too; these are the transparency of his scores, the choice distribution of parts, clarity of sound and the clarity of his harmony."

Although Fine never studied with Copland, he has had a social acquaintance of long standing with him. Since the latter has a general interest in all composers, Fine has shown him almost everything he ever wrote. Almost every young composer who has had any contact with Copland manages to show him his music at some time or other and, although Copland is not an active teacher, Fine stated that he has almost a more direct contact with young writers than any other composer in the country. "Since he has a genuine interest in what's going on," continued Fine ,"young composers wish to test him for reaction to their works. Copland spends an evening every once in a while looking over the music of young composers in the New York area." In listening to a composer's work Copland reacts strictly to the musical-expressive content and not from the technical point of view. In addition to himself, Fine named other composers who have been influenced by Copland as the following: Arthur Berger, Harold Shapero, Alexei Haieff, Lukas Foss, Leonard Bernstein, and Robert Palmer.

In his own music Fine cites his *Choral New Yorker* and *Design for October*, which "are distinctly like Copland in mood and harmony." Noting a Copland influence in his *Violin Sonata,* Fine also senses that in his recent wood-wind *Partita* there is an influence of *Appalachian Spring*. The coda from the *Partita* has a

kind of peaceful landscape quality that Fine believes is like Copland, but no one else seems to think so.

Turning to other opinions, Donald Fuller has noted a strong
Copland influence on the younger generation and even on some
of his contemporaries, "especially when the theatre is involved,
where Copland's folk style is most suitable because it is direct
and expressive without complexity." [27] He cited the stage works
of Marc Blitzstein and Leonard Bernstein, Lukas Foss (*The
Prairie*), Leo Smit (ballet), Virginia Sampler and Walter Hendl
(*Dark of the Moon*) as reflecting a Copland imprint.

In a review of Benjamin Britten's *Serenade* for tenor, horn,
and strings, Arthur Berger stated that that work "affords striking
evidence that at least one composer abroad is as profoundly conscious of the Copland style as so many young men here are. This
is unprecedented for an American composer, perhaps because
no one of us has ever had so individual a manner—something
specific . . . to emulate." [28] Berger pointed out that Britten's
"Prologue" for French horn practically duplicates the initial English horn solo of the "Interlude" from *Music for the Theatre*. Thus
we have specific evidence of a Copland influence in European
music.

That there exists a Copland influence on the young composers
of Israel is indicated in the article of Peter Gradewitz sent to
the New York *Times* from Tel Aviv, which told of the "real pio-
neering task" performed by the American. In the spring of 1951,
Copland flew over from Rome to conduct a five-day composers'
conference, attended by thirty-two of Israel's leading composers,
during which some fifty Israeli works were played, analyzed,
and discussed, and the problems of national and regional music
debated. Of the younger composers, according to the *Times*,
Copland showed special interest in three: Ben-Zion Orgad, who
had continued to develop since his studies at Tanglewood in
1949; Haim Alexander, whose *Six Israeli Dances* for piano created a favorable impression at the recent local I.S.C.M. concert;
and Yehoshua Lakner, whose *Sonatina for Flute and Piano* was
reputed to be one of the most valuable works produced in Israel
recently.

Making his debut at the Ein Gev Festival as a choral director, Copland conducted his large Biblical work, *In the Beginning*, on the shores of Lake Tiberias, in a structure that is a replica of the Berkshire Music Shed. [29] Thus the composer's influence appears to be growing impressively throughout the world.

An indication that the Copland influence is definitive among the works of the young American composers of serious music is evident in the review of the first of two "Evenings of New Works by Young Composers," sponsored by the League of Composers, which took place at the Museum of Modern Art on April 20, 1952. Of this concert the *Times* critic wrote:

> The Bright Young Men of the Twenties and Thirties now being patriarchs of modern music, it is to composers such as those performed last evening that one must look for new trends in music. If last night's concert is a trustworthy guide, what we are to hear is more of the same. . . . The influence of Hindemith and Copland was much in evidence.[30]

Returning to the problem, which is the crux of this entire study, the determination of Aaron Copland's position in, and contribution to, American music, I am convinced that this study has presented adequate proof of the following conclusions.

Approaching the two-hundredth anniversary commemorating the establishment of the United States as a nation, which latter time marks its beginnings of world leadership among the Family of Nations, it is significant that the art of music, recognizably slower in a country's development than its literature, painting, and sculpture, has produced, in Aaron Copland, its first definitive American composer.

Although Copland's immediate musical ancestry goes back no further than Goldmark and Dvořák, there seems little aesthetic transmission of influences by these men to the younger man beyond their devotion to the formal aspects of music and the tendency to incorporate Negro and Indian themes into their work.

The American musical ancestry from which Aaron Copland could have been derived, of which there are reflections manifested in his music, appears to be from a line of composers whose fundamental achievements were the following: William Billings, our first important hymnodist; Stephen Foster, who created an authentic folk music; Louis Moreau Gottschalk, our first composer to use Creole and Latin-American melodies in his compositions; Edward MacDowell, the first American to develop a mastery of the composer's technical craft, who gave American music a European standing; Henry F. Gilbert, whose use of Negro music as material was novel and fresh; Charles Griffes, the first American to write "modern music"; Charles Ives, our most daring innovator and a leading polytonalist; George Gershwin, who produced a "jazz" treatment of the Negro folk idiom; and Virgil Thomson, whose aesthetic of "simplicity" has shaped American music since 1935.

By mastering the tools of composition, acquired from a combination of his American and European study, Aaron Copland speaks the tonal language of his day. In this he has achieved a synthesis of the aims of MacDowell, Griffes, and Ives. Thoroughly aware of Gershwin's jazz production, by virtue of this mastery of the composer's craft, Copland achieved (where Gershwin was only able to aspire) an American idiom in which jazz is an ingredient in the style of his "serious" or absolute works. In his casting about for, experimenting with, and testing of contemporary discoveries such as polyrhythmic, polytonal, quarter-tone, and atonal materials, Copland reflects the innovative tendencies of both Griffes and Ives. By adopting Virgil Thomson's aesthetic of writing more relaxed and easygoing compositions for popular consumption, and in turning to American folk sources for materials, Copland realized a synthesis of the manifestations of Thomson, Billings, Foster, Gottschalk, and Gilbert, and became our first composer to exhibit true greatness in his theater and absolute works.

In respect to his "modern" musical expression which, as this study has indicated, stems from a European origin, Copland appears to be the lineal descendant of Debussy, Scriabin, Fauré, Mahler, Stravinsky, Schoenberg, Bartók, Milhaud, and the Mexican, Chávez.

Having determined Aaron Copland's national and contemporary roots which, taken together, establish his historical position in American music, let me briefly summarize his contribution to our music, the major achievements of which may be listed as follows: his distinguished and original musical production, totaling more than sixty-five scores, in many forms, which reflect not only his use of twentieth century discoveries in music materials but its discoveries in new musical media, the radio, phonograph, and film; his *Gebrauchsmusik* production for the vast audiences that were created as a result of these inventions, including his music written for performance by high-school students, which forms an important part of our creative cultural stream; his three books and approximately sixty-five published critiques which are important contributions to our scanty contemporary critical literature, the books functioning in our college, university, and music-school libraries as authoritative texts on the growth and materials of contemporary music, the critiques presenting an authentic record of the development of contemporary music in America; his organizational activities in behalf of American music including the Copland-Sessons Concerts, Yaddo Festivals of American Music, American Composers' Alliance, and his activities in the League of Composers, all of which have contributed to the advancement of music in America; his travels to Mexico and Latin-American countries which are not only reflected in his music but have resulted in an inter-American relationship whose significance is more than artistic; finally, his realization that the transmission of an American musical tradition is a continuous process for which the younger composers must be fittingly prepared as future guardians of a heritage to which he has contributed so much. These contributions offer final proof that, in the work of Aaron Copland, America has produced her first great composer.

ADDENDUM

"Pointillism" Applied to Music

KEEPING in mind Virgil Thomson's recent admonition that while nothing in contemporary music may be regarded as "fixed," it is nevertheless an essential duty in a study of this nature to crystallize for practical purposes any new term or extension of an idea that may prove of value to musical criticism or musical techniques.

Although the term "pointillism" and its musical connotation as advanced by Dr. Vincent Jones in his classes of Aesthetics and Musical Criticism at New York University during the latter 1940's and early 1950's was perfectly clear to him and to us (his students), I have since discovered that its musical analogy is vague to many musicians and that its implications in Copland's music appear even more obscure.

Since the musical application of "pointillism" is still so new that it has not, as yet, found its way into musical dictionaries, I have asked Dr. Jones to provide us with a brief explanation. His communication, sent from Los Angeles and dated March 16, 1955, reads as follows:

> Pointillism is a system of applying pigment, usually pure colors, in measured strokes (often merely dots) which was evolved by the French painter, Georges Seurat (*c.* 1885).
>
> It is possible to suggest a parallel in music where the tones of a melody are distributed among several instruments. Thus there is a rapid succession of different timbres rather than one prevailing color in the melodic line.
>
> Anton Webern's technique of "atomizing" a melody, a procedure stimulated by Schoenberg's theory of *Klangfarbenmelodien* (tone-color melodies) suggests the analogy with pointillism in painting.

Grove's *Dictionary of Music and Musicians*, Supplementary Volume, 1944, p. 667, notes that Webern's *Six Bagatelles* for string quartet (1913) and *Three Little Pieces* for violoncello and piano (1913) "are still more highly concentrated, still more transparent and pointillistic in texture" (than Schoenberg's *Piano Pieces*, Op. 11). Erwin Stein, writing in *The Chesterian* (October, 1922), asserted that "almost every note of a melody [in the *Bagatelles*] is given to a different instrument, and each one in a different tone-colour (harmonics, *pizzicato, col legno*, etc.)" Further, Grove notes that in "Wiese im Park," the first of the *Four Songs*, Op. 13, "Webern clung to his pointillistic instrumental technique, though even here the voice part, despite its hideously unvocal intervals, provides a slight thread of continuity."

A clear example of the use of the pointillistic instrumental technique in the work of Copland is noted in his *Short Symphony*, *Sextet* version quoted here (Example 1). The opening theme of the first movement is heard in recapitulation, in a setting distributed between timbres of piano, and strings and clarinet.

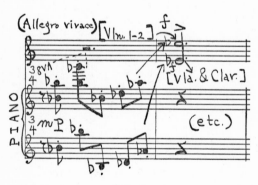

Ex. 1

The above example affords another aspect of the musical implications of "pointillism." Borrowing a rule from Ernst Křenek's *Studies in Counterpoint*, I quote: "In the twelve-tone technique, only the order of succession of the tones in the twelve-tone series is relevant, regardless of their register." [1] Thus, to refer again to Copland's music, according to the above rule, Example 1 and Figure A are considered identical.

Fig. a

Pursuing Dr. Jones's analogy of pointillism in painting with timbre (or tone color) in music, let us consider briefly Aaron Copland's first published book, *What to Listen for in Music*,[2] specifically Chapter 7, devoted to "Tone Color." He differentiates between the "tone color" or timbre of the principal four sections of the orchestra—strings, woodwinds, brass, percussion— and the characteristic timbres of each individual instrument. Of pertinent interest to us here is his stress of importance to composers of the three different registers of the cello tone, each of which produces a different timbre or color: the upper register he designates "very poignant and touching"; middle register, "smooth, baritone quality of sound"; and the low register, "sonority . . . of sober profundity." *

Violinists all agree that although the violin has its own characteristic timbre, it has many gradations of tone color. For example, the E string has an absolutely different timbre from the G string.

Turning briefly to the instrument that has been correctly, if humorously, termed the "maid of all work," the piano, and its manifold reservoirs of timbres, we know that the superior instruments of today, in the hands of an imaginative performer, can, in the upper register (with a judicious use of pedal) evoke, or re-create the soft, dulcet sounds of a celeste; without pedal, using sharp, metallic finger strokes, the sound of a xylophone; and that

---

* As early as 1867, B. Silliman, Jr., in *Physics*, p. 284, observed that "the essential difference between the bass and tenor voices, and between the contralto and soprano, consists in the tone or timbre which distinguishes them even when they are singing the same note." *New Standard Dictionary of the English Language* (New York and London, Funk & Wagnalls, 1916).

a harp effect can be realized by almost any amateur. Even intervals of perfect fourths and fifths in the middle register used in fanfare style suggest the timbre of hunting horns (so effectively used by Mendelssohn and Schumann in their piano works), while the lower tones, sounded staccato and dry, realize the grotesque quality of the bassoon in the same register. In addition to the many timbres the piano can conjure up, the instrument has its own especial characteristic timbres, a singing cantilena, brilliance, masses of tone, et cetera, and, with the tasteful use of pedals, in conjunction with an ultrasensitive touch and more "modern" harmonies, the impressionistic palette came into being, which greatly enriched the scope of its many-hued timbres.

All of which leads to my final adaptation of the term "pointillism" to contemporary piano writing, in the expanded meaning we gave to it at New York University. In proceeding from one note of a melody to the next (on keyboard instruments as well as from one instrument to another in the orchestra), without confines of register, composers have opened for themselves new vistas of the conception of melody writing, a technique we have termed "pointillism." In utilizing the term "pointillism" to describe the widened scope of twentieth century melody writing, we are providing a useful word to musical criticism and a colorful addition to our steadily growing contemporary vocabulary.

APPENDIX I

List of Musical Works

UNPUBLISHED JUVENILIA*
(Brooklyn, 1916–1921)

CAPRICCIO: for violin and piano (circa 1916).

MOMENT MUSICALE: a tone poem for piano (May 28, 1917).

MELANCHOLY: A song "à la Debussy" for voice and piano, text by Jeffrey Farnol (September 14, 1917).

SPURNED LOVE: for voice and piano, text by Thomas B. Aldrich (November 2, 1917).

AFTER ANTWERP: for voice and piano, text by Emile Cammaerts (December 10, 1917).

DANSE CHARACTERISTIQUE: for piano, four hands, (March, 1918).

WALTZ CAPRICE: for piano (1918).

THREE SONGS (to lyrics of Aaron Schaffer): (1) "A Summer Vacation": (2) "My Heart Is in the East," for high voice and piano (both dated May, 1918); (3) "Night Song": for mezzo-soprano and piano, (Marlboro, N. Y., July-December 16, 1918); manuscripts with Aaron Schaffer.

POÈME: for cello and piano (December 29, 1918).

SONNET I: for piano (September 21, 1918; included later in *Three Sonnets*).

SIMONE: for voice and piano (text by Remy de Gourment) (January-September 16, 1919).

LAMENT: for cello and piano (unfinished, circa 1919).

PRELUDE (I): for violin and piano (August-November, 1919).

SONNET II: for piano (April 19, 1919).

MUSIC I HEARD: for voice and piano (text by Conrad Aiken) (April 7, 1920).

SONNET III: for piano (March 13, 1920). First performance by composer, Salle Gaveau, Paris, September 23, 1921.

* Manuscripts with the composer unless otherwise designated.

PRELUDE (II): for violin and piano (February, 1921).

TROIS ESQUISSES (Moods): for piano (1) amertume (November 14, 1920); (2) pensif (January 8, 1921); (3) jazzy (November 3, 1921). First performance by composer, Fontainebleau concert, Salle Gaveau, Paris, September 23, 1921.

SONATA (Class of Rubin Goldmark): for piano (1920–1921).

CATALOG OF PUBLISHED AND UNPUBLISHED WORKS

(1) SCHERZO HUMORISTIQUE (Le Chat et la Souris): for piano, (Brooklyn, March 19, 1920). Published in 1921, by Durand & Cie; U. S. Edition published by Boosey and Hawkes, N. Y. First performance by composer, Fontainebleau Graduation Concert, September 23, 1921, Salle Gaveau, Paris. Duration 4 minutes.[t]

(2) OLD POEM (translated from the Chinese by Arthur Waley): for high voice and piano (Brooklyn, June, 1920). Published, in 1923, by Maurice Senart; now published by Salabert, N. Y. First performance by Charles Hubbard and the composer, Salle des Agriculteurs, Paris, January 10, 1922. Duration 2½ minutes.

(3) PASTORALE (translated from Kafiristan by E. Powys Mathers): for high voice and piano (Brooklyn, April 4-12, 1921). Unpublished: manuscript with John Kirkpatrick. First performance by Charles Hubbard and the composer, Paris, January 10, 1922. Duration 2¼ minutes.

(4) FOUR MOTETS (Text arranged from the Bible, by the composer): for mixed chorus, *a cappella* (1) *Adagio ma non troppo;* (2) *Allegro (molto ritmico);* (3) *Molto adagio;* (4) *Vivo* (Paris, fall, 1921). First performance, Fontainebleau School, by Melville Smith, conducting the Paris-American-Gargenville Chorus, fall of 1924. Second performance, Paris, 1937, chorus conducted by Nadia Boulanger. Unpublished; duration 8 minutes.

(5) PASSACAGLIA: for piano (Paris, Dec., 1921-Jan., 1922). First perf., Société Musicale Indépendante, Paris, by Daniel Ericourt, Jan., 1923. Pub., in 1922, by Maurice Senart; now pub. by Salabert. Duration 5 min.

(6) RONDINO (On the name of Gabriel Fauré): for string quartet (Paris, spring, 1923). First perf., Fontainebleau, Sept., 1924.

[t] Time duration is only approximate.

Second perf., New York, May 6, 1928, Copland-Sessions Concerts, by a quartet composed of Wolfe Wolfinsohn, Edwin Ideler, Herbert Borodkin, and Lucien Schmitt. Pub., by Arrow Music Press, N.Y. Duration 6 min.

(7) GROHG: ballet (Paris, 1922–1925). Excerpts: (1) *Cortège Macabre* (winter, 1922–1923). First perf., by Howard Hanson and the Rochester Philharmonic Orch., Rochester, N.Y., May 1, 1925. Unpublished: manuscript-score and parts with American Music Center, N.Y. Duration 9 min. (2) *Dance Symphony*: Orchestral Suite (N.Y., 1930). First perf., by Stokowski and the Philadelphia Orch., Academy of Music, Phil., Apr. 15, 1931. Pub., by Cos Cob Press, N.Y. Duration 18 min.

(8) As IT FELL UPON A DAY (to poem of Richard Barnefield): for voice, fl., clar. (Vienna, summer, 1923). First perf., Société Musicale Indépendante, Paris, by Ada MacLeish and others, Feb. 6, 1924. Pub. by New Music Edition, N.Y. Duration 5½ min.

(9) SYMPHONY FOR ORGAN AND ORCHESTRA: (1) Prelude; (2) Scherzo; (3) Finale (Paris and N.Y., May-Nov., 1924). First perf., by Walter Damrosch and the N.Y. Symphony, Aeolian Hall, N.Y., Jan. 11, 1925. Unpublished: manuscript-score and parts with American Music Center, N.Y. Duration 25 min.

(9a) FIRST SYMPHONY: scherzo movement only in orchestral version (1927). First perf., by Fritz Reiner and the Philadelphia Orch., Carnegie Hall, N.Y., Nov. 4, 1927. Pub., in *First Symphony*, by Cos Cob Press. Duration 10 min.

(9b) FIRST SYMPHONY: orchestral version of the above organ and orchestra work, without organ (1928). First perf., in this version, by Ernest Ansermet and Berlin Sym. Orch., Berlin, Dec., 1931. Pub., by Cos Cob Press. Duration 25 min.

(10) TWO CHORUSES FOR WOMEN'S VOICES: (1) "The House on the Hill" (to text of Edward Arlington Robinson): Four-part *a cappella* (S.S.A.A.); (2) "An Immorality" (Ezra Pound): Three-part (S.S.A.), with sop. solo and piano accom. (Jan., 1925). First perf., by Gerald Reynolds and Women's University Glee Club, Engineering Building, N.Y., Apr. 24, 1925. Pub., by E. C. Schirmer, Boston. Duration 9 min.

(11) MUSIC FOR THE THEATRE: suite for small orch. (1) Prologue, (2) Dance; (3) Interlude; (4) Burlesque; (5) Epilogue (N.Y., MacDowell Colony, Lake Placid, May-Sept., 1925). First perf., by Koussevitzky and Boston Symphony Orch., Boston, Symphony

Hall, Nov. 20, 1925. First time in New York (same group), Town Hall, Nov. 28, 1925. Pub., by Cos Cob Press. Duration approx. 25 min.

(12) TWO PIECES FOR VIOLIN AND PIANO: (1) "Nocturne"; (2) "Ukelele Serenade" (N.Y. and Paris, Jan.-Apr., 1926). First perf. (according to *Boston Sym. Program Notes,* 1926–1927), Société Musicale Indépendante, Paris, with Samuel Dushkin and the composer, May 5, 1926. Pub., by B. Schott's Söhne, Mainz. Duration 7 min.

(13) SENTIMENTAL MELODY: for piano (Guethary, Basses Pyrénées, Aug., 1926). First perf., by the composer, for Ampico Recording, 1927. Pub., by Schott & Co., London, in *The New Piano Book,* Vol. III. Duration 1 min.

(14) CONCERTO FOR PIANO AND ORCHESTRA (in one movement—two parts): for large orch. (N.Y. and Guethary, Jan.-Nov., 1926). First perf., with the composer, Koussevitzky, and the Boston Sym. Orch., Symphony Hall, Boston, Jan. 28, 1927. Pub., in two versions: (1) Orchestral score and parts; (2) In a two-piano (four-hand) arrangement by John Kirkpatrick, by Cos Cob Press. Duration 18 min.

(15) SONG (poem of E. E. Cummings): for voice and piano (Königstein, Aug., 1927). First perf., by Ethel Luening and the composer, at the New School for Social Research, N.Y., Oct. 11, 1935. Pub., by Cos Cob Press. Duration 2 min.

(16) LENTO MOLTO: for string quartet (N.Y., Feb.-Apr., 1928). First perf. (with "Rondino"), Copland-Sessions Concerts, Edyth Totten Theatre, N.Y., May 6, 1928. Pub. with "Rondino" as *Two Pieces for String Quartet,* by Arrow Music Press, N.Y. Duration 5 min; both pieces 11 min.

(16a) TWO PIECES FOR STRING ORCHESTRA: a str. orch. version of the above str. quartet pieces, by the composer (Peterborough, Aug.-Sept., 1928). First perf., in this version, by Koussevitzky and the Boston Sym. Orch., Symphony Hall, Boston, Dec. 14, 1928. Pub., by Arrow Music Press. Duration 11 min.

(17) VOCALISE: for voice and piano (Santa Fé, N.M., June, 1928). First perf. on New Music Recording, with Ethel Luening and the composer. First perf. in N.Y., by Ethel Luening and the composer at the New School for Social Research, Oct. 11, 1935. Pub., by Alphonse Leduc, Paris; available in America at M. Baron Co., N.Y. Duration 4 min.

(18) Vitebsk (study on a Jewish theme): for piano, vln., and cello (N.Y. and Santa Fé, 1928). First perf., by W. Gieseking, O. Onnou, and R. Maas, League of Composers, Town Hall, N.Y., Feb. 16, 1929. Pub., by Cos Cob Press. Duration 11 min.

(19) Symphonic Ode: for large orch., in one movement (Königstein, Santa Fé, Peterborough, Briarcliff Manor, N.Y., Juziers, France, N.Y. City, Aug., 1927-Sept., 1929). First perf., Koussevitzky and the Boston Sym. Orch., Symphony Hall, Boston, Feb. 19, 1932. Unpublished: manuscript-score and parts with American Music Center. Duration 20 min.

(20) Piano Variations: for solo piano (Bedford, Yaddo, and N.Y. City, Jan. to fall, 1930). First perf., by the composer, League of Composers, Art Center, N.Y., Jan. 4, 1931. Pub. by Cos Cob Press. Duration 11 min.

(21) Miracle at Verdun (incidental music to Hans Chlumberg's play): for small orch. (N.Y., Jan.-Feb., 1931). First perf., Martin Beck Theatre, N.Y., Mar. 16, 1931. Unpublished manuscript-score and parts with composer.

(22) Elegies: for violin and viola (Mexico City, summer, 1932). First perf., by Charlotte and Ivor Karman, League of Composers, French Institute, N.Y., Apr. 2, 1933. Withdrawn.

(23) Short Symphony: for orchestra (I) Allegro vivace; (II) Lento; (III) Finale (N.Y., Paris, Berlin, Morocco, London, Mexico, Friend's Lake, N.Y., 1932–1933). First perf., by Carlos Chávez and the Orquesta Sinfónica de México, Mexico City, Nov. 23, 1934. Pub., by Boosey and Hawkes. Duration 15 min.

(23a) Sextet (reduced version of the Short Symphony): for string quartet, clarinet, and piano (N.Y., 1937). First perf., in this version, by P. Winter, H. Rosoff, E. Vardi, B. Greenhouse; A. Christman, clarinetist, and Judith Sidorsky, pianist, Town Hall, New York, Feb. 26, 1939. Pub., by Boosey and Hawkes. Duration 15 min.

(24) Statements: for large orch. (I) "Militant"; (II) "Cryptic"; (III) "Dogmatic"; (IV) "Subjective"; (V) "Jingo"; (VI) "Prophetic" (Yaddo, Mexico City, Friend's Lake, Bemidji, Minn., Cambridge, Mass., Peterborough, June, 1932–summer, 1935). First perf. (two movements only), by Ormandy and Minneapolis Sym. Orch., Jan. 9, 1936. First perf. (full version), by Mitropoulos and N.Y. Philharmonic-Sym. Orch., Carnegie Hall, N.Y., Jan. 7, 1942. Pub., by Boosey & Hawkes. Duration 18½ min.

(25) HEAR YE! HEAR YE! (ballet): for full orch. (Lake Bemidji and Chicago, July-Oct., 1934). First perf., by Ruth Page & Co. with Rudolph Ganz, conductor, Chicago Opera House, Nov. 30, 1934. Unpublished: manuscript-score and parts with composer. Duration 35 min.

(26) WHAT DO WE PLANT (junior high-school chorus): for three-part treble voices with piano accom. (Peterborough, summer, 1935). Pub., by Boosey & Hawkes. Duration 2 min. and 20 sec.

(27) TWO CHILDREN'S PIECES: for piano (1) "Sunday Afternoon Music"; (2) "The Young Pioneers" (Peterborough, N.H., Aug., 1935). First perf., by the composer, N.Y., Feb. 24, 1936. Pub., by Carl Fischer. Duration 2½ min.

(28) EL SALÓN MÉXICO: for large orch. (N.Y., Peterborough, Tlax-cala, Mex., 1933–1936). First perf., by Chávez and Orquesta Sinfónica, Mexico City, Aug. 27, 1937. Pub., by Boosey and Hawkes. Duration 10 min.

(28a) EL SALÓN MÉXICO: version for two pianos (arr. by Leonard Bernstein). Pub., by Boosey & Hawkes. Duration 10 min.

(28b) EL SALÓN MÉXICO: version for piano solo (arr. by Leonard Bernstein). Pub., by Boosey and Hawkes. Duration 10 min.

(29) THE SECOND HURRICANE: play-opera for high-school perf. (li-bretto by Edwin Denby) (N.Y., Tlaxcala, Mex., Jan.-fall, 1936). First perf., by the Music School of Henry Street Settlement, Leh-man Engel, cond., at the Playhouse, N.Y., Apr. 21, 1937. Pub., by C. C. Birchard, Boston. Perf. time, approx. 90 min.

(30) MUSIC FOR RADIO (Saga of the Prairie): for chamber orch. (N.Y., Mexico, fall, 1937). First perf., by Howard Barlow and Columbia Sym. Orch. in CBS network's "Everybody's Music" series, July 25, 1937. Pub., by Boosey and Hawkes. Duration 12 min.

(31) BILLY THE KID: ballet (N.Y., London, Paris, Peterborough, N.H., June-Sept., 1938). First perf., with Eugene Loring and Ballet Caravan, Chicago, Oct., 1938. Duration 35 min.

(31a) BILLY THE KID: orchestral suite from the ballet, for large orch. (1) "The Open Prairie"; (2) "Street in a Frontier Town"; (3) "Card Game at Night"; (4) "Gun Battle"; (5) "Celebration after Billy's Capture"; (6) "Billy's Demise"; (7) "The Open Prairie Again." Pub., by Boosey and Hawkes. Duration 20 min.

(31b) BILLY THE KID (excerpt, "Prairie Night" and "Celebration"): for fl., oboe, 2 clar., bassn., 2 hrns., 2 trump., 2 trom., timp., perc., piano. Pub., by Boosey & Hawkes. Duration 3, 2 min. respectively.

(31c) BILLY THE KID (a) "Waltz"; (b) "Celebration": (Arr. for band, by Philip Lang. Pub., by Boosey & Hawkes. Duration 6 min. (Also arr. for violin and piano; cello and piano by the composer.)

(31d) BILLY THE KID (excerpts from the ballet): for piano solo (arr. by Lukas Foss) (I) "The Open Prairie"; (II) "Street Scene in a Frontier Town": A. Cowboys amble by; B. Mexican dance and finale; (III) "Billy and His Sweetheart"; (IV) "Celebration after Billy's Capture." Pub., by Boosey & Hawkes. Duration 8 min.

(31e) BILLY THE KID (excerpts from the ballet): for two pianos (four hands), arr. by the composer. Pub., by Boosey & Hawkes. Duration 12 min.

(32) AN OUTDOOR OVERTURE: for large orch. (N.Y., Oct. 18-Nov. 5, 1937). First perf., by Alexander Richter and High School of Music and Art Orch., School Auditorium, N.Y., Dec. 16, 1938. Pub., by Boosey & Hawkes. Duration 9½ min.

(32a) AN OUTDOOR OVERTURE: the above arr. for band, by the composer (N.Y., 1941). First perf., in this version, by the Goldman Band, conducted by the composer, June, 1942. Pub., by Boosey & Hawkes. Duration 9½ min.

(33) LARK (poem of Genevieve Taggard): for four-part chorus of mixed voices, a cappella and baritone solo (Peterborough, N.H., Aug.-Sept., 1938). First perf., by Robert Shaw and Collegiate Chorale, Museum of Modern Art, N.Y., Apr. 13, 1943. Pub., by E. C. Schirmer. Duration 5 min.

(34) THE FIVE KINGS (incidental music to composite of plays by Shakespeare, arr. by Orson Welles): for five instruments. First perf., by the Mercury Theatre, Boston, Feb. 27, 1939. Unpublished: manuscript-score and parts with composer.

(35) QUIET CITY (incidental Music for Irwin Shaw's play): for clar., sax., trump. and piano (N.Y., Jan.-Feb., 1939). Unpublished: manuscript-score and parts with the composer.

(35a) QUIET CITY (arrangement of the principal music from the play as a concert piece): for strings, trump., and Eng. hrn. [or oboe] (Lenox, Mass., Sept., 1940). First perf., in this version, by Daniel Saidenberg and the Saidenberg Little Sym., Town Hall, N.Y., Jan. 28, 1941. Pub., by Boosey & Hawkes. Duration 8½ min.

(36) FROM SORCERY TO SCIENCE (music for a puppet show): for orchestra, mechanically recorded (N.Y., Feb., 1939). First perf., Hall of Pharmacy, N.Y. World's Fair, May 12, 1939. Unpublished: manuscript-score and parts with the composer.

(37) THE CITY (music for a documentary film): for chamber orch. (N.Y., spring, 1939). First perf., conducted by Max Goberman, Little Theatre of the World's Fair Science and Education Bldg., May 26, 1939. Two excerpts from the film are to be found in the orchestral suite, *Music for Movies*.

(38) OF MICE AND MEN: musical score for a Hal Roach film by John Steinbeck (Hollywood, Oct.-Dec., 1939). Film *première* at Roxy Theatre, N.Y., Feb. 16, 1940. One excerpt from the film appears in the concert suite, *Music for Movies*.

(39) JOHN HENRY: for chamber orchestra (N.Y., complete on Feb. 25, 1940). First perf., a broadcast by Howard Barlow and Columbia Broadcasting Sym., Mar. 5, 1940. (Revised version, 1952.) Pub., by Boosey and Hawkes. Duration 3 min.

(40) OUR TOWN: music for a United Artists film by Thornton Wilder (Hollywood, Mar.-Apr., 1940). Film *première,* Radio City Music Hall, N.Y., June 13, 1940. One excerpt from the film appears in the concert suite, *Music for Movies*.

(40a) OUR TOWN (music from the film score): for large orch., in one extended movement (N.Y., 1940). First perf., in this version, by Howard Barlow and Columbia Broadcasting Orchestra, June 9, 1940. Pub., by Boosey & Hawkes. Duration 9 min.

(40b) OUR TOWN: three piano excerpts from the film score, by the composer (N.Y., 1944) (I) "Story of Our Town"; (II) "Conversation at the Soda Fountain"; (III) "The Resting-place on the Hill." Published, by Boosey & Hawkes. Duration 7 min.

(41) EPISODE: for organ (Lenox, Mass., Aug. 20, 1940). First perf., by William Strickland, Mar. 9, 1941. Pub., by H. W. Gray Co., N.Y. Duration 4 min.

(42) PIANO SONATA: *Molto moderato; Vivace; Andante sostenuto* (Woodstock, Hollywood, N.Y., Tanglewood, South America, 1939–1941). First perf., by the composer, for La Nueva Musica, Buenos Aires, Oct. 21, 1941. First perf. in New York, by John Kirkpatrick, Town Hall, Jan. 9, 1943. Pub., by Boosey & Hawkes. Duration 23 min.

(43) LAS AGACHADAS: (The Shakedown Song): for solo group and eight-part mixed chorus *a cappella* (N.Y., 1942). First perf., by

Hugh Ross and Schola Cantorum, Carnegie Hall, N.Y., Mar. 25, 1942. Pub., by Boosey & Hawkes. Duration 6 min.

(44) LINCOLN PORTRAIT: for speaker and large orch. (N.Y., Feb.-Apr. 16, 1942). First perf., by André Kostelanetz and Cincinnati Sym. Orch., with William Adams, speaker, Cinn., May 14, 1942. Pub., by Boosey & Hawkes. Duration 14 min.

(45) RODEO: ballet (Stockbridge, Mass., May-Sept., 1942). First perf., by Agnes de Mille and Ballet Russe de Monte Carlo with Franz Allers, conductor, Metropolitan Opera House, N.Y., Oct. 16, 1942. Duration 22 min.

(45a) RODEO: suite for large orchestra, extracted from the ballet, in four dance episodes (1) "Buckaroo Holiday"; (2) "Corral Nocturne"; (3) "Saturday Night Waltz"; (4) "Hoe-down" (N.Y., fall and winter, 1942). First perf., of three episodes, by Arthur Fiedler and Boston "Pops" Orch., May 28, 1943. First complete perf., in this version, by Alexander Smallens and N.Y. Philharmonic-Symphony Society, Lewisohn Stadium, N.Y., June 22, 1943. Pub., by Boosey & Hawkes. Duration 17 min.

(45b) RODEO ("Hoe-down" only): for str. and optional piano. Pub., by Boosey & Hawkes. Duration 3½ min.

(45c) RODEO ("Hoe-down" only): for violin and piano. Pub., by Boosey & Hawkes. Duration 3½ min.

(46) MUSIC FOR MOVIES: for small orchestra (1) "New England Countryside"; (2) "Sunday Traffic," both excerpts from the film The City; (3) "Barley Wagons"; (4) "Threshing Machines," both excerpts from the film Of Mice and Men; (5) "Grovers Corners," excerpt from the film Our Town (Oakland, N.J., fall to Dec. 19, 1942). First perf., by Daniel Saidenberg and the Saidenberg Little Sym., Town Hall, N.Y., Feb. 17, 1943. Unpublished, manuscript-score and parts with Boosey & Hawkes. Duration 16 min.

(47) DANZÓN CUBANO: for two pianos—four hands (Oakland, N.J., fall, 1942). First perf., by the composer and Leonard Bernstein, League of Composers, Town Hall, N.Y., Dec. 9, 1942. Pub., by Boosey & Hawkes. Duration 6 min.

(47a) Danzón CUBANO: transcription for large orchestra by the composer (1945). First perf., in this version, by Reginald Stewart and Baltimore Sym. Orch., Baltimore, Feb. 17, 1946. Published by Boosey & Hawkes. Duration 6 min.

(48) FANFARE FOR THE COMMON MAN: for brass and percussion

(Oakland, N.J., fall, 1942). First perf., by Eugene Goossens and Cincinnati Sym. Orch., Cinn., Mar. 14, 1943. Pub., by Boosey & Hawkes in *Ten Fanfares by Ten Composers*. Duration 2¼ min.

(49) NORTH STAR: music for a Samuel Goldwyn film by Lillian Hellman (Hollywood, Feb.-Sept., 1943). Première in N. Y. at two theaters, the Victoria and Palace, Nov. 4, 1943.

(49a) NORTH STAR (two choruses): (a) "Younger Generation" (S.S.A. or S.A.T.B.), also arr. by the composer for solo voice and piano; duration approx. 2½ min; (b) "Song of the Guerrillas" (for male chorus, with baritone solo and piano accom.); duration approx. 3½ min. Both choruses published, in all forms, by Boosey & Hawkes. "Song of the Guerrillas" is also available with orchestral accompaniment, score, and parts on rental from the publishers.

(50) SONATA FOR VIOLIN AND PIANO (I) *Andante semplice;* (II) *Lento;* (III) *Allegretto giusto* (Oakland, N.J., Hollywood, N.Y., 1942–1943). First perf., by Ruth Posselt and the composer, Times Hall, N.Y., Jan., 17, 1944. Pub., by Boosey & Hawkes. Duration 17 min.

(51) LETTER FROM HOME: for large orch. (Tepoztlan, Mex., summer, 1944). First perf., by Paul Whiteman and Philco Radio Orch. over ABC, Oct. 17, 1944. Unpublished: score and parts with Boosey & Hawkes. Duration 5 min.

(52) APPALACHIAN SPRING, ballet: for 13 instruments (Oakland, N.J., Hollywood, N.Y., 1943–1944). First perf., by Martha Graham and Co., Louis Horst, conductor, Library of Congress, Wash., D.C., Oct. 30, 1944. Duration 34 min.

(52a) APPALACHIAN SPRING: concert version, arr. for medium large orchestra, by the composer (Bernardsville, N.J., spring, 1945). First perf., in this version, by Artur Rodzinski and N.Y. Philharmonic Sym. Society, Carnegie Hall, N.Y., Oct. 4, 1945. Pub., by Boosey & Hawkes. Duration 20 min.

(53) JUBILEE VARIATION (on a theme by Engene Goossens): a single variation for large orch. (N.Y., Jan., 1945). First perf., by Goossens and the Cinn. Sym., Cinn., March, 1945. Unpublished: score and parts (including the variations of 10 other composers) with Cinn. Orch. Duration of Copland's variation 3 min.

(54) THE CUMMINGTON STORY (musical score for a documentary film produced by the Overseas Unit of the U.S. Office of War Information): for chamber orch. (N.Y., Jan., 1945).

(55) THIRD SYMPHONY: for large orch. (I) *Molto moderato;* (II) *Allegro molto;* (III) *Andantino quasi allegretto;* (IV) *Molto deliberato* (Tepoztlan, Mex., N.Y., Bernardsville, N.J., Ridgefield, Conn., Peterborough, N.H., Stockbridge and Richmond, Mass., July, 1944-Sept., 1946). First perf., by Koussevitzky and Boston Sym. Orch., Symphony Hall, Boston, Oct. 18, 1946. Pub., by Boosey & Hawkes. Duration 39 min. (approx.)

(56) IN THE BEGINNING (text from Genesis): for mixed chorus, *a cappella,* with mezzo-soprano solo (Boston, Feb.-Apr., 1947). First perf., by Robert Shaw and Collegiate Chorale, Cambridge, Mass., Harvard Memorial Church, May 2, 1947. Pub., by Boosey & Hawkes. Duration 17 min.

(57) THE RED PONY: music for a Republic film based on tales by John Steinbeck (Hollywood, Feb.-Apr., 1948). *Première* showing, Mayfair Theatre, N.Y., Mar. 8, 1949.

(57a) THE RED PONY (children's suite for concert use): for large orch. (I) "Morning on the Ranch"; (II) "The Gift"; (III) "Dream March and Circus Music"; (IV) "Walk to the Bunkhouse"; (V) "Grandfather's Story"; (VI) "Happy Ending" (Palisades, N.Y., and Richmond, Mass., April-Aug., 1948). First perf., by Efrem Kurtz and Houston Sym. Orch., Auditorium, Houston, Oct. 30, 1948. Pub., by Boosey & Hawkes. Duration 21 min.

(58) FOUR PIANO BLUES: for piano solo (1) Freely poetic (1947); (2) Soft and languid (1934); (3) Muted and sensuous (1948); (4) With bounce (1926). First perf., by Leo Smit, League of Composers Concert, Carl Fischer Hall, N.Y., Mar. 13, 1950. First perf. of Blues No. 4 (originally called Blues No. 2) by Hugo Balzo, Montevideo, Uruguay, May 7, 1942. Pub., by Boosey & Hawkes. Duration 8 min.

(59) CONCERTO FOR CLARINET AND STRING ORCHESTRA (with harp and piano): Slowly and expressively; Cadenza; Rather Fast (N.Y., Mexico City, Richmond, Mass., South America, Hollywood, Sneden's Landing, Palisades, N.Y., spring, 1947-Oct., 1948). First perf., on the air, by Benny Goodman, with the NBC Sym. Orch. conducted by Fritz Reiner, Nov. 6, 1950. First concert perf., by Ralph McLane and Philadelphia Orchestra, conducted by Ormandy, Academy of Music, Phil., Nov. 23, 1950. Pub., by Boosey & Hawkes. Duration 17½ min.

(60) THE HEIRESS: music for a Paramount film by Ruth and Augustus Goetz, based on the novel *Washington Square,* by Henry James

(Hollywood, Nov.-Dec., 1948). *Première* showing, Radio City Music Hall, N.Y., Oct. 6, 1949.

(61) PREAMBLE FOR A SOLEMN OCCASION: for narrator and large orch. (Sneden's Landing, Palisades, N.Y., Aug. 16-Sept. 5, 1949). First perf., by Leonard Bernstein and Boston Sym. Orch., Carnegie Hall, N.Y., Dec. 10, 1949. Pub., by Boosey & Hawkes. Duration 6 min.

(62) TWELVE POEMS OF EMILY DICKINSON (song cycle): for mezzo-soprano with piano accom. (Sneden's Landing, Mar., 1949-Mar., 1950). First perf., by Alice Howland and the composer, Columbia University's Sixth Annual Festival of Contemporary American Music, McMillin Academic Theatre, N.Y., May 18, 1950. Pub., by Boosey and Hawkes. Duration 28 min. (Five of these songs are pub. separately.)

(63) OLD AMERICAN SONGS (newly arranged): for voice and piano accom. (First Set): (1) "The Boatmen's Dance"; (2) "The Dodger"; (3) "Long Time Ago"; (4) "Simple Gifts"; (5) "I Bought Me a Cat" (Sneden's Landing, Sept.-Oct., 1950). First perf., by Peter Pears and Benjamin Britten, Aldeburgh Festival, England, Oct. 29, 1950. First perf. in America, by William Warfield, accom. by Otto Herz, Town Hall, N.Y., Jan. 28, 1951. Pub., by Boosey & Hawkes. Duration 13 min.

(63a) OLD AMERICAN SONGS: the above with piano accom. arr. for small orch. by the composer.

(63b) OLD AMERICAN SONGS: the above arranged for mixed voices, with piano accom., by Irving Fine.

(63c) OLD AMERICAN SONGS: the above arranged for male chorus, with the exception of No. 3, arr. by Irving Fine.

(64) OLD AMERICAN SONGS (newly arranged): for voice and piano accom. (Second Set): (1) "The Little Horses" (Lullaby); (2) "Zion's Walls" (Revivalist Song); (3) "The Golden Willow Tree" (Anglo-American Ballad); (4) "At the River" (Hymn Tune); (5) "Ching-a-ring Chaw" (Minstrel Song). First perf., by Donald Dame and Otto Seyfert, Town Hall, N.Y., Mar. 2, 1954. Pub., by Boosey & Hawkes. Duration 12 min.

(65) QUARTET FOR PIANO AND STRINGS: for piano, violin, viola and cello (I) *Adagio serio;* (II) *Allegro giusto;* (III) *Non troppo lento* (Sneden's Landing, June-Oct. 20, 1950). First perf., by the New York Quartet, Mieczyslaw Horszowski, piano, Alexander Schneider, Milton Katims, and Hermann Busch, Library of Con-

gress, Coolidge Festival, Wash., D.C., Oct. 29, 1950. Pub., by
Boosey & Hawkes. Duration 23 min.

(66) THE TENDER LAND: Opera in two Acts (Libretto by Horace
Everett) (Ossining, N.Y., 1952–1954.) First perf., by N.Y. City
Center Opera Co., Apr. 1, 1954, Thomas Schippers, cond. Revised version in three Acts (1954–1955). First perf. of this version at Oberlin Conservatory, Oberlin, Ohio, May 20, 1955. Pub.,
by Boosey & Hawkes. Perf. time, approx. 110 min.

(67) DIRGE IN WOODS: for voice and piano. Text by George Meredith (Ossining, N.Y., June, 1954.) First perf. at Fontainebleau
School of Music, summer, 1954. Manuscript. Duration 3½ min.

(68) CANTICLE OF FREEDOM: for chorus and orch. Text by John Bar-
bour (died circa 138?) (Ossining, March, 1955). First perf. by
Orchestra and Chorus of Massachusetts Institute of Technology,
Cambridge, Mass., May 8, 1955. Manuscript. Duration 16 min.

ADDRESSES OF MUSIC PUBLISHERS

American Music Center, 250 W. 57 St., New York City

Arrow Music Press, 250 W. 57 St., New York City

C. C. Birchard Company, 285 Columbus Ave., Boston, Mass.

Boosey and Hawkes, 30 W. 57 St., New York City

Cos Cob Press, same address as Arrow Music Press

Carl Fischer, Inc., 165 W. 57 St., New York City

H. W. Gray Co., 159 E. 48 St., New York City

Alphonse Leduc—U.S. representative, M. Baron Co., 8 W. 45 St.,
New York City

New Music Edition—Distributed by American Music Center (See above).

Salabert, Inc., 23 E. 26 St., New York City

E. C. Schirmer, 221 Columbus Ave., Boston, Mass.

B. Schott, Mainz, and B. Schott, London—U.S. representative, Associated
Music Publishers, 25 W. 45 St., New York City

List of Recordings*

ALLEGRO RECORD
   Sonata for Violin and Piano
      Fredell Lack, violin, and Leonid Hambro, piano. 33 ⅓ rpm
      (1950). AL-33.

AMERICAN RECORDING SOCIETY RECORDS
   Appalachian Spring (suite from the ballet)
      American Recording Society Orch., Walter Hendl, cond.
      33 ⅓ rpm (1953). American Recording Society 26.
   Music for the Theatre
      American Recording Society Orch., Walter Hendl, cond.
      33 ⅓ rpm (1952). American Recording Society 12.

ARTIST RECORD
   Quiet City
      (In album entitled *Four American Landscapes*) Janssen
      Symphony Orch., Werner Janssen, cond. 33 ⅓ rpm (1950).
      Artist 100. (Originally released by Artist, 1949, on 78 rpm
      discs in album JS-13).

BOOSEY AND HAWKES RECORDS
   "Hoe-down" from *Rodeo*
      New Concert String Ensemble, Jay Wilber, cond. 78 rpm
      (1948), BH-116A.
   Outdoor Overture (arr. for band)
      Band of the Irish Guards. 78 rpm (1948). BH-2142.

CAPITOL RECORD
   Rodeo: Four Dance Episodes (from the ballet)
      Ballet Theatre Orch., Joseph Levine, cond. 33 ⅓ rpm
         (1953). Capitol P-8196, Cap. 8238, Cap. L-8198.
   Quiet City
      Concert Arts Orch., Golschmann, cond. 33 ⅓ rpm (1954).
      Cap. P-8245.

* The numbers in parenthesis indicate year of release of each recording.

COLOSSEUM RECORD
   Old American Songs (First Set)
      Randolph Symonette, bass-baritone. 33⅓ rpm (1951).
      In *Americana,* Colosseum 1008.

COLUMBIA RECORDS
   From *Billy the Kid* (suite from the ballet):
      "Prairie Night" and "Celebration Dance"
         New York Philharmonic Symphony Orch., Stokowski,
         cond. 78 rpm (1949). Columbia 19011-D, Columbia
         A-1516, Columbia ML-2167.
      "The Open Prairie" (arr. as piano solo by Lukas Foss)
         Oscar Levant, piano. 78 rpm (1949). Col. album-set
         MM-251.
   Concerto for Clarinet and String Orchestra (with harp and piano)
      Benny Goodman, soloist, and Columbia String Orch., Aaron
      Copland, cond. 33 ⅓ rpm (1951). Columbia ML-4421.
      (With *Quartet for Piano and Strings*).
   El Salón México
      Columbia Symphony Orch., Leonard Bernstein, cond. 33 ⅓
      rpm (1951). Columbia ML-2203.
   Lincoln Portrait
      Kenneth Spencer, speaker, and New York Philharmonic
      Symphony Orch., Rodzinski, cond. 78 rpm (1946). In album
      Columbia MX-266. Also released in 33⅓ rpm (1949). Co-
      lumbia ML-2042.
   Old American Songs (First Set)
      William Warfield, baritone, Aaron Copland, piano. 33 ⅓
      rpm (1951). Columbia ML-2206.
   Piano Variations
      Aaron Copland, piano. 78 rpm, in album (1935). Columbia
      X-48 (Collector's item).
   Quartet for Piano and Strings, New York Quartet, 33 ⅓ rpm
   (1951). Columbia ML-4421. (With *Clarinet Concerto*).
   Sextet for String Quartet, Clarinet and Piano
      Juillard String Quartet, with Leonid Hambro, piano, and
      David Oppenheim, clar. 33 ⅓ rpm (1953). Columbia
      ML-4492.
   Twelve Poems of Emily Dickinson
      Martha Lipton, mezzo-soprano, and Aaron Copland, piano.

33 ⅓ rpm (1955). Columbia (Record number unknown at this time).

Two Pieces for String Quartet ("Lento molto," "Rondino")
Dorian String Quartet. 78 rpm (1940). Columbia 70092-D (Collector's item).

Two Pieces for Violin and Piano
"Nocturne"
Jacques Gordon, violin, and Aaron Copland, piano. 78 rpm, with *Piano Variations,* (1935). Columbia album X-48 (Collector's item).
"Ukelele Serenade"
Jacques Gordon, violin, and Aaron Copland, piano. 78 rpm, with *Vitebsk* (1937). Columbia album X-68 (Collector's item).

Vitebsk (Study on a Jewish Theme), trio
Ivor Karman, violin, David Freed, cello, and Aaron Copland, piano. 78 rpm, in album (1937). Columbia X-68 (Collector's item). (This album also contains the "Ukelele Serenade" from *Two Pieces for Violin and Piano*.)

CONCERT HALL SOCIETY RECORDS
Concerto for Piano and Orchestra
Leo Smit, soloist, and Rome Radio Orch., Aaron Copland, cond. 33 ⅓ (1952). Concert Hall Society F-4.

Danzón Cubano
Leo Smit and Aaron Copland, duo-pianists. 78 rpm (1947). Concert Hall AL. Also released in 33 ⅓ (1951). Concert Hall CHC-51.

Two Blues (from *Four Piano Blues*) and *Sentimental Melody*
Leo Smit, piano. 33 ⅓ rpm (1951). Concert Hall CHC-51.

Our Town (suite from the film score)
Leo Smit, piano. 33 ⅓ rpm (1951). Concert Hall CHC-51. (Originally released in a set of 78 rpm, with the *Piano Sonata,* in album-set A2 [limited edition], collector's item.)

"Hoe-down," from *Rodeo* (arr. for violin and piano)
Louis and Annette Kaufman. 33 ⅓ rpm (1951). Concert Hall CHC-58. (From a collection entitled *Americana,* which includes the "Ukelele Serenade" from *Two Pieces for Violin and Piano,* and short works by other leading contemporary composers).

Sonata for Violin and Piano
> Louis Kaufman, violin, and Aaron Copland, piano. 78 rpm with album (1949). Concert Hall C-10 (Collector's item).

Two Pieces for Violin and Piano
"Nocturne"
> Louis Kaufman, violin, and Aaron Copland, piano. 78 rpm, included in an album-set with the *Violin Sonata*, (1949). Concert Hall C-10 (Collector's item).

"Ukelele Serenade"
> Louis and Annette Kaufman, 33 ⅓ rpm (1951). Concert Hall CHC-58. (With "Hoe-down" from *Rodeo*).

DECCA RECORDS

Our Town (suite from the film score)
> Little Orchestra Society, Thomas Scherman, cond. 33 ⅓ rpm (1952). Decca DL-7527.

Red Pony (suite from the film score)
> Little Orchestra Society, Thomas Scherman, cond. 33 ⅓ rpm (1952). Decca DL-9616.

Sonata for Violin and Piano
> Joseph Fuchs, violin, and Leo Smit, piano. 33 ⅓ rpm (1950). Decca DL-8503.

H M V RECORD

Old American Songs (First Set)
> Peter Pears, tenor, and Benjamin Britten, piano. 78 rpm (1952). HMV DA-7038-9.

LONDON RECORD

Four Piano Blues
> Aaron Copland, piano. 33 ⅓ rpm (1951). LPS-298. (Also released in England on 78 rpm disc.)

MERCURY RECORDINGS

Quiet City
> Eastman-Rochester Sym., Hanson, cond. 33 ⅓ rpm (1953). MERCURY-40003.

Third Symphony
> Minneapolis Symphony Orch., Antal Dorati, cond. 33 ⅓ rpm (1953). MERCURY-50018.

M G M RECORDINGS

El Salón México ["Fantasia Mexicana" from the film *Fiesta;* arr. for piano and orch. by Johnny Green.] MGM Symphony Orch., Macklin Marrow, cond., Leonid Hambro, piano. 78 rpm (1947). MGM 30016A.

Episode

In "Organ Music by Modern Composers," Richard Ellsasser, organ. 33 ⅓ rpm (1953). Album E 3064.

Music for the Theatre

MGM Symphony Orch., Izler Solomon, cond. 33 ⅓ rpm (1954). MGM-3095.

Two Children's Pieces for piano: *Sunday Afternoon; The Young Pioneers.* In "Piano Pieces for Children by Modern American Composers," Marga Richter, piano. 33⅓ rpm (1955). Album E 3147

Two Pieces for String Orchestra: Lento molto; Rondino. MGM String Orch. Izler Soloman, cond. 33⅓ rpm (1954). E 3117.

NEW MUSIC QUARTERLY RECORDING

Vocalise

Ethel Luening, soprano, and Aaron Copland, piano. 78 rpm (1935?) New Music Quarterly Record 1211 (Collector's item).

RCA VICTOR RECORDINGS

Appalachian Spring (suite from the ballet)

Boston Symphony Orch., Koussevitzky, cond. 78 rpm, in album (1946). RCA Victor DM-1046. (Also released in 33⅓ rpm (1953) RCA Victor LCT-1134).

Billy the Kid (suite from the ballet)

RCA Victor Symphony Orch., Leonard Bernstein, cond. 33⅓ rpm (1950). RCA Victor LM-1031. (Also 45 rpm, RCA Victor WDM-1333, and 78 rpm, RCA Victor DM-1333.) Each of the sets contains Copland's "Jingo," No. 5, from *Statements.*

"Waltz"

Dallas Symphony Orch., Antal Dorati, cond. Both 45 rpm and 78 rpm (1948). In RCA Victor WDM-1214 and DM-1214 (Rodeo album-set). Also Victor LM-32.

"Celebration Dance," "Billy's Demise," "The Open Prairie

Again" Whittemore and Lowe, duo-pianists. 33 ⅓ rpm (1952). RCA Victor LM-1705, (*20th Century Music for Two Pianos*).

El Salón México

Boston Symphony Orch., Koussevitzky cond. 78 rpm, in album (1939), RCA Victor DM-546. Also released in 33 ⅓ rpm (1953). RCA Victor LCT-1134.

Al Goodman's Orch. 78 rpm (1947). RCA Victor 28-0419. (Also 45 rpm, 1950, shortened version under title "Fantasia Mexicana," RCA Victor 52-0065.)

Lincoln Portrait

Melvyn Douglas, speaker, and Boston Symphony Orch., Koussevitzky, cond. 78 rpm in album (1947). RCA Victor DM-1088.

Music for the Theatre

Eastman-Rochester Symphony Orch., Howard Hanson, cond. 78 rpm, in album (1941). RCA Victor (Collector's item).

Piano Sonata

Leonard Bernstein, piano. 78 rpm, in album (1949). RCA Victor DM-1278.

Rodeo: Four Dance Episodes (from the ballet)

Dallas Symphony Orch., Dorati, cond. 78 rpm, in album (1948). RCA Victor DM-1214. (Also 45 rpm, in album, 1950, RCA Victor WDM-1214; and 33⅓ rpm, 1950, RCA Victor LMX-32). Both album-sets include the "Waltz" from *Billy the Kid*.

Scherzo Humoristique: The Cat and the Mouse

Jesús Maria Sanroma, piano. 78 rpm (1940). RCA Victor 15861 (Collector's item). Included in album-set, RCA Victor M-646, entitled *Piano Music of the Twentieth Century*.

Statements: No. 5 "Jingo" only

RCA Victor Symphony Orch., Leonard Bernstein, cond. 45 rpm, included in album-set (1950). RCA Victor WDM-1333. (Also 78 rpm, in RCA Victor album-set DM-1333.) *Billy the Kid* (suite) is the principal work in both sets.

UNIVERSITY RECORDING

Vitebsk (trio)

University of Oklahoma Trio, Robert Gerle, violin, Gabriel

Magyar, cello, Keith Wallingford, piano. 33 ⅓ rpm (1953). XTV 19349-1A.

URANIA RECORDING
Appalachian Spring
Berlin Radio Symphony Orch., Rother, cond. 33 ⅓ rpm, (1946). Urania URLP-7092.

VANGUARD RECORDING SOCIETY RECORD
Appalachian Spring and El Salón México
Vienna State Opera Orch., Franz Litschauer, cond. 33 ⅓ rpm (1953). Vanguard 439.

VOX RECORDINGS
"An Immorality"
Vienna State Academy Chamber Chorus, Ferdinand Grossman, cond. 33⅓ rpm (1953). Vox PL-7750 (in *Concert of American Music in Schoenbrunn.*) (Collector's item).
"Story of Our Town"
Andor Foldes, piano. 78 rpm, album-set (1947). Vox 174 (in a collection entitled *Contemporary American Piano Music*). (Collector's item).
"Ukelele Serenade and Hoe-down" (for violin and piano)
Louis Kaufman, violin, and Annette Kaufman, piano, in *Album Americana*. Album No. 627. (Collector's item).

WALDEN RECORDING
Passacaglia; Sonata; Variations
Webster Aitken, piano, (1953). Walden 101.

WESTMINSTER RECORDING
Appalachian Spring; El Salón México; Billy the Kid (shortened version); *Fanfare*
National Symphony Orchestra, Howard Mitchell, cond. 33⅓ rpm (1954). WESTMINSTER 5286.

YOUNG PEOPLE'S RECORDS
The Music of Aaron Copland
Musicians from New York Philharmonic Orch., Walter Hendl, cond., with Madeline Lee and Adelaide Klein. Written by Raymond Abrashkin and includes excerpts from *The Red Pony* and other works. 78 rpm (1948). YPR-408A & B.

Chronological List of Copland's Critical Works

BOOKS

What to Listen for in Music. New York: McGraw-Hill Book Co., 1939.
Our New Music. New York: McGraw-Hill Book Co., 1941.
Music and Imagination. Cambridge: Harvard University Press, 1952.

TRANSLATIONS OF BOOKS PUBLISHED

What to Listen for in Music
>GERMAN Translation: *Lerne Musik Horen,* Pub. by Edition Kasparek, Munich.
>SWEDISH: *Att Lyssna till Musik,* Pub. by Hugo Gebers Förlag, Stockholm.
>ITALIAN: *Come Ascoltare La Music*a, Pub. by Garzanti, Milan.
>HEBREW TRANSLATION in preparation, Tel-Aviv.
>SPANISH Translation in preparation, Mexico.

Our New Music
>SPANISH Translation: *Musica y Musicos Contemporaneos,* Pub. by Editorial Losada, Buenos Aires.
>GERMAN: *Musik von Heute,* Pub. by Humboldt Verlag, Vienna.
>GERMAN: *Unsere Neue Musik,* Pub. by Edition Kasparek, Munich.

Music and Imagination
>SPANISH Translation in preparation.

PERIODICAL AND NEWSPAPER ARTICLES

"Gabriel Fauré: A Neglected Master," *Musical Quarterly,* Oct., 1924, pp. 573–586.
"George Antheil," *The League of Composers' Review,* Jan., 1925, pp. 26–28.
"Letter in Defense of Mahler," New York *Times,* Apr. 5, 1925.
"America's Young Men of Promise," *Modern Music,* Nov-Dec., 1926, pp. 13–20.
"Playing Safe at Zurich," *Modern Music,* Nov.-Dec., 1926, pp. 28–31.
"Jazz Structure and Influence," *Modern Music,* Jan.-Feb., 1927, pp. 9-14.

"Forecast and Review" (Baden-Baden Festival), *Modern Music,* Nov.-Dec., 1927, pp. 31-34.

"Stravinsky's 'Oedipus Rex'," *The New Republic,* Feb. 29, 1928, pp. 68–69.

"Music Since 1920," *Modern Music,* Mar.-Apr., 1928, pp. 16–20.

"Carlos Chávez—Mexican Composer," *The New Republic,* May 2, 1928, pp. 322–323.

"The Lyricism of Milhaud," *Modern Music,* Jan.-Feb., 1929, pp. 14–19.

"From a Composer's Notebook," *Modern Music,* May-June, 1929, pp. 15–19.

"A Note on Nadia Boulanger," *The Fontainebleau Alumni Bulletin,* Vol. V, May, 1930.

"Modern Orchestration Surveyed by Wellesz," *Modern Music,* Nov.-Dec., 1930, pp. 41–44.

"Contemporaries at Oxford, 1931," *Modern Music,* Nov.-Dec., 1931, pp. 17–23.

"Stravinsky and Hindemith Premieres," *Modern Music,* Jan.-Feb., 1932, pp. 85–88.

"The Composer and His Critic," *Modern Music,* May-June, 1932, pp. 143–147.

"The Composer in America, 1923–1933," *Modern Music,* Jan.-Feb., 1933, pp. 87–92.

"One Hundred and Fourteen Songs," *Modern Music,* Jan.-Feb., 1934, pp. 59–64.

"Scherchen on Conducting and Ewen on Composers," *Modern Music,* Jan.-Feb., 1935, pp. 94–96.

"The American Composer Gets a Break," *The American Mercury,* Apr., 1935, pp. 488–492.

"Active Market in New Music Records," *Modern Music,* Jan.-Feb., 1936, pp. 45–47.

"Pioneer Listener" (review of Paul Rosenfeld's *Discoveries of a Music Critic*), *The New Republic,* Apr. 15, 1936, pp. 291-299.

"Our Younger Generation—Ten Years Later," *Modern Music,* May-June, 1936, pp. 3–11.

"New Scores and Records," *Modern Music,* Nov.-Dec., 1936, pp. 97–99.

"Mexican Composer—Silvestre Revueltas," New York *Times,* May 9, 1937.

"Thompson's Musical State" (Book Review), *Modern Music*, Oct.-Nov., 1939, pp. 63–65.

"The Aims of Music for Films," New York *Times*, Sunday Music Page, Mar. 10, 1940.

"Second Thoughts on Hollywood," *Modern Music*, Mar.-Apr., 1940, pp. 260–275.

"The Composers Get Wise," *Modern Music*, Nov.-Dec., 1940, pp. 18–21.

"The Musical Scene Changes," *Twice a Year*, V-VI (1940-41), pp. 340–343.

"Some Notes on my 'Music for the Theatre'," *Victor Record Review*, Mar., 1941, pp. 6, 18–21.

"Five Post-Romantics," *Modern Music*, May-June, 1941, pp. 218–224.

"The Composers of South America," *Modern Music*, Jan.-Feb., 1942, pp. 75–82.

"Latin-Americans in Music," *WQXR Program Book*, June, 1942, p. 1.

"From the '20's to the '40's and Beyond," *Modern Music*, Jan.-Feb., 1943, pp. 78–82.

"Serge Koussevitzky and the American Composer," *Musical Quarterly*, Apr., 1944, pp. 255–269.

"On the Notation of Rhythm," *Modern Music*, May-June, 1944, pp. 217–220.

"The American Composer Today," U.S.A. (Government Publication) Vol. II, No. 10 [n.d.] pp. 23–27.

"Fauré Festival at Harvard," New York *Times*, Sunday Music Page, Nov. 25, 1945.

"Neglected Works: A Symposium," *Modern Music*, winter, 1946, pp. 3–12.

"Memorial to Paul Rosenfeld," *Notes*. (Mar., 1947), pp. 147–148. Reprinted under title of "A Verdict," *Paul Rosenfeld, Voyager in the Arts*. New York: Creative Age Press Inc., 1948, pp. 166–169.

"Review of Benjamin Britten's 'The Rape of Lucretia'," *Notes*. (Mar., 1947), pp. 190–191.

"Influence, Problem, Tone," *Dance Index*. Vol. VI, Nos. 10, 11, 12, 1947. (Special issue devoted to "Stravinsky in the Theatre"), p. 249.

"Composer's Report on Music in South America," New York *Times*, Sunday Music Page, Dec. 21, 1947.

"The New 'School' of American Composers," New York *Times*, Magazine Section, March 14, 1948.

"The Art of Darius Milhaud" (Review of recording of *First Symphony*), *Saturday Review of Literature*, June 26, 1948, p. 43.

"Stefan Wolpe: Two Songs for Alto and Piano" (Music Review), *Notes*, Dec., 1948, p. 172.

"What Is Jewish Music?" (Review of Peter Gradenwitz's *The Music of Israel*), New York *Herald Tribune*, Book Review Section, Oct. 2, 1949.

"Tip to Moviegoers: Take Off Those Ear-Muffs," New York *Times*, Magazine Section, Nov. 16, 1949.

"The World of A-Tonality" (Review of René Leibowitz's *Schoenberg and His School*), New York *Times*, Book Review Section, Nov. 27, 1949.

"The Personality of Stravinsky" (in Edwin Corle, ed., *Igor Stravinsky*), New York; Duell, Sloan & Pearce, 1949. pp. 121–122.

"A Modernist Defends Modern Music," New York *Times*, Magazine Section, Dec. 25, 1949.

"Duo for violin and piano by Leo Kirchner" (Music Review), *Notes*. June, 1950, p. 434.

"The American Musical Scene," *Musik Olympiad*. Salzburg, Vol. I, No. 1.

"Fourth String Quartet by William Schuman" (Music Review), *Musical Quarterly,* July, 1951, pp. 394-396.

"An Indictment of the Fourth B," New York *Times*, Magazine Section, Sept. 21, 1952.

"Creativity in America," *Proceedings, National Institute of Arts and Letters, Series II, No. 3* New York: The Spiral Press, 1953. pp. 33–40 (Blashfield Address).

"Notes Without Music by Darius Milhaud" (Book Review), New York *Times*, Book Review Section, Feb. 22, 1953.

"The Life and Music of Béla Bartók by Halsey Stevens" (Book Review), New York *Times*, Book Review Section, May 3, 1953.

"The Measure of Kapell," Memorial Article on William Kapell, *The Saturday Review*, Nov. 28, 1953, p. 67.

"Festival in Caracas," New York *Times*, Sunday Music Page, Dec. 26, 1954.

"Music: As an Aspect of the Human Spirit," from *Man's Right to Knowledge: Second Series*. New York: Columbia University Press, 1955. (Reprinted in *Musical Courier*, Feb. 1, 1955.)

"Modern Music: 'Fresh and Different'," New York *Times*, Magazine Section, March 13, 1955.

Notes

CHAPTER ONE

[1] Aaron Copland, *Our New Music* (New York: McGraw-Hill Book Co., 1941), p. 132.

[2] "Portrait of an American Composer," New York *Times*, August 24, 1941.

[3] Copland, *op. cit.*, p. 213.

CHAPTER TWO

[1] Quoted from Ronald F. Eyer, in "Meet the Composer," *Musical America*, Dec. 10, 1943, p. 7.

[2] *Ibid.*

[3] Aaron Copland, *Our New Music* (New York: McGraw Hill Book Co., 1941), p. 214.

[4] Copland, *op. cit.*, p. 215.

[5] Aaron Copland, "Memorial to Paul Rosenfeld," *Notes*, March, 1947, pp. 147-151.

[6] *Musical Courier*, September, 1946, p. 14.

CHAPTER THREE

[1] Aaron Copland *Our New Music* (New York: McGraw-Hill Book Co., 1941), pp. 71-79.

[2] Nicolas Slonimsky, *Music Since 1900* (New York: Coleman-Ross Co., 1949), p. 216.

[3] Copland, *op. cit.*, pp. 217-219

[4] Copland, *op. cit.*, pp. 218-219.

[5] Herbert Elwell, "Nadia Boulanger: A Tribute," *Modern Music*, January-February, 1938, pp. 76-77.

[6] "The Music of Aaron Copland", *Music Quarterly*, October, 1945, p. 444.

[7] Moses Smith, *Koussevitzky* (New York: Allen, Towne & Heath, 1947), p. 110.

[8] Paris-New York *Herald*, January 11, 1922. The original program of Hubbard's recital, provided by John Kober for this study, indicates that Arthur Berger's listings for the first performances of "Old Poem" and of Pastorale" as February, 1922, are both incorrect. See *Aaron Copland* (New York: Oxford University Press, 1953), p. 99.

[9] Claude Delvincourt, February 15, 1924.

[10] February 17, 1924.

[11] Slonimsky, *op. cit.*, pp. 247-249.

[12] Smith, *op. cit.*, p. 118.

[13] Copland, *op. cit.*, p. 222.

CHAPTER FOUR

[1] Aaron Copland, "Jazz Structure and Influence," *Modern Music,* January-February, 1927, pp. 9-14.

[2] *Ibid.*

[3] "The Newest American Composers," *Modern Music,* March-April, 1938, p. 153.

[4] *Bulletin of the Symphony Society of New York,* Vol. XVIII, No. 8, unpaged.

[5] New York *Times,* January 12, 1925 (unsigned review).

[6] New York *Herald Tribune,* January 12, 1925.

[7] "Musical Chronicle," *The Dial,* March, 1925, pp. 258-259.

[8] *Koussevitzky* (New York: Allen, Towne and Heath, 1947), p. 186.

[9] New York *Herald Tribune,* May 2, 1925.

[10] *Musical Courier,* September, 1946, p. 14.

[11] " 'The Six' of American Music," *Christian Science Monitor,* Magazine Section, March 17, 1937, p. 8.

[12] December 19, 1925.

[13] *Boston Symphony Orchestra Programs and Notes (1926–1927),* p. 1110. The date of the first performance is at variance with that given by Berger, as April 19, 1926 (see "The Music of Aaron Copland," *Musical Quarterly,* October, 1945, p. 444) and John Kirkpatrick (see "On Copland's Music," *The Fontainebleau Alumni Bulletin,* May, 1928, p. 3), both of whom were undoubtedly given that date by the composer. Since Kirkpatrick's listing of the first performance of these pieces did not appear until 1928 and Berger's not until 1945, it is presumed that the *Boston Notes,* prepared during the same year as the first performance of the violin pieces, are likely to be more accurate. Berger continues to hold to the "erronius" April date in his book *Aaron Copland, op. cit.,* published in 1953.

[14] *The Fervent Years* (New York: Alfred A. Knopf, 1950), pp. 13-14.

[15] *Boston Symphony Orchestra Programs and Notes (1926–1927),* p. 1110. In listing the date of February 3, 1927, as the first performance of the *Piano Concerto,* Kirkpatrick is in error.

[16] January 29, 1927.

[17] January 29, 1927.

[18] January 29, 1927.

[19] *Letters of Composers,* Gertrude Norman and Miriam Lubell Shrifte, eds. (New York: Alfred A. Knopf, 1946), p. 401.

[20] *Boston Transcript,* February 7, 1927.

[21] Oscar Thompson, *Great Modern Composers* (New York: Dodd, Mead & Co., 1941), p. 44.

[22] "A Festival that Failed," *Modern Music,* November-December, 1927, pp. 34-38.

[23] "Forecast and Review," *Modern Music,* November-December, 1927, pp. 31-34.

[24] Thompson, *op. cit.*, p. 46.

[25] June 26, 1927.

[26] *New York Times,* September 16, 1928.

[27] February 4, 1929.

[28] May 24, 1929.

[29] June 19, 1929 (unsigned review).

[30] June 22, 1929 (unsigned review).

[31] June 22, 1929.

[32] "Premieres and Experiments—1932," *Modern Music,* March-April, 1932, pp. 122-123.

[33] "Style," *The Hound and Horn,* September, 1930, pp. 106-110.

[34] "The earmark of Copland's music is leanness, slenderness of sound, sharpened by the fact that it is found in connection with a strain of grandiosity." *One Hour with American Music* (Philadelphia: J. B. Lippincott Co., 1929), p. 128.

CHAPTER FIVE

[1] *One Hour With American Music* (Philadelphia: J. B. Lippincott Co., 1929), p. 129.

[2] *The Fervent Years* (New York: Alfred A. Knopf, 1950), p. 289.

[3] Arthur Berger, "The Music of Aaron Copland," *Musical Quarterly,* October, 1945, p. 432.

[4] *New York Sun,* February 18, 1929.

[5] January 5, 1931 (unsigned review).

[6] J. D. B. (Jerome D. Bohm), January 5, 1931.

[7] Linton Martin, *the Philadelphia Inquirer,* April 16, 1931.

[8] April 16, 1931.

[9] "America in Berlin," *Modern Music,* January-February, 1932, p. 90.

[10] "America in London," *Modern Music,* January-February, 1932, pp. 92-93.

[11] Moses Smith, *Koussevitzky* (New York: Allen, Towne & Heathe, 1947), pp. 217-218.

[12] February 20, 1932.

[13] L. A. S., February 20, 1932.

[14] February 20, 1932.

[15] *New York Herald Tribune,* March 4, 1932.

[16] Slonimsky, *Music Since 1900* (New York: Coleman-Ross Co., 1949), p. 346.

[17] New York *Times,* April 4, 1932.

[18] "A Musical Tournament," *The New Republic,* June 15, 1932, pp. 119-121.

[19] New York *Herald Tribune,* October 2, 1933.

[20] September 5, 1932.

[21] September 23, 1932.

[22] July 2, 1933.

[23] *Letters of Composers,* Gertrude Norman and Miriam Lubell Shrifte, eds. (New York: Alfred A. Knopf, 1946). pp. 393-394.

[24] New York *Herald Tribune,* January 8, 1942.

[25] New York *Times,* January 8, 1942.

INTRODUCTION TO CHAPTERS VI, VII, VIII

[1] New York *Herald Tribune*, October 2, 1933.

[2] In Germany, Hindemith stated his *Gebrauchsmusik* creed as follows: "It is [regrettable] that . . . so little relationship exists today between the producers and consumers of music. A composer should write today only if he knows for what purpose he is writing. . . . The demand for music is so great that composer and consumer ought . . . to come at last to an understanding." Oscar Thompson, *Great Modern Composers* [New York: McGraw-Hill Book Co., 1941], p. 116.

[3] *Our New Music* (New York: McGraw-Hill Book Co., 1941), pp. 228-229.

[4] *This Modern Music* (New York: Thomas Y. Crowell Co., 1942), pp. 158-159.

CHAPTER SIX

[5] Lawrence Gilman, "An Opera for School Children to Sing," New York *Herald Tribune*, April 4, 1937.

[6] "High-Brows Wow Local Public," *Modern Music*, May-June, 1937, pp. 233-237.

[7] April 22, 1937.

[8] New York *Times*, November 5, 1950.

[9] April 14, 1943.

[10] "America's No. 1 Composer," *Esquire*, April, 1948, p. 57.

[11] "A Symphonist Goes to Folk Sources," *Musical America*, February, 1948, p. 29.

[12] "To Order, for Radio," *Modern Music*, November-December, 1936, pp. 12-13.

[13] New York *Times*, July 18, 1937.

[14] *Modern Music*, November-December, 1937, p. 48.

[15] "Coolidge-Fiesta in Mexico," *Modern Music*, November-December, 1937, pp. 37-40.

[16] "Through the World of Music," *Excelcior*, August 29, 1937.

[17] *El Universal*, August 31, 1937.

CHAPTER SEVEN

[1] "A Symphonist Goes to Folk Sources," *Musical America*, February, 1948, p. 29.

[2] New York *Times*, April 4, 1932.

[3] "Copland's *Hear Ye! Hear Ye!*" *Modern Music*, January-February, 1935, pp. 86-88.

4 New York *Times*, May 25, 1939.

5 "With the Dancers," *Modern Music*, November-December, 1942, pp. 53-54.

6 New York *Times*, October 17, 1942.

7 "Mrs. Coolidge's Birthday Party," *Modern Music*, November-December, 1944, p. 42.

8 "The Neo-Baroque," *Modern Music*, March-April, 1945, pp. 152-165.

9 *The Fervent Years* (New York: Alfred A. Knopf, 1950), p. 289.

10 (New York: W. W. Norton and Co., 1937), p. 120.

11 Copland, *Our New Music* (New York: McGraw-Hill Book Co., 1941), pp. 236-275.

12 "The Aims of Music for Films," New York *Times*, March 10, 1940.

13 "What Music Has Charms?" New York *Times* (Hollywood dateline), June 23, 1940.

14 Aaron Copland, "The Aims of Music for Films," New York *Times*, March 10, 1940.

15 June 14, 1940.

16 New York *Times*, June 16, 1940.

17 New York *Times*, November 5, 1943.

18 November 2, 1948.

19 Lawrence Morton, "An Interview with George Antheil," *Film Music Notes*, November-December, 1950, p. 5.

20 *Ibid.*, p. 6.

CHAPTER EIGHT

1 Oscar Thompson, *Great Modern Composers* (New York: Dodd Mead & Co., 1941), p. 46.

2 Copland, "From the '20's to the '40's and Beyond," *Modern Music*, January-February, 1943, pp. 78-82.

3 New York *Herald Tribune*, August 17, 1951.

4 Buenos Aires *Herald* (English Edition), September 28, 1941.

5 December 21, 1941.

6 New York *Times*, January 10, 1943.

7 New York *Times*, February 20, 1949.

8 Gertrude Norman and Miriam L. Shrifte, *An Anthology of Letters of Composers* (New York: Alfred A. Knopf, 1946), pp. 403-404.

9 *Ibid.*

10 "Tanglewood in Retrospect," *Modern Music*, Fall, 1946, p. 300.

11 "Copland's New Symphony," New York *Herald Tribune*. Nov. 24, 1946.

12 New York *Times*, May 20, 1947.

13 June 23, 1947.

14 Aaron Copland, "Composer's Report on Music in South America," New York *Times*, Sunday Music Page, December 21, 1947.

15 New York *Times*, November 17, 1947.

16 New York *Times*, April 13, 1954.

17 Peggy Glanville-Hicks.

18 New York *Times*, March 29, 1955.

CHAPTER NINE

[1] *The League of Composers' Review,* January, 1925, pp. 26-28.
[2] *Modern Music,* November-December, 1925, pp. 13-20.
[3] *Ibid.,* November-December, 1926.
[4] *Ibid.,* March-April, 1928, pp. 16-20.
[5] *The New Republic,* May 2, 1928, pp. 322-323.
[6] *The Fontainebleau Alumni Bulletin.* Vol. 5, May, 1930.
[7] Modern Music, May-June, 1932, pp. 143-147.
[8] *Ibid.*
[9] *Ibid.,* January-February, 1933, pp. 87-92.
[10] *Ibid.,* (January-February, 1934), pp. 59-64.
[11] *The American Mercury,* April, 1935, pp. 488-492.
[12] *Modern Music,* May-June, 1936, pp. 3-11.
[13] New York *Times,* May 9, 1937.
[14] *Modern Music,* November-December, 1940, pp. 18-21.
[15] *Ibid.,* January-February, 1942, pp. 75-82.
[16] *WQXR Program Book,* June, 1942, p. 1.
[17] *Modern Music,* January-February, 1943, pp. 78-82.
[18] *The Musical Quarterly,* April, 1944, pp. 255-269.
[19] "The American Composer Today," in USA (government publication) Vol. 2, No. 10 (n. d.) pp. 23-27.
[20] *Notes,* March, 1947. Reprinted under the title of "A Verdict," *Paul Rosenfeld, Voyager in the Arts* (New York: Creative Age Press, Inc., 1948), pp. 166-169.
[21] New York *Times,* Magazine Section, March 14, 1948.
[22] *Ibid.,* November 16, 1949.
[23] *Ibid.,* December 25, 1949.
[24] *Proceedings American Academy of Arts and Letters,* Second Series, Number Three (New York: Spiral Press, 1953), pp. 33-40.
[25] *Man's Right to Knowledge, 2nd Series.* New York: Columbia University Press, 1955. pp. 99-106.
[26] New York *Times,* Sunday Magazine Section, March 13, 1955.
[27] "A Symphonist Goes to Folk Songs," *Musical America,* February, 1948, pp. 29, 256, 397.
[28] "Scores and Records," *Modern Music,* April-May, 1945, p. 200.
[29] "Copland in Israel," New York *Times,* Sunday Music Page, May 13, 1951.
[30] J. B., New York *Times,* April 21, 1952.

ADDENDUM

[1] (G. Schirmer, Inc., 1940), p. 1.
[2] (New York: McGraw-Hill Book Co., 1939), pp. 78-100.

Index

Index

Casella, Alfredo, 265
Castro, Jose Maria, 249, 274
Castro, Juan Jose, 229
Cazden, Norman, 273
Chabrier, Emanuel, 275
Chanler, Theodore, 115, 128, 268
Charpentier, Raymond, 61
Chavez, Carlos, 107, 111-113, 137, 142-143, 145, 147, 150, 155, 174, 180, 200, 247, 267, 270, 274, 276, 279, 286, 287, 293
Chlumberg, Hans, 133, 198-199
Chopin, Frederic, 21
Churchill, Mary Senior, 156
Citkowitz, Israel, 111-113, 146-147, 268, 273, 285
Claflin, Avery, 266, 272
Clurman, Elsie Abrams, 37
Clurman, Harold, 37, 43, 46, 48, 50, 56, 60, 65, 88, 90, 120, 149, 199
Coates, Albert, 104, 127
Cocteau, Jean, 40
Cogan, Alice, 101
Columbia Broadcasting System, 169, 177, 178, 204, 281
Columbia Phonograph Co., 271
Committee for Inter-American Cultural Relations, 228
Cone, Edward, 275
Confrey, Zez, 67
Connelly, Marc, 247
Coolidge, Elizabeth Sprague, 180, 194, 253, 261, 270
Copland, Aaron
critical works, 66, 263-294
   Music and Imagination, 264
   Our New Music, 228, 264, 270
   What to Listen for in Music, 182, 264, 297
Copeland, Aaron
musical works
   "Allegro for Spring Quartet" (on theme by Paul Vidal), 44
   Appalachian Spring, 56, 150n, 194-198, 215-216, 235
   "As it fell upon a day," 54, 58-59, 61, 89, 173
   Billy the Kid, 56, 168, 172, 175, 179, 183, 187-190, 229
   "Blues, No. 2," 250; *see also Four Piano Blues*
   Canticle of Freedom (chorus and orchestra), 262-263
   City, The, (film score), 201, 202, 203
   Concerto for Clarinet and String Orchestra, 222, 250-252

Copland, Aaron, (*continued*)
musical works (*continued*)
   Concerto for Piano and Orchestra, 66, 91-96, 104, 108, 109-110, 126-127, 174, 201-202, 250
   Cortège Macabre, 54-56, 62-63, 82
   Cummington Story, The, (film score), 201, 208, 240
   Dance Symphony (*Grohg*), 64, 108, 123, 124, 133-134, 206, 251
   Danzón Cubano, 176-177, 194
   "Dirge in Woods," for voice, 262
   El Salón México, 165, 167, 173, 174-177, 180, 181, 182, 183, 198, 284
   "Elegies" for violin and viola, 148, 158
   "Episode" (organ), 172, 228
   Fanfare for the Common Man, 222, 223, 226-227
   First Symphony (Symphony for Organ and Orchestra), 66, 75-83, 99, 106, 108, 136, 143, 150-151, 172, 239
   Five Kings, The (music for a play), 199-200
   "Four Motets," 47, 48, 59, 73
   Four Piano Blues, 222, 249-250
   From Sorcery to Science (music for puppet show), 199-20
   Grohg, 50, 54, 60, 63, 65, 106, 187; *see also Dance Symphony*
   Hear Ye, Hear Ye!, 56, 155-156, 185, 186-187
   Heiress, The (film score), 201, 208, 212-216
   "House on the Hill, The" 66, 80, 143
   "Immorality, An," 66, 80, 81, 143, 144
   In the Beginning, 222, 245-247, 292
   John Henry, 168, 169-170, 177, 179, 204
   Jubilee Variation, 222, 240
   Juvenilia, 29, 35-36; *see also* List of, Appendix I
   "Lark," 171-172
   "Las Agachadas," 170
   "Lento Molto," 96, 97, 101-103, 105; *see also Two Pieces for String Quartet* and *Two Pieces for String Orchestra*
   Letter from Home, 177, 179, 222, 239
   Lincoln Portrait, 163, 167, 191, 207, 222, 224-225
   Miracle at Verdun (music for play), 133, 199

Index

Index

Index